Macedonian Greece

Macedonian Greece

John Crossland
and
Diana Constance

B. T. Batsford Ltd, London

ISBN 0 7134 3809 6

Printed in Great Britain by
Butler & Tanner Ltd
Frome Somerset,
for the publishers
B.T. Batsford Ltd
4 Fitzhardinge Street
London W1H OAH

Contents

List of Illustrations

The authors and publishers would like to thank the following individuals and organizations for the use of their photographs. Professor Andronicos (royal tomb at Vergina, in colour; nos. 27 and 28); The British Museum (no. 15); The Institute for Macedonian Studies (no. 29).

Unacknowledged photographs are by Diana Constance; nos. 33 and 35 are from her collection.

The maps are by Patrick Leeson.

Acknowledgment

Our first debt of gratitude is to Professor Manolis Andronicos for his patient help in our research and for giving us such freedom of access to the tombs at Vergina. Without such generosity (and we include here his assistants Panagiotis Faklaris and Mrs Chrysoula Paliedeli) this book would not have been possible.

We wish to thank other members of the Greek Archaeological Service in Macedonia: Mrs Mary Siginidou, Ephor for Edessa and Pella; Mrs Nicholidou, Ephor for Byzantine Works, Thessaloniki, and her assistant, Mrs Anastasia Tourta; Dr Nikonanos, of the Byzantine Art Service; Mrs Katerina Koukuli-Chrysanthaki, Ephor of Kavala; Professor Demetrios Pandermalis of Thessaloniki University.

Our thanks are also due to Professor Jean Maffre and his colleagues from the French School of Athens who are bringing to light the rich heritage of Thasos.

So many others have eased the path of this enterprise with their kindness: Professor Robert Browning, until recently Professor of Classics at Birkbeck College in the University of London; Mrs Eleni Cubitt of the Greek Embassy, London; Miss Margaret Tyrrell; Mrs Louisa Laouda; Professor Mitsakis and the staff of the Balkan Institute; Mr Simeophrides, Mayor of Kastoria, and his staff; Dr Aris Poulianos; the Macedonian Tourist Police, particularly in Kastoria, Edessa and Lithokoron; Miss Healey of the Institute of Archaeology library in Gordon Square, London; Zoe Argyropoulos and her husband, Kleanthis, at Gerakina Beach (their information on Halkidiki and Greek wines was invaluable.

Our greatest thanks go to the Macedonians themselves. Despite centuries of invasion and occupation, they have retained their good humour, great generosity and sense of identity.

Introduction

Macedonia has meant many things to many men in its 3000 years of recorded history. Its present-day nature is the subject of a dispute on cultural and historical grounds which we do not intend to go into. For the purposes of this book, we are describing the Macedonia of Philip II, a historical reality which, in the fourth century BC, changed the course of history. We are all, in some way, affected by that history. In 25 short years, Philip of Macedon took this land of mountain fastnesses, surrounding rolling, windswept plains, from being a politically insignificant border state to the leadership of all Greece, and to the brink of world dominion.

This extraordinary man answered the jibes of Demosthenes, that Macedonia was peopled with barbarian riff-raff and led by a king who lacked a good Greek pedigree, in the most comprehensive way possible. He mobilized Greek patriotism in a cause which his heir would transform into a far-reaching crusade, mingling the ancient civilization of the East with the luminosity and questioning of Hellenism into one stream which the Romans were to direct, with the help of Christianity, to the West.

Recently the importance of fourth-century Macedonia has been dazzlingly reaffirmed by the discovery of the royal tombs of Vergina. The prize was the large, unlooted tomb attributed to Philip, which proved to be a veritable time-capsule of t he Macedonian civilization, caught at the outset of Alexander's great adventure.

We have used the tomb discovery as both the linchpin and departure point for this book. We have set out, if you like, to track down Philip and his land. We are not concerned with modern politics; the Greeks themselves, having surmounted the prejudices of Demosthenes, rest their case on Macedonia as it was known in the king's time, and so do we.

Strabo, the geographer, pointed out that it formed almost a parallelogram. He described the Roman boundaries; the Adriatic, the Via Egnatia, the Rhodope Mountains and the Hebros river. Philip would have spoken of Olympos and the Vale of Tempe as the southern boundary, the Pindus as the western, and probably the Strymon and Neapolis (modern Kavala) as the eastern limit.

Macedonia lies at the northern limits of the Aegean, which for many visitors from northern Europe gives it a decided advantage over the baking heat of the southern islands. The few degrees' difference in temperature can be a real boon in July and August. Winds, such as the Vadaris and Melteme, an inevitable hazard along the edge of this mountainous continental mass, can give this cooler temperature a decidedly chilly edge, but in summer they die as rapidly as they rise. Swimming can be guaranteed from April until as late as October.

It is no more than a four-hour drive from the beaches of Halkidiki, at one end of the region, to the cool mountain ranges at the other. These envelop the plains of what Homer called 'Lovely Emathia' in a great semi-circle, from Olympos in the south, up through the Pierian massif to join the main Balkan chain.

Emathia still lives up to its epithet − it is the Greek fertile crescent. For instance, the route to the wine-making country of Naoussa and to the tombs of Lefkadia runs through peach and apple orchards. Macedonian apples are large, dusky-pink in colour and sweet as honey. As with its history, the country is easily amenable to superlatives. The highest mountain in Greece guards its southern border and its lakes lie across the northern border zone like inland seas, mirror-smooth or troubled and dark with the Balkan storms.

The quest for Macedonia's archaeological remains has really only picked up momentum in the past few years. All the evidence emerging − which can be seen either on site or in the museums − points to a civilization which had no mere nodding acquaintance with Hellenic culture but was thoroughly imbued with it.

In our search for Philip, we visited Pella, the city founded and embellished by his ancestor, Archelaus, with the best of Greek craftsmanship and arts; the training ground and sacrificial centre of his army at Dium and cities which he either founded, such as Philippi, or destroyed, for example Olynthos.

Olynthos was one of a confederation of wealthy cities in Halkidiki, which battened on the trade roots of the northern Aegean. Today, of course, increasingly, the triple-pronged peninsula is a playground, offering spacious beaches and an unpolluted sea as well as a ruggedly attractive interior region sprinkled with villages where folk arts and culture are being revived. Incongruously, the holiday coast has grown up cheek-by-jowl with one of the most exclusive communities on earth − in fact an autonomous republic within the republic of Greece − Mount Athos, the Holy Mountain.

Macedonia also has its own verdant island moored just offshore − Thasos. This golden isle of the ancients, where new discoveries have confirmed the accuracy of stories by Herodotus and others about its wealth, offers the advantages of the region in miniature. Here, first-class bathing beaches are less than half an hour by car from a mountain village; perhaps the best formula for a stay on the island.

Most visitors will get their first and last glimpse of the north, touching down at, or taking off from Thessaloniki airport. The long, gentle curve of the head of the Thermaic Gulf and the natural amphitheatre of hills make a good setting for the second city of Greece. A girdle of crenellated walls and a pattern of squares and avenues, making their way down the slopes to the sea, give a reassuring impression from the air which is amply fulfilled on closer acquaintance.

Here we jumped nearly 300 years from the Macedonia of Philip to see what remained of the legacy of his heirs in conquest, the Romans, and of the civilization that perpetuated his son's work — Byzantium. Thessaloniki is one of the richest surviving repositories of Byzantine art and although when we were last there some of it was denied to the visitor because of the grievous damage caused by the 1978 earthquake, it was hoped that renovations would soon be completed.

JUGOSLAVIA

Florina

Edessa

Naoussa

Kastoria

Veria

Vergina

Siatista

Kozani

Katerini

Litohoron

0	10		30 miles
10		50 km	

BULGARIA

D E O K I A
N

⊙ Serres

Kavala

Thasos

⊙ Langadas

THASOS

Thessaloniki

Arnea

Poligiros

13

1. Philip II's Background

Attend, noble Karanos, and set my words in your mind. Forsake Argos and Hellas of the fair women and go to the waters of Aliakmon, and wherever you first see goats grazing, then you are to dwell in happiness, you and all your offspring.

Oracle on the foundation of Macedonia

A common sight in Macedonia is the solitary shepherd, surrounded by extravagantly horned Judas goats. He stands, wrapped in old greatcoat or blanket, or if the weather is inhospitable, enveloped by the black canopy of his umbrella.

A wave, and the seamed, weather-beaten face breaks into a self-conscious smile. This has been the shepherd's home and his way of life from beyond recorded history, long before a part of the Balkan massif known as Macedonia became a pressing political question or a bone to be contended for between the powers. As one watches the shifting pattern of Satanic-eyed goats against the hillsides, and listens to the wind's amplification as it eddies around the rock faces, it is not hard to accept that this man's lineal ancestor first settled the area.

He was called Karanos, and the legend has it that he followed a herd of wild goats through the mountains until he reached the Emathian plain. Those first Macedonians founded a settlement known as Aigai ('the place of goats') which, as we know from the tomb discoveries, became a cult centre and royal necropolis.

The source of the myth was the great Dorian migration of the thirteenth century BC which established a new breed of Greek. Unfortunately the physical characteristics of these settlers, as with so much else about them, is conjectural, and the lack of firm information tended to perpetuate the myth. This was particularly so with the early Macedonians, who had been late invaders of the Greek peninsula and, finding Argos and the south over-populated, apparently retraced their steps and settled in the most northerly fertile area, Emathia, huggermugger with the other Indo-European tribes, the Illyrians and the Thracians.

It is not necessary to take seriously Demosthenes' dismissive words about the 'Macedonian riff-raff', led by a man who not merely did not belong, and was not related to the Greeks, but was not even of respectable foreign descent. Herodotus stated quite clearly that Perdiccas, the first recorded king of Macedonia, and his descendants were Greeks and there is no reason why we should not take the Father of History's word on this fundamental point.

No, the division between Greeks and Macedonians was not ethnic but cultural. The acid test of Greekness to a Greek was two-fold: the ability to speak what to him was the only civilized language, and, a concomitant of this, to live in the city-state (the *polis*), where the virtues inculcated by the clarity of that form of communication were practised.

Macedonian was a form of dialect spoken along with Greek and which Alexander himself is said to have used under stress. More importantly, however, Macedonia retained an antiquated tribal society based on king-ship. Such a society, with no democratic system, was a tyranny and therefore could not be said to be a true Greek state.

What kind of society bred 'the uncivilized intruder' who dragged Greek civilization out of the narrow confines of the *polis* and made possible its exportation, with such far-reaching results?

The kings claimed descent from Heracles and by their aggressive, sanguine behaviour, seemed constantly to be trying to live up to it. To the Greeks, what happened on their northern borders must have seemed like some archaic epic, Homer to the life. These tribal chieftains brawled, banqueted and hunted — of the big game which they went after, bears and wild boar still roam the northern mountains. They were also patrons of the arts; Philip's ancestor, Archelaus, who transferred the capital from the ancient centre of rule, and as we now know, royal necropolis at Vergina, to Pella at the end of the fifth century BC, attracted a circle of the foremost names in the arts.

Euripides, exiled from Athens in old age, ended his days in Pella, where he flattered his host by writing a tragedy, *Archelaus*. It was presented in the theatre, the site of which is still undiscovered, and was perhaps followed by a banquet in the old palace, also awaiting the archaeologist's spade, where the work of the painter, Zeuxis, and the poet, Agathon, may well have been admired.

Archelaus died indulging his other passion, hunting, in the same year that the great Socrates took poison, 399 BC. Philip's father Amyntas seized the throne after the ten-year interregnum which followed Archelaus' death. He held his territories with difficulty and was actually driven out by the Illyrians at one point, before being restored by an alliance with the Spartans.

Philip was fortunately removed from the Macedonian political scene in the disturbed aftermath of his father's death. His eldest brother Alexander was assassinated and the murderer, Ptolemy, took the regency on behalf of the second son, Perdiccas. Ptolemy, perhaps fearing the potential in the lad, sent Philip as hostage to Thebes, the most powerful city-state of the time, where he came under the influence of Epaminondas, one of the true innovators of military history.

The young hostage would while away the hours watching the Theban hoplites practising the drill which had put the Greek states in awe of them and their general after the battle of Leuctra. At Leuctra, Epaminondas had taken the standard formation of a Greek citizen militia, the phalanx, and refined it into a devastating weapon.

By the time that Philip was returned to Macedonia after his three-year exile, one can imagine that his budding military talent had received a tremendous formative thrust. His skill and ideas were badly needed. In 359 the Illyrians debouched from the mountains around Prespa and Ochrid and, in trying to stem the invasion, Perdiccas was killed, together with 4000 of his men.

With the very survival of Macedonia at stake, the succession lay between four claimants: seemingly the one with the strongest case, Amyntas, Perdiccas' son, being an infant. A regency could not be contemplated seriously at this time. National security demanded strong leadership and Philip did not hesitate to seize the initiative. Macedonia was an elective kingship, but one restricted to members of the House of Temenidae, the Greek 'descendants of Heracles'. The choice lay with the Assembly of the Macedonians, the council of chieftains, and was usually a foregone conclusion. Philip would have been generally acclaimed king 'as the only one who had been borne to that hope'. He would then have donned royal robes, and received the royal signet.

The true transfer of power, as opposed to ritual, came when the royal guard, the Companions, stepped up to flank the sphinx-embellished throne and, clashing their spears on their shields, shouted 'we will fight to the death against the king's enemies'. Fight indeed they now had to, but thanks to Philip's ruthlessness against invaders and not in a civil war. Archelaus, his half-brother, was executed; his younger brothers escaped and Amyntas, being too young to form a focus for rebellion, was allowed to live on at court as a dignitary and roving ambassador, until Alexander disposed of him.

Philip enjoyed rare advantages for an opportunistic young general. At only 24 he commanded a feudal levy, which though turbulent, gave him a reservoir of manpower with which to work out the ideas gained in an excellent academy, and what was more it saved him the expense of relying heavily on mercenaries, despite the allegations of later writers. He did use mercenaries too, and would find the gold to pay them.

Mercenaries were not only a drain on the exchequer but their well-developed sense of self-preservation often led to battles being thrown away. The new king's plan was to get maximum efficiency out of his own countrymen on the battlefield and no more effective model existed than the phalanx, as developed by Epaminondas, but he added his own refinements. From that master Philip had learned the tactic of massing his infantry, between eight and 16 ranks deep, against one point in the enemy's line and throwing it back by overwhelming local superiority, instead of trying to wear it down by attrition, as in the past.

There was a flaw in this. Philip's levies were poor shepherds and farmers, unable to afford the expensive arms and armour of the citizen soldiers of a *polis* such as Thebes. However, he did possess the nucleus of a splendid natural cavalry, feudatory chieftains who took a Homeric pride in their fiery Thracian horses and gold-embellished equipment. They were to be greatly augmented when he expanded into the horse-breeding lands of Thessaly. These 800 Companions, so called because they combined the functions of royal servants and commanders with sharing the king's debauches, would form the hard point of the weapon Philip was now shaping.

The phalanx would form a bristling hedgehog of points, a flexible form-ation which could be either stacked in depth into a column for weight or thinned out to envelop the enemy in a 'pincer'. Its main purpose, however, was to provide a mobile strong-point from the shelter of which the cavalry could charge at break-neck speed and decide the battle.

The basic component of a phalanx was the *dekad*, which despite the root, came to mean a formation of 16 men. These were formed into companies of 250 which in turn marched in brigades known as *taxis*. The *taxis* was recruited regionally to create an esprit de corps. The biggest and strongest men were specially selected, as in all armies down the ages, for the royal foot guards, the *pezhetairoi basilikoi*. Instead of joining up for the duration of a campaign or when the farming year permitted, they signed on for a stated number of years. By spirit, training and their arms, they became the cream of an army that was itself an elite.

The *pezhetairoi*, later called the *hypaspists*, would have worn full armour, the *thorax* ('cuirass'), of overlapping strips of iron or bronze, with broad shoulder pieces, fastened to the corslet, and a conical helmet, the type of equipment shown on the façades of the Lefkadia tombs.

Their poorer brethren, in the line of battle, probably did not even wear armour, apart from the ubiquitous Epirot or Macedonian helmet, a circular 'pot'-type helmet, but with a comb. Their lack of personal defence did not matter unduly because their standard weapon was designed to keep the enemy at a distance. It was the 18-foot *sarissa* ('pike'), a weapon which was to establish such a reputation for itself, that drill books were still being devoted to its use in Elizabethan England, citing Philip's battles.

On the dusty parade grounds around Aigai, and later on Dium, in the shadow of Mount Olympos, these elements — Companions, *hypaspists* and other, varied skirmishing troops — were welded into a machine.

The classical authors noted with awe the strict regimen imposed. The troops were put through gruelling route marches 'fully armed, with helmets, shields, greaves, sarissas, and as well as their arms, rations and the gear they needed from day to day'. On top of that, regular reviews were held so that the king could check progress. A general found luxuriating in warm water was severely punished.

Less than a year's training was enough to bring this new model army to the pitch where it eliminated the Illyrian menace in one pitched battle, Philip leading the royal guards in person. It was not his style to command from the rear, and in 22 years of an embattled career he was scarred from tip to toe, losing an eye and becoming lame in one leg.

His empire-building was not only achieved by war. The marriage tie and astute diplomacy played quite as big a part, but his positively Henrician tastes in marriage were to prove most inconvenient, not to say fatal.

As for diplomacy, Isocrates, the nonagenarian philosopher, in calling on the king to unite the Greek states in a national ravanchist war against Persia, said that although in the past Philip might have thought himself less of a diplomat than some, 'after his recent achievements he must think himself more so than most'. Philip's diplomacy was aimed at winning for Macedonia a place in the sun of the Hellenic world. That could only be achieved at the expense of Athens, the other Greek state with 'imperial' pretentions. With its new army, Macedonia could expand to the north and west without fearing any sophisticated opposition. In fact the 'kings' of the mountain tribes in what is today southern Yugoslavia and Albania benefited from a strong protecting hand, which replaced their endemic warfare, and were honoured to enlist among Philip's Companions.

Towards the sea, however, the rising power was blocked by Athens. Macedonia has a short coastline and only two good natural harbours, in Thessaloniki — in Philip's day insignificant Therme — and Kavala, formerly known as Neapolis. It was a coastline dominated 2300 years ago by former colonies and client cities of Athens, the main naval power in the eastern Mediterranean. Yet Athens imported the majority of the timber she needed to build her triremes, the cornerstone of her power, from Macedonia, then as now the most verdant part of Greece.

As if this was not enough of a provocation to an expansionist-minded ruler like Philip, the main source of gold, and not a little of the silver in the Aegean area, lay tantalizingly just out of his reach, in the Thracian marches, again in an area where Athenian naval mobility and mercantile acumen could exploit them.

Philip desperately needed money. His pastoral, and by Greek standards backward, society could not support military adventure without large amounts of it. There is always a temptation with a standing army to use it rather than simply to let it stand, and Philip succumbed without too many qualms, setting it off eastwards towards Mount Pangeon, the mountain of gold. The mountain's gold reefs had been exploited for the Athenians, including Thucydides, and before them the inhabitants of the island of Thasos, a few miles away across the Gulf of Kavala. Despite the savagery of the hinterland, inhabited by the warlike Thracians, with their horse cults, the coastal strip had developed a rich lifestyle thanks to the mines.

Philip took them, the city of Amphipolis, which they supported, and he staked out a new eastern frontier anchored on the Nestos river and protected by a new colony named in his honour, Philippi.

War with Athens was almost inevitable after such a challenge. Amphipolis had been an Athenian colony which they had lost in the Peloponnesian War with Sparta. Philip bought time by distracting the Athenians with proposals to hand over the city to them, as 'rightful' possessors, if they would give him the key city of Pydna in return.

Pydna guarded the only pass round the flank of Mount Olympos, Macedonia's natural guard to the south. As soon as Amphipolis was in the bag, he double-crossed the Athenians by taking Pydna and, for good measure, the Athenian city of Potidea, which commanded the Kassandra peninsula (and the ruins of which visitors nowadays pass as they cross the narrow spit of land at its neck, en route to their luxury hotels). Philip is supposed to have received the news of the city's fall on the same day that Alexander's birth was announced and his horse won a race at Olympia.

He relentlessly pursued his game of guile, coupled with shows of strength. He made, and then reversed, alliances with an insouicence worthy of a Ribbentrop. States, or combinations of states, made what they had thought to be common cause with him only to find they had been out-flanked. One voice consistently gave warning of the outcome of trying to do a deal with Philip, but Demosthenes' words were disregarded until it was too late.

The struggle between Philip and the Greek states, and especially Athens, was one between two political systems. Macedonia represented a system which to Athens was already 200 years out of date, a monarchy and one that was moving towards absolutism at that. It was a system that could fairly easily be geared to war and the pursuit of empire. Athens, on the other hand, maintained the form of democracy, but where citizenship was restricted to a minority and became an inherited thing oligarchy was bound to take over. Athens was in a decadent state, and her unwillingness to take the measures necessary for self-defence was mercilessly probed by Demosthenes.

Philip is dead? comes one report. 'No, he is ill' from another. What difference does it make? Should anything happen to Philip, Athens, in her present frame of mind, will soon create another Philip. This one's rise was due less to his own power than to Athenian apathy.

The occasion of this outburst, the first 'Philippic' of 352 BC was Philip's debut in Greek affairs, the invasion of Thessaly, using the so-called Sacred War as a pretext. The war had started three years earlier over the alleged desecration of sacred ground at Delphi by the city of Phocis in central Greece. The council with responsibility for protecting the shrine had fined and declared war on the city, which retaliated by seizing the treasury at Delphi and raising a mercenary army on the proceeds.

Philip was drawn into the conflict, ostensibly as a devout duty and to protect his southern frontier, but despite early defeats at the hands of Phocis he came out on top and was able to pose as protector of Thessaly, whose *archon* ('leader') he became. He was very much alive, despite suffering from wounds including the loss of an eye while taking yet another Athenian city. He probably decided to rest on his laurels at this point and confined himself to the mere threat of an advance against the Athenian outposts at Thermopylae.

In fact he didn't have to threaten them, since he was doing a very good job of out-manoeuvring them on their own element, the sea. Macedonian privateers raided Athenian garrisons in the Aegean, carried off the

Athenian state galley in a cheeky descent on Marathon and, more seriously for a heavily populated city-state, intercepted food convoys coming from the Chersonese (modern Gallipoli) with wheat and stock-fish.

Our refusal to seize the fleeting moment, and our assumption that the future will look after itself, have effectively turned Philip into the greatest monarch who has ever appeared in Macedonia. Now at last we have our opportunity in Olynthus. It has come to us unsought, and it is the greatest in our history.

Demosthenes, 1st Olynthiac 349

The Athenians failed to rise to the 'great opportunity'. Philip had thrown down the gage yet again, turning on his former allies in the league of Halkidikian cities and especially Olynthus. This city, ideally situated to exploit the trade of the Thermaic Gulf, had established quite close links with Macedonia when it was announced that it was seeking an alliance with Athens and sheltering Philip's two refugee half-brothers.

Philip's revenge was terrible. He had a fifth column already in Olynthus and as the Macedonians approached, many of the more prominent citizens left the city. Philip's war engines — this is believed to be the first use of torsion weapons such as ballistae — pounded the fortifications. Even today the massive fortifications give some idea of their strength. When the city finally fell, Philip decreed that it should be obliterated and the inhabitants sold into slavery. The 4000-odd coins found on the site during excavations before the Second World War were mute testament to what happened. There was not one dated later than 349 BC.

The smoke rising from burning millet fields and the shattered walls of Halkidiki was the clearest warning yet that Philip had the power to impose his will on the Greek world and the clearest evidence that neither alliance nor the Athenian military establishment was sufficient proof against it. As the saying went, Athens was like a boxer, which instead of clinching with its opponent, clutched the last place it was hit.

Philip was now ready for a truce to consolidate his gains and take stock. First he treated those profaners of a holy place, the Phocians, as he did the Olynthians, destroying their cities and usurping their vote in the Sacred Council. He also gave the Thebans, who had been the driving force behind the Sacred War, a lesson in who really was now the arbiter of Hellas. He capped this run of success by re-consecrating the holy places of Delphi and presiding at the Pythian Games.

What is your greatest desire? Freedom? Then is it not obvious that Philip's very titles are diametrically opposed to it? Every king and every tyrant is an enemy of freedom and an opponent of law. Take good care that in your eagerness to avoid war you do not acquire a despot.

Demosthenes, 2nd Philippic 341 BC

It did not need an oracle to predict the future course of events. Attempts had been made in the previous 50 years to agree on a general formula for peace keeping among city-states, a so-called *koine eirene* ('a general peace'). It was one solution to the problem of unity which perhaps was never a real starter because of hubris on the part of the city-states. Now a seemingly inexorable fate seemed to be dictating the alternative — union under one man.

Once-powerful Thebes accepted alliance, as a junior partner, with its former hostage and apprentice at war. Philip used the peace to expand into the eastern Aegean and particularly towards the Hellespont and the grain basket of the Chersonese.

Demosthenes, from his place in the Ecclesia, lashed his peers, asking them if Philip had to land at Piraeus before they recognized him as their deadly enemy.

The seizure of the Athenian grain convoy, soon to be followed by the granary itself, did precipitate a renewal of war, but it was not these incidents which sealed the fate of the city-states.

An 'incident' was apparently engineered, again over the alleged violation of a sacred place, and Philip, with his voting power on the Sacred Council, was able to show Amphissa, an Athenian client, and Athens itself, to have been in the wrong. This time neither the Thermopylae barrier, nor indeed Boetia and Thebes itself, were respected. Thebes was thrown into the arms of an Athens, waking up very late in the day.

The allied army met Philip in pitched battle in front of Thebes at Chaeronea in the August of 338 BC. With benefit of hindsight it could be said that the Athenians should have fought it a decade earlier in Halkidiki. As it was, an outnumbered Macedonian army caught the allies with a ruse similar to the one William the Conqueror used at Senlac. They pretended to withdraw, then, at a pre-arranged signal, they turned and charged, yelling their battle cry.

It was a copybook example of the mobility of the Macedonian phalanx. Alexander himself led the assault on the Theban Sacred Band, the elite body of Epaminondas' old army, and they fought to the last, bearing all their wounds in front. Athenian losses alone totalled more than 1000 and the corpses of the Sacred Band were separately honoured with a large stone lion which still surveys the battlefield.

Chaeronea was the swan-song of a military career spanning two decades, that had taken a remote border state to the threshold of world power. The train of events started, within a few months of final victory, that would lead to the enterprise of Persia. But the young cub who had covered himself with glory at Chaeronea was fated, as in some Greek drama, to garner those laurels. The old lion took the fatal steps which were to lead to his grave . . . and to Andronicos' dazzling discovery.

2. The Royal Tombs

The noble Temenidae have royal rule over a wealthy land; for it is the gift of aegis-bearing Zeus. But go in haste to the Bouteid land of great flocks, and wherever you see gleaming-horned, snow-white goats deep in sleep, sacrifice to the gods and found the city of your state on the level ground of that land.

We discovered Philip of Macedon as the news circulated of the discovery of a fabulous new treasure trove and a civilization revealed in all its splendour. Reports had appeared in the British press of the uncovering of a tomb, which was being tentatively associated with the father of Alexander the Great.

We were establishing at that stage no more than an acquaintance with Macedonia but as we were only an hour and a half away from Vergina, the tiny cotton-farming community where the finds were being made, we decided to drive out and experience this archaeological wonder for ourselves.

Driving from Thessaloniki, we made Veria our base, the Beroea of the Bible, and today an attractive agricultural and skiing centre. Vergina lies about 12 kilometres to the west, just where the Pierian massif gives way to the rolling Emathian plain. We could see the distant topography of Vergina from the splendid look-out at the tourist pavilion on the belvedere at Veria. The road, at that time badly sign-posted and pot-holed, snaked down the side of the escarpment to the village of Lofos Vikellis. It was a hot day, the Vardaris was whipping up a dust cloud and we constantly had to keep an eye open for mules or regiments of geese which seemed to have established a right-of-way across the road.

We had not even an introduction to Professor Manolis Andronicos, the discoverer of the royal tomb, or the first idea of where the site was located. After crossing the barrage of the Aliakmon — the dark, serpentine river, edged with reeds and here flowing through a mountain canyon, which Philip's ancestors were supposed to have followed to their new home around Vergina — the village sign came up quite quickly.

We looked in vain for the mound which the first newspaper reports had mentioned as covering the tomb. All we saw was a typical Greek village about siesta time with the older men sitting in the cafés drinking seemingly interminable cups of metrio. We were eventually taken in charge by a group of boys and with the help of tugs and gestures moved towards what looked like a building site. A still huge section of mound dominated an extensive area of churned-up ground. Pine trees hung precariously on the edge of the cut. The whole site was wired off and in the foreground large pieces of corrugated iron seemed to be covering pits, the actual entrances of which were buttressed with polystyrene blocks covered with sacking.

This was it, the royal necropolis of Macedonia that people were identifying with Philip II. At that moment a young man appeared and asked if he could help. He turned out to be Panagiotis Faklaris, Professor Andronicos' personal assistant, and he directed us to a two-storeyed house at the back of the site which the professor rents during the summer months, while he is excavating.

Professor Andronicos received us courteously, showing us out to the balcony of his study while Greek coffee was ordered. He is a man of quick, almost nervous, gestures and a ready wit. His eyes twinkle as he recounts anecdotes about archaeology, often at the expense of the pompous or foolishly credulous and since his discovery he has had more than his share of these types to deal with. He has come to be regarded as something of an archaeological guru, being approached by those who claim to know the whereabouts of Alexander's body or to be able to lead him to a buried bronze chariot.

That day at Vergina he recounted the story of his search for the royal tombs, a detective story replete with all the red herrings, dashed hopes and triumphant but still inscrutable conclusion that one would expect. It has been told partially since, but we were privileged to hear it at its fount, with a wealth of personal detail and insight.

Andronicos first came to Vergina as a second-year student in 1937 with his professor, Constantine Rhomaios. Together they excavated the palace up on the ridge behind the village and he little realized as he uncovered the ground plan of late Hellenistic royal apartments that he was establishing a connexion, the importance of which would only become clear years later.

One other archaeological feature fascinated Andronicos — an earthen tumulus 12.5 metres high and nearly 100 metres in circumference, which reared over the far end of the village. Heuzey, the French archaeologist who first uncovered a Macedonian tomb there, marked the huge mound on his map as 'le grand tumulus'.

But there was only time to uncover a small tomb of classical structure in the Ionic order, in white marble, before war intervened in Andronicos' career for the first time. While he was serving with the Free Greek forces in the Middle East his tumulus became a military objective — and the very thought of what might have happened still makes him shudder. The Germans sowed mines on it to prevent partisans using it as an observation post.

It was six years before Andronicos could return to the mysterious mound and then he found that he could not take up exactly where he left off. He was appointed curator of antiquities at Veria while war engulfed Macedonia once again, this time civil war. The Greek army, too, appreciated the advantages of the tumulus as a look-out and it was while digging trenches that they stumbled on the first of the clues to unlocking its secrets. They came across fragments of marble, painted tombstones and news of their find could not have been reported to more receptive ears than Andronicos'. As soon as the fighting ended, he returned to the site and found a crater on top of the tumulus, concealing a barrel-vaulted tomb, which had collapsed.

The damage had probably been done by thwarted grave robbers, but their frustrations could hardly have matched that of Andronicos in the years to come. Money was in short supply in post-war Greece, certainly for anything as esoteric as archaeology, and as the first trial trenches established nothing beyond the fact that the mound was not an Iron Age barrow but had been raised for some special purpose in the Hellenistic era, Andronicos returned to the palace which had been dated to the time of Antigonos Gonatas.

Antigonos II, surnamed Gonatas (283-239 BC) was the grandson of one of Alexander's most successful generals. He made good his grandfather's dynastic pretensions and one of his gestures to establish his credentials as an heir of the great rulers of Macedon was to build the palace up on the hill which Andronicos excavated.

Here the archaeologist uncovered a magnificent mosaic floor in polychrome pebbles and similar to Pella, but far bigger and displaying an elaborate tendril design surrounded by a Greek key. Simultaneously he excavated an early Iron Age tumulus cemetery, which yielded iron swords and bronze ornaments, and compensated him for his frustration over his long-term objective.

In 1962, a decade after his first attempt, Andronicos returned to his old adversary, the great mound. He dug down from the centre to a depth of 11 metres but without success.

Season succeeded season with trial trenches, and although there was no sign of any tomb, more painted gravestones began to turn up. Andronicos was nonplussed. Why ballast an apparently empty tumulus with broken stele and who would desecrate a Greek graveyard? It was unthinkable that such a crime could have been committed by a Greek. Shrines were sacred in ancient times and wars were fought to avenge their desecration. This had obviously been the work of barbarians. But who?

About this time Andronicos attended a lecture given by Professor Nicholas Hammond in which he heard the British classical scholar put forward for the first time his theory that Aigai, the traditional sacred centre and old capital of the Macedonians, was not Edessa as was originally supposed, but Vergina. One of the pieces of evidence used to deduce this was the *De Ventis* of the naturalist Theophrastus, who had noted of Aigai: 'There also occurs a backlash of winds so that they blow back against themselves when they flow against high places and cannot rise above them. Therefore the clouds sometimes move in the opposite direction to the winds as in the neighbourhood of Aigai in Macedonia, when north wind blow against north wind.' Hammond noted the same rare phenomenon at

Vergina. Andronicos was not yet convinced and in his publication of the painted stele, said as much.

The dating of the gravestones to the fourth century BC, i.e. before Alexander broke the tradition of royal burial at Aigai and certainly before Gonatas, made Andronicos ponder, however, and Hammond's next piece of textual evidence turned him from a sceptic into a believer. He pointed out a reference in Plutarch's *Life of Pyrrhus* to the desecration of the Macedonian royal necropolis by Gaulish mercenaries of the Epirot king, who in 274 BC, had temporarily driven Antigonos Gonatas from the country. Plutarch wrote: 'As a race the Gauls possess an insatiable appetite for money, and they now dug up the tombs of the rulers of Macedon who are buried there, plundering the treasure and insolently scattering the bones.'

It all now fitted into place: the cause of the desecration, given by a near-contemporary authority and the date, which established who had thrown up the vast mound, and why it had been done.

Gonatas regained Macedonia in the next year, 273 BC. As the consolidator of one of the great dynasties of the country, the Antigonids, he had a special reason to honour the remains of his predecessors – and ensure the continued repose of his own mortal remains. He would have had it in his mind to try to confuse any would-be tomb robber. An archaeologist would have reason to suspect a diversionary ploy in the lay-out of the tumulus. The king, in fact, reconsecrated the necropolis and then took the most practical step to accomplish his aim – he threw up the great tumulus, but off-set it from the smaller tumuli covering the tombs, both desecreated and undesecrated. Of course Andronicos' weary years of search are the best possible testament to its success.

Two small problems now remained for the professor, to find a tomb and the money to excavate it. Andronicos took a terrible risk with his professional reputation when, in 1976, he suggested that the site could yield an incredible reward in the royal necropolis of Macedonia.

The next season's digging started on a note of nervous excitement. Would this be the year when, in the words of his favourite poet, Seferis, Andronicos would actually touch his history? The fates were coquettish; the trenches sunk below ground level, revealed nothing. It occurred to Andronicos that in making the centre of the mound his target he might just be making the same mistake as the tomb robbers it was designed to confuse. He tried to put himself in the place of Gonatas, concocting a 'blind' to give the best possible insurance of security. Those recurring painted stele came forcibly to mind.

Then it all seemed to clarify. Gonatas' ploy to off-set the mound indicated to Andronicos that the necropolis must be somewhere around the periphery, and he realized that the stele, the debris of those vandalized graves, would have been scattered about the mound to convince the robbers that any tombs it might have concealed had already been looted.

Andronicos now seemed to have the plan of the vault; all that was needed was to find the combination to unlock it. In fact that season was a time of frustration and anguish such as he had never known before. He was much more concerned than he chose to reveal. Money was running out and he had made his faith in the existence of a tomb or tombs a matter of public commitment.

Digging conditions were good as the archaeologists toiled away into August, but the weather was not likely to hold out indefinitely . . . no longer than the funds, and Andronicos began to think of his teaching at the University of Thessaloniki. Perhaps, though, he would try one last trench. Already 40,000 tons of earth had been removed in the season's digging without any result, but there was no harm in pushing out a trench towards the south-western buttress of the mound, which had not been explored before.

Andronicos identified the distinctive shape of a smaller mound which had been cocooned by the greater one. He sank a trench and very quickly came upon a low, secondary wall of sun-dried bricks which had been roughly plastered and which turned out to be part of the tomb attributed to Philip. Nearby were the remains of what had probably been a Heröon. Two more days' digging revealed the wall of what has been called the tomb of Persephone. The painting alone indicates its richness and we can now only conjecture on the treasures it contained before it was looted.

It was late September. They were now involved in a race against time; autumn rains were due and funds were dwindling. Andronicos made a last great effort to bring the season's digging to a successful conclusion. He had as yet no inkling that he was practically standing on the roof of an un-plundered tomb and he first turned his attention to the small Persephone tomb.

The fairly small chamber (2.09 x 3.50 metres) had been stripped of the gold and silver women's finery which it must have contained before Pyrrhus' Gauls arrived, but the underground picture gallery, which was revealed in the beam of Andronicos' torch, quickly banished any pangs of disappointment.

He had uncovered the finest surviving painting from ancient Greece — the prize occupying the whole 3.50-metre width of the north wall. The subject of this fresco was the Rape of Persephone, a masterly group of figures in predominant tones of alizarin, gold-brown and flesh pink. The pigment still enlivens the surprisingly loose and vital drawing; a sombre Pluton drives his four-horse chariot (the *quadriga*), while Persephone, a mane of hair streaming in the wind, her eyes staring in terror, struggles to escape.

On the east wall sits the grieving Demeter, Persephone's mother, a powerful piece of impressionistic painting in monochrome. Whose hand do we see here? There are so few surviving examples of Greek painting that we have no means of making a firm attribution. We do know that Hellenistic painting of the fourth century was widely celebrated and from the small band of itinerant painters we know of, one name stands out — Nicomachus, son of Aristeus, and he is the one Andronicos favours. The Roman historian Pliny mentions 'a Rape of Persephone, a picture that was formerly in the temple of Minerva in the Capitol' as one of Nicomachus' masterpieces.

Presumably it was a panel painted in tempera which formed part of the Roman plunder from Greece, as the donor was Lucius Plancus, Mark Antony's deputy there.

The other clue given by Pliny is that 'no painter ever worked with greater rapidity than Nicomachus'. Undoubtedly, the paintings in the chamber tomb indicate rapid execution, but by someone able to freeze an action with an absolute economy of line, while investing it with great emotion.

Andronicos now turned to the rough-plastered wall they had found first. They had already found evidence of a pyre near by, and now the spades and mattocks slowly revealed a curved roof, about 4 metres down under the central cap of the small mound.

Slowly, painstakingly, the work crept into another month and the tomb began to slough off the earthern mantle of centuries. As it did so another surprise was in store for the archaeologists. As they uncovered the front of the tomb, a glistening white façade emerged, 9.10 metres wide, resembling a temple, barred along the bottom of the entablature with vivid cobalt blue and scarlet. Even after 2300 years' burial the pigment looked as though it had just been applied.

What stretched across the upper part of the façade made Andronicos gasp. Although ravaged by the earth's natural processes of decay, a fresco, unique in classical painting, had survived as a kind of proscenium for the tomb. Again, the hand of a great master was obvious — Andronicos thinks that of Philoxemus of Eritria, a pupil of Nicomachus — and it is possible that the subject matter was deliberately chosen as befitting him for whom the tomb was intended. For it depicts a hunt in winter. The paint is used with the same sureness and liveliness that we know so well from Greek sculpture. From the left the fresco shows a stag wounded by a javelin, hurled by a huntsman who we see in three-quarters rear view. Various huntsmen move between the leafless trees, one of them, a horseman, being taller than the rest. He appears to be in the prime of life, and is wearing a laurel wreath and riding a brown horse.

There are ten huntsmen in the frieze and an orgy of killing is in progress. Yet the rider on the brown horse dominates the design — he is even given the noblest of prey to spear, a lion. His features are indistinct, but there is enough similarity to the figure of Alexander in the famous battle mosaic in Naples to add a fascinating piece of circumstantial evidence towards a solution of the mystery of the tomb's donor — and occupant.

At the very least Andronicos knew, as he looked down on the emerging structure that October day, that he had found no common grave. However, he had no reason to think that the tomb had not been plundered as almost all the others found in northern Greece. The doors of the tomb were hidden behind a porous limestone wall built to prevent the great pressure of earth above from crushing them. Keeping his impatience in check, Andronicos took a weekend off to catch up on his chores and to take his car in to Veria for servicing.

On the Saturday morning the telephone rang at the garage. It was one of his two women assistants, Dr Stella Droughou, and she announced calmly:

'I have found the doors and they are still closed'.

The car was retrieved, service half completed, and Andronicos drove off at speed for Vergina. He told us of the doubts he had had: 'I was always sure that beneath 13 metres of earth of the great tumulus it would have been difficult for a tomb to have been despoiled. But I was thinking of a tomb at the centre and not one at the periphery. And even this belief couldn't be maintained when alongside the great tomb we had found a small tomb empty of its contents . . .' But as he added: '. . . archaeological research always reserves surprises for its workers' — something of an under-statement in the circumstances.

The question now was: should the tomb be opened up in view of the late season, and if so, how? The door lintel had cracked under the centuries of pressure from the tons of earth above and any attempt to open the doors might bring down the whole façade.

Andronicos decided that it would not be safe to leave the tomb exposed to the elements throughout the winter. Whatever lay inside, behind the great curvature of honey-coloured tufa, would have to be reached by the age-old robbers' route — highly inconvenient for conservators hauling bulky equipment, but there was no alternative. It involved removing the keystone from the last arch of the back wall, leaving a space no more than 34 centimetres wide. First, though, the roof of the tomb had to be cleared and even this tedious operation contributed to the growing awareness of the discovery's importance.

Lying directly over the keystone and serving obviously as a valediction when the tomb was sealed, was a heap of sun-dried bricks which had once been an altar. There were traces of a pyre and in the middle of the charred heap intriguing evidence of a barbaric sacrifice straight out of *The Iliad*. Iron swords, iron fragments of horse harness and the point of a Macedonian spear (*sarissa*), all bearing signs of burning, would seem to have been brought there, as a symbol of his power, directly from the dead man's funeral pyre.

Here was a tangible link with Homer's world of heroes, as described in the funeral of Patroclus:

. . . the mourners piled up the wood and made a pyre of 30½ metres each way, and upon it they laid the body. . . . Four horses [Achilles] laid carefully on the pyre, groaning aloud. Nine dogs the prince had, that fed from his table, two of these Achilles took and cut their throats and laid them beside him. The 12 noble Trojans he slew without mercy. Then he applied the relentless fire to consume all.

Scorched pottery found in the ashes dated to the time of Philip.

Andronicos decided to open the tomb on Tuesday, 8 November. This was the earliest date he could assemble the technicians who would be needed to start conserving whatever it contained, as soon as the air of 2300 years was rudely disturbed.

That day, he woke, he says, with the tensest expectancy. 'I myself, who had written a year earlier that the excavations at Vergina could bring the most incredible reward, didn't dare to believe that this prospect was being realized beyond any hope'. Gathered together overlooking the tomb were two architects, technician restorers, a photographer, Andronicos' students and assistants, and, giving the historic moment official sanction, the Prefect of the Nome ('county') of Veria.

The keystone was slowly lifted by the chief technician and his son, and Andronicos climbed onto the vault, torch in hand, for the crowning point of his life's work.

The beam swung around a square, coarsely stuccoed chamber. The floor seemed to be bare. He was deeply disappointed; there wasn't even any evidence of the floral decorative motifs which brightened other Macedonian tombs. The impression was of hasty completion.

But then the onlookers became aware of an exciting development. Andronicos had leaned farther into the dark shaft and pointed his torch directly downward. Immediately he saw what appeared to be a mass of disintegrated furniture — and the gleam of gold and the luminous whiteness of ivory.

In as calm a voice as he could manage, he relayed the news that everyone had hoped for, but none had dared to expect: '. . . on the right I see a bronze shield and greaves. There is one marble sarcophagus and on the left silver vessels.'

Someone secured a rope and easing himself through the opening into the chamber put up a ladder to enable Andronicos to descend. Andronicos spoke later of how deeply stirred and awe-struck he was as the richly wrought objects came into focus amid the mass of decomposed matter. 'I touched the metals, bronze and silver, the armour that was untouched from the centuries, from the moment when the marble doors had been shut after the last rites for the dead.' With the help of Takis Mathios, the chief restorer of Thessaloniki museum, and another, Andronicos now slid off the lid of the white marble sarcophagus. It was a moment comparable to Carter's unveiling of the remains of Tutankhamen — when he first looked upon the golden mask of the Pharoah. Andronicos said of it: 'There shone straight into our eyes the gleam of a gold casket with the star on its lid.'

It would probably be more correct to call the insignia a sunburst — another pointer to a regal occupant. Again a classical source, Herodotus, gives a credible pointer. In fact it is a delightful story, of three exiles from the Argive Court, one of whom was the first king of Macedonia, Perdiccas. They sought shelter at the court of the Illyrian king and earned their keep as common herdsmen. The Illyrian queen did the baking, for in Herodotus' words 'in olden times the royal families and not only the common people were lacking in money'. She discovered that the loaves she baked for Perdiccas regularly rose to twice the size of the others. Told of this, the Illyrian king feared a rival and expelled the exiles. Perdiccas alone had the courage to claim his wages and the king pointed to the circle of light shed by the sun slanting through the post hole of the roof. 'That's the wage you deserve and that's what I give you.' Perdiccas said immediately, 'we accept what you give, oh king', and cut a circle round the beam with his knife and scooped it into the fold of his cloak. The brothers came to live 'close to the gardens of Midas, in which roses grew of their own accord and in which the Silenus was caught'. . . . Dionysos will crop up again and again . . . and Mount Pangeon is renowned for its roses to this day.

Whose were these bones which lay in the gold casket, 'pure white but bearing traces of the purple cloth in which they had been wrapped?' First there had been the royal sun-burst emblem. Now Andronicos carefully lifted a beautiful foliate wreath composed of delicate oak leaves and sprouting with acorns. The oak . . . sacred tree of Zeus and symbol in the Graeco-Roman world of extraordinary military prowess. Pliny called the oak wreath 'the most glorious reward that can be bestowed for valour.' But he also pointed out that Homer had awarded crowns only to the gods or to an entire army.

This garland is both trophy and, fashioned as it is of incorruptible metal, a diadem. A diadem for a god? Philip did after all, allow himself to be portrayed as the thirteenth deity in the Macedonian pantheon. The full significance of that golden larnax and its contents only began to hit Andronicos after he had scaled the ladder and emerged into the light.

He and his team walked silently back to his small house to rest and eat. Exciting possibilities came to mind. 'What had we found, what had we held in our hands? It was beginning to enter my head that these were the bones of the king who prepared the road along which his son swept to the ends of the earth'.

Within an hour or so the gold larnax, perched on Takis Mathios' lap, was on its way by car to the security of the Thessaloniki archaeological museum, where it and the other treasures can now be seen. Security became a problem from the moment the limestone blocks were lifted from in front of the doors and the keystone was revealed. The weather could not be expected to hold so late in the year and although an overnight guard was mounted by local policemen, there was no way of guaranteeing the safety of these riches in such a relatively remote place without a complex logistical operation.

Andronicos was in fact back on site with an advanced guard of technicians to conserve his finds early on 9 November. He drove back from Thessaloniki through a steady stream of voters making for the polls. 'The Greeks were obsessed with the last of the elections. Everyone was fighting his own fight and we were fighting to save our own treasure'.

Truly, the treasure was a valedictory offering fit only for a king. The decomposed matter which had formed the base ground for the treasure in the state Andronicos had first seen it had apparently been a wooden couch, with a gold-embroidered coverlet, sprinkled with tiny golden discs, again displaying the sun-burst motif. The framework of the couch had been decorated with glass palmettes and ivory. It probably had the horse's head finials of the headrest common in Macedonian couch decoration.

In the semi-circle lay marvellously wrought objects, all of which, without any stamp or signature, seemed to proclaim 'here lies the first man of his age'. As they gleam in their cases in the archaeological museum at Thessaloniki, it takes no great effort of imagination to visualize the scene as they were placed reverently in the tomb — the sumptuous couch providing the touch of gracious intimacy beloved of the Macedonians.

Contrasting with this domesticity, Andronicos saw the military panoply of the dead man. Between two pairs of leg greaves lay a real prize — the first Macedonian-styled helmet ever found. It was of iron, with cheek pieces and a high, curved comb. The images of Athene Nike, goddess of war, stared out from the front plate.

Nearby were symbols of kingship, a silver-gilt diadem with adjustable band, similar to those depicted on coins and medallions of Philip and his successors, and a sword. Again, a unique artefact of the great age of Hellenism had come to light. Despite the decay of its scabbard and part of the hilt, it retained the ivory decoration on tip and hilt, which was also decorated with gold rings and palmettes. One object stood out among the dust-covered artefacts, a great, dully gleaming bronze disc. Closer inspection showed that it was not a shield but a shield cover. The shield itself had apparently been made of wood and leather, which had disintegrated.

What remained was enough to convince Andronicos that it had been the single most beautiful piece in the tomb. The silver cruciform grip had survived, each arm decorated with Nikes, poised on tip-toe like ballet dancers — and, in contrast, snarling lions. The ivory boss had the figures of a young man and a woman. When found, the figures were badly corroded and the woman, in particular, lacked limbs. They were found in the debris and a fascinating jigsaw puzzle was set, with technicians trying the delicate ivory limbs in various positions to arrive at a design which was at once harmonious and plausible.

Andronicos' trained eye had very soon spotted the importance of these tiny decorative details and it was to lead him to the most striking single piece of evidence linking the tomb with Philip.

With Stella Droughou he looked down that morning through the opening at the debris scattered on the floor of the funeral chamber. He clambered down to take a closer look at the pieces of ivory gleaming among the baser material. He could see that they were tiny heads and limbs. 'I took one of them in my hands and looked at it. I was on my hands and knees. I opened my eyes and put the piece down again. I am no longer a child hearing voices, but none the less I heard a trumpet blast. I didn't think I was making a mistake; so far as I knew it was the man himself, in the prime of life, bearded, looking slightly tired, his cast of features noble and decisive — it was the demon of Demosthenes! I put it down and spread my hands out for a second ivory . . . . I was afraid that perhaps it was an error of perception. I closed my eyes and opened them again — yes, it was he with the long neck, slightly twisted to one side, moist eyes, no beard. It was the son of the other one — the son whose fame spread throughout the world.'

If he was correct, he had in front of him a gallery of the Temenidae of the fourth century, the ruling house at the very apogee of Macedonian glory. He found himself spinning a connexion with the Philippeion at Olympia, the shrine to which the conqueror dedicated ivory portraits of his family made by the sculptor Leochares.

After the riches of the main chamber, what might the antechamber reveal? A direct approach through the marble doors was out of the question as there was a crack in the lintel and the fragility of the finds in the main chamber would not allow any extensive fresh work to be undertaken. Andronicos decided to remove one of the blocks from the party wall, leaving just enough room to crawl through. He emerged into an unexpectedly large room (3.66 x 4.46 metres) with finely stuccoed walls in red and white. Not only was it more finished than the adjacent room but it bore all the signs of having been built separately; the vaulting was not continuous and the flaking stucco seemed to indicate that the tomb had been buried very soon after completion and before the stucco had had time to dry.

Another white marble sarcophagus was standing by the south wall (1.10 x 0.56, 0.068 metres high). The top had apparently been covered with an offering which included feathers and the floor of the antechamber bore ample evidence of the riches which had been left to honour the second tenant of the tomb. That identity offered an intriguing possibility, if one accepted that the sarcophagus next door was that of Philip.

There was evidence aplenty of a connexion with the warrior of the main chamber; a splendid gold *gorytus* (combined bow and arrow case) almost identical to the Scythian examples found in southern Russia, a gilded fish-scale pectoral (armoured piece) to protect the throat above the rim of the cuirass, and, another link in the trail of evidence leading back to Philip, a pair of gilded bronze greaves, one bigger than the other. It was known that Philip was lamed by a battle wound on the left leg and this left greave was 3.50 centimetres shorter than the other. It had also been made to allow for a deformity of the knee.

But there was other evidence, evidence of a feminine influence; and foremost a delicate golden wreath of myrtle leaves and a golden diadem with fluttering birds, and flowers, the latter a host to tiny bees which had been frozen in the act of sucking nectar. This stephane, dedicated to Aphrodite, goddess of love, is one of the finest examples of a goldsmith's work from antiquity. The diadems were actually lying among the debris on the floor.

There were also fragments of richly decorated furniture, particularly of a wooden couch with a gold veneer and embellished with ivory plaques depicting human figures and floral designs in relief, and circular glass insets.

The moment of greatest wonder for Andronicos and his team in the whole excavation was when they slid away the covering slab to see another gold larnax, slightly smaller than the first and less elaborate, but with the same regal sunburst on the lid. This yielded easily on its finely crafted hinges and revealed instead of the blanched bones alone, the soft gleam of gold embroidery on a dark ground of purple material.

The bones were wrapped in an exquisite trapezoidal cloth which had already turned to butter-like consistency. The restorers worked their skills, however, and now the cloth can be appreciated in all its glory in the archaeological museum in Thessaloniki. It has a design of a large calyx sprouting acanthus leaves, with a surround of flowers, through which swallows are flying.

Andronicos felt he was safe in associating the antechamber burial with a woman, and a regal figure at that. If the bones in the next chamber were those of Philip it would be reasonable to identify these remains with those of a consort sharing the very apogee of the king's power. There was one strong contender, Cleopatra, Philip's last and fatal love.

Analysis of the bones certainly confirms that they were of a woman aged between 23 and 27, about Cleopatra's age. It has to remain conjecture, but if they are her bones, of what a tragedy are they evidence. She and her infant son by Philip were the blood sacrifices exacted by Olympias in the aftermath of the king's murder. The mother was forced to watch while the child was dragged over a brazier of live coals and was then obliged to hang herself.

Whether Olympias instigated or connived at Philip's murder we can never know but she certainly did not benefit from it. Irritated by her constant interference in state affairs, Alexander is reputed to have said: 'No one ever had to pay so high a price for nine months' lodging!' She made Antipater's vice-royalty of Macedonia, in Alexander's absence, as difficult as possible and the antipathy was extended to the viceroy's son, and incidentally her own son-in-law, Cassander, the founder of Thessaloniki.

It was, perhaps, only fitting that retribution should come from this family connexion. After a civil war Cassander penned her up in Pydna where she surrendered. He put her on trial, in Macedonian fashion, before a council of the army, which sentenced her to death. The soldiers were so in awe of her that they could not be trusted to carry out the sentence, so it was left to the relatives of her former victims.

So died a woman whose image is only known to us from a gold medallion in Thessoloniki museum but whose personality still holds a fascination over the space of two and a half millenia. She ensnared Philip's affections when they were both initiated into the rites of the Cabiri on Samothrace. Theirs was an ambiguous relationship, in which two passionate personalities contended for dominance, and it was a struggle that took a dark and devious course to this tomb.

Little is known about the rites of the Cabiri but they are recorded as having taken place at night, attended by Dionysic excesses. The cult was very old, probably Phoenician in origin, and was rooted in nature worship as was that of Dionysos. The mysterious ritual was conducted by torchlight, and initiates are thought to have paid their vows to gods whom Herodotus described as 'resembling pygmies, made like Haphaestos, who is said to have been their father'. Just the sort of exotic exclusivity calculated to appeal to a 24-year-old like Philip. But the ritual would have had a very different effect on Olympias. As a princess of Epirus, site of the ancient oracle of Dodona, she would have been familiar with the mysticism of the cults of the northern and western borderlands of the Greek world.

She was in fact a priestess of Dionysos and led her followers in orgiastic rites in which snakes apparently played a major part. One ancient author wrote of her habit of taking tame snakes out of baskets of ivy and allowing them to curl themselves around the thyrsis of the women 'so as to terrify the men'. Philip became so nervous about his wife's taste in religious obser-vances that according to Plutarch, his passion for her weakened and affection cooled 'so that from that time on he seldom came to sleep with her. The reason for this may either have been that he was afraid she would cast some evil spell or charm upon him or else that he recoiled from her embrace because he believed that she was the consort of some higher being.'

The truth was that the couple had become alienated. Philip spent most of his time campaigning and, according to the vagaries of his passions or political expediency, took many mistresses and five other wives. Olympias compensated for her frustrations by weaving fantasies about Alexander's origins, telling him that he had been fathered by a god, and urging him to be worthy of his divine parentage. The psychological warfare of a failed marriage is familiar and in this case it was to counterpoint, or according to some theories, actually set in train, an act of regicide. It still provides one of the perenially fascinating 'Whodunnits?' of history.

Alexander was 18 and a war hero with his laurels still fresh when his father, Philip, the uniter of Greece and newly elected *hegemon* ('captain') of the Greek states, decided to marry again — officially for the seventh time. He was 45 and his intended bride was a good 20 years younger — but she was a Macedonian and her family, like so many Howards or Seymours at a Tudor Court, were in the ascendant. There is no firm evidence at this stage that Philip intended to divorce Olympias; she still held the official title of queen. Alexander even went to the wedding banquet; an evening which must have started on a strained note and very rapidly degenerated into a full-scale Temenidae family rift. As it turned out the breach proved un-bridgeable.

Attalus, uncle and guardian of Philip's new wife, Cleopatra, called for a toast; that the happy couple would give Macedonia a legitimate heir. Shouting: 'Do you take me for a bastard then?' Alexander flung his goblet at Attalus' head. Philip intervened and after an exchange of words with his son, drew his sword and charged across the room. Blind drunk and lamed by the wound to which that greave is such eloquent testimony, he collapsed on the floor. Alexander snarled contemptuously: 'See — he who would cross from Europe into Asia cannot even pass from couch to couch.'

The invasion of Asia was certainly well advanced in planning. It would be the culmination of Philip's plans for a united Greece; a cause to bring together the Hellenes, as the philosopher Isocrates had urged for so long. The Persians, themselves having dynastic problems, were well aware of Philip's plans and it is logical to assume that they would have taken precautionary measures. Diplomacy, attempts to confirm old allies and gain new ones, would certainly have high priority. But there is some evidence that murder was being considered also.

Some time after Philip's death the orator Aeschines indirectly accused

Demosthenes of being an accessory before the fact. He told the Athenians: 'This was the man, fellow-citizens . . . who when informed through Charidemus' spies that Philip was dead, before anyone else had been told, made up a vision for himself and lied about the gods, pretending he had had the news not from Charidemus but from Zeus and Athene.' Demosthenes certainly seems to have had remarkably rapid intelligence of his old enemy's death. Did he have privileged information about a Persian-inspired plot, the instrument of which would have been at that banquet . . . smiling . . . but murdering (or planning to murder) while he smiled?

Pausanius was one of Philip's bodyguards, his Companions, who Demosthenes dismissed as an 'entourage of bandits and flatterers, capable of taking part in drunken revelry which I hesitate to describe'. In fact Pausanius would have started his career as a royal page, as he was from a noble family from Orestis in the mountainous Pindus area. According to Diodorus he was 'beloved by the king because of his beauty. When he saw the the king was becoming enamoured of another Pausanius, he addressed him with abusive language, accusing him of being a hermaphrodite and prompt to accept the amorous advances of any who wished.'

The second Pausanius confided in Attalus then, overcome with shame, found death in the front rank of battle against the Illyrians. Attalus engineered an act of revenge. He invited the first Pausanius to a banquet, 'plied him till drunk with unmixed wine, then handed his unconscious body over to the muleteers to abuse in drunken licentiousness.' Pausanius appealed to Philip but the king would not indict his future-in-law on a criminal charge. Nor did he feel that he could risk the command of the spearhead of the forthcoming Persian expedition — for which Attalus was under consideration — over such a comparatively trivial issue.

Pausanius hung about at court nursing a grievance which grew with Attalus' advancement. Alexander could afford to be more open about his anger. He stormed out of the court, taking Olympias with him, and they rode over the Pindus to the court of the queen's brother, Alexandros of Epirus. Alexander himself rode on north into Illyria, a disagreeable exile from which he was rescued by a mutual friend of his father.

He returned to Macedonia with Olympias, but found the atmosphere if anything more oppressive than before. The Attalids were now the collective influence behind the throne and Alexander became so unsure of himself that he allowed Olympias and others to influence him in an absurd course of action. Philip was negotiating a match for his backward bastard son, Arridaeus, with the daughter of the Satrap of Caria, a state lying across the Persian province in Asia Minor. Alexander, thinking that this was the first step to supplanting him in the succession, sent his own envoy to Caria suggesting that he should be the suitor instead. Philip, thwarted in his diplomacy, banished Alexander's circle of friends, who were thought to have encouraged him in the plot.

The drama now moved swiftly to its climax. All the actors were in place. Philip's well-developed sense of self-preservation seemed to be deserting him for he made light of the dangerously heightened emotions and grievances let loose in the royal household as a result of his own unbridled behaviour, and concentrated solely on the forthcoming war. The Delphic oracle was consulted and pronounced: 'Wreathed is the bull. All is done. There is also the one who will smite him.'

Self-love and a sense of a destiny on its way to fulfilment combined to create the hubris that any Greek would have recognized as an essential ingredient in the drama. In his current mental state Philip was only capable of one interpretation of the oracle's words; Persia was about to feel the edge of his sword.

Before embarking, however, the king decided to secure his base by a political marriage. He arranged a match between his brother-in-law, King Alexandros, and his daughter, another Cleopatra. At the same time he announced his decision to divorce Olympias.

No grosser insult could have been offered to the woman who, in contrast to the others recruited to his harem, was a princess in her own right. But what is more she claimed descent from Achilles and the house of King Priam of Troy. To such a woman, a Dionysic priestess with a strong sense of the mystic, and certainly possessing a will to match Philip's, this lineage would be no mere family tradition. We know how she constantly urged her son to recognize his divine origins.

Set aside for a mere girl from the squirearchy, Olympias must now have conceived a cold hatred for Philip, if she had not done so already. She may well have worked on Pausanius, as Plutarch, for one, stated: 'she was believed to have encouraged the young man and incited him to take his revenge'. Did she go further and actually plan the murder? The Roman historian Justin, who wrote a history of Philip, epitomizing earlier versions, says baldly that she prepared the get-away and when she heard the deed was done, 'put a crown of gold on the head of Pausanius, as he was hanging on a cross. A few days later she burnt the body of the assassin, when it had been taken down, upon the remains of her husband and made him a tomb in the same place; she also provided for yearly sacrifices to be made to his name'. She is also said to have consecrated the murder weapon under the name of Myrtale, her own name as a child.

Whether or not she guided the sword, the assassin was already sufficiently primed for the deed. The combination of revenge and Persian gold could not have been more happily fortuitous for her.

Philip now committed the ultimate blasphemy of pride — he had himself shown as a god. The wedding was planned, in the June of 336, as a public relations exercise. Philip 'was determined to show himself to the Greeks as an amiable person and to respond to the honours conferred on him when he was appointed to the supreme command, with appropriate entertainment'. The Macedonian nobility and guests from the various Greek city-states flocked to Aigai to be regaled with 'brilliant musical contests and lavish banquets'. The climax of the festival, some sort of games, were scheduled to be held in the theatre. (Together with the city of Aigai, it is a longer-range target for Andronicos.) Diodorus says:

The Royal Tombs

While it was still dark, the multitude of spectators hastened into the theatre and at sunrise the parade formed. Along with lavish display of every sort, Philip included statues of the 12 gods wrought with great artistry and adorned with a dazzling show of wealth to strike awe into the beholder, and along with these was brought a thirteenth one, suitable for a god, that of Philip himself, so that the king exhibited himself enthroned among the 12 gods.

Every seat was taken when the king, preceded by the two Alexanders, but otherwise walking alone, 'since he wanted to show publicly that he was protected by the goodwill of all the Greeks', entered the theatre.

The lame, scarred old warrior was simply dressed in a white tunic and cloak. His one good eye must have gleamed with pride. The whole of Greece was represented here, paying homage to the one man who had been strong enough to unite them. Shortly the great war against Persia would start; Athenian would march with Theban and Macedonian to avenge the desecration of the shrines of the Athenian acropolis in the Persian wars. . . . He walked through the parodos, the open wings of the Greek theatre; the murmur of the crowd swelled to a roar of acclamation. The Captain of the Guard suddenly appeared behind him, his hand beneath his cloak. It was all over in seconds. . . . Pausanius thrust a Celtic sword into the king's ribs 'and stretched him out dead'. The assassin then sprinted for the gates of the city where horses were apparently waiting. He caught his foot in a trailing vine and fell. His pursuers caught up and killed him on the spot with their javelins, according to one version.

If anyone else was involved it was fortunate indeed that the assassin's lips were so quickly sealed. Of course, if Justin's account is believed, Pausanius would have died slowly — by a cross, involved staking out and slow starvation — and perhaps efforts were made to force the names of any accomplices from him. But if so the chronicles are silent. The ancient chronicles reveal a tantalizing mystery and a mystery it must remain. The tombs put us in direct touch with this turbulent world — it is after all, as Andronicos said, our tangible history. But the objects are mute; they keep the secrets of the grave. There are no names, as in the tomb of Lyson and Kallikles, to identify the dead, much less answer the questions posed by Plutarch, Diodorus and Justin.

Soon after his discovery of the presumed tomb of Philip, Andronicos came across another unplundered tomb. It contained the bones of two young people; one, according to anthropological research, a boy aged about 12, and the other a young woman of about 20. As in the Persephone tomb, it is a profitless exercise to try to identify the dead; (there are theories that they could be Adatha, a Thracian mistress of Philip, and one of his illegitimate sons). The decoration is enough; you simply marvel at another miracle of classical Greek painting which has survived the ages.

A fresco of a chariot race runs round the upper band of the chamber. The artist set out to create a sense of movement, and largely succeeded, by varying the perspective. Horses are seen plunging and curvetting, head-on or from the side; hooves seem to flail the ground and the wheels have the illusion of spinning fast. The forms have been strengthened and the three-dimensional effect enhanced by subtle use of shading. The tomb contained 39 silver vases, an ivory mask and part of a ceremonial couch carved with figures or Pan and a Silenus in a Dionysic rout, holding a woman around the waist with one hand and waving a torch in the other.

When we were last at Vergina a proud government was beginning to pour funds into conserving these unique treasures. Andronicos, his finds now on sets of Greek stamps, could not help but reflect on the vagaries of fate as his every wish for ways of bringing ancient Macedonia back to life seemed to be instantly gratified. One of his dearest wishes was to see the site at Vergina returned as nearly as possible to the state in which it appeared as the glistening tomb was unwrapped from its earthen shroud. In fact he wanted visitors to capture something of the magic of his discovery, through a re-constructed, and sectioned tumulus (although on rather a smaller scale!) Perhaps one day his wish will be granted.

3. The History of Thessaloniki

Almost nothing remains of Cassander's city. His Thessaloniki quickly developed into an important trade entrepôt, dealing in the wealth of the Macedonian empire, of Seleucian Syria and Ptolemaic Egypt. Traces of this period, in the shape of shrines to Isis and Serapis, were uncovered in the clearing-up operations after the fire of 1917. The wealth and hubris of the Macedonian state brought it into rivalry and then direct conflict with the burgeoning Roman republic. After wars lasting on and off for more than a decade the Romans crushed Macedonia with the help of a tactic they had learnt from Hannibal, the elephant charge.

But far from applying a policy of *delenda* (complete destruction of the enemy cities and enslavement of their populations), the Romans merely abolished the kingship, and in place of the rather shabby pretensions of the successors of Philip's royal line, raised a system of four autonomous regions, each run by a council of the people. Even when, after rebellion, Macedonia was reduced to provincial status, it received special consideration. Thessalonica, as it was called by the Romans, was created a *civitas libera* ('free city') in control of its own *regio* ('district'), and after the abandonment of Pella and the building of the Via Egnatia to secure Rome's communications with the eastern Mediterranean its importance grew enormously. A fine forum and public buildings were tangible proof of a fresh security and civic pride noted by Strabo when he called the city the metropolis of Macedonia.

The civil wars of the dying years of the Roman republic failed to halt the progress even though the contending armies marched past it, and it had a narrow call when Brutus offered the sack of the city to his troops as an incentive. Religious cults flourished in such a cosmopolitan centre. We already know that Egyptian deities were worshipped, and continued to be well into imperial Roman times, but so, also, were Greek deities, Pythian Apollo, Pallas Athene and the mysterious Cabiri, whom we have already met in relation to Philip.

The concept of the One, Unseen God came with the Jews, possibly less than a decade after the city's foundation, and Christianity borne on the same wind of Eastern mysticism followed in the middle of the first century AD. In the winter of 49-50 the former rabbi, Paul of Tarsus, and his companion Silas took the Egnatian Way to Thessalonica after founding the first church in Europe at Philippi. Following an almost invariable rule, Paul first visited his own people in the synagogue. The Jews of Thessalonica were fairly Hellenized — they even used Greek inscriptions on their gravestones — and for three successive Sabbaths Paul had an attentive audience and even began to make converts.

They met in the house of the Apostle's host, Jason, who was a Greek. But as we know from the *Acts of the Apostles* a reaction soon set in and members of the synagogue 'hired idlers from the market place' to harass the preachers and charged Jason and other converts before the magistrates with sedition, alleging that 'the men who have thrown the entire world into a tumult have come here too.'

Jason and his friends were granted bail and the same night set Paul and Silas on the road to Veria. Jason and two other founding members of the church in the city, Secundus and Aristarchus, remained faithful to their charge and were so successful in proselytizing that Paul wrote to them in his *First Epistle to the Thessalonians*; 'So that ye were examples to all that believe in Macedonia and Achaea. For from you sounded out the word of the Lord, not only in Macedonia and Achaea, but also in every place your faith to God's word spread abroad, so that we need not to speak any thing.' Jason's feast day in the Orthodox Church is 29 April, that of Secundus 28 December and Aristarchus' 14 April and 27 September.

It was a church which, however, had to operate clandestinely for much of the first two and a half centuries of its existence. The Emperor Galerius Maximinianus is remembered as one of its most implacable enemies. He was one of the Quadrumvirate which for a time reversed the process of decline in the Roman empire by using their military skills to shore up the frontiers, by overhauling the administration, and as a concomitant of this, by dividing it up into spheres of influence and thus eliminating the risk of civil war. Both Diocletian and his son-in-law Galerius, who divided up the East between them (although Diocletian remained senior partner in the whole empire with the title of Augustus) were practical, probably uncouth, men of the world, and certainly their busts and coins are very revealing portraits. Even with more enlightened rulers, sects which preached a higher authority than the emperor would have been courting trouble. The emperors of the East saw Christianity as a subversive force to be eradicated at all costs. Galerius was, if anything, keener than his father-in-law to crush the sect. Christians were forbidden to practise or confess their faith and those that did so courted death.

The stage was set for the confrontation of two of the key figures in Thessalonica's story, Demetrius, the young subaltern, of aristocratic stock, who seemed to his contemporaries one of the most tragic victims of the persecution, and his tormentor, the bull-necked, crew-cut soldier who was determined to enforce uniformity of religious observance.

Demetrius was probably imprisoned, with other Christians, in the bath-house and gymnasium where his basilica now stands. Whether his military record would have saved him we can never know, for a gladiator sponsored by Galerius, Lyaios by name, issued a general challenge to single combat.

In the highly charged atmosphere of the time it must have seemed too good an opportunity to miss striking a blow at Galerius through a surrogate. Nestor, a friend of Demetrius, accepted the challenge, first asking Demetrius for his blessing. Lyaios was killed and Galerius, who was in the imperial box, issued orders for the execution of Nestor, a known Christian, and as the story of the benediction had become known, of his friend too. Soldiers descended the narrow, vaulted passages of the bath-house and speared the young man to death.

Within a decade of his death, the cult of Demetrius was growing apace, with miracles being reported. He had, it was said, healed the sick, opened prison doors, and naturally, provided the necessary financial liquidity for a shrine, fitting his new position in the city's life. Half a mile away to the east the great brick rotunda built by Galerius as a resting place appropriate to the bones of Augustus— the title he held briefly after Diocletian's retirement — remained empty.

With the death of Constantius Chlorus, Caesar of the West, at Eboracum (York), and Diocletian's retirement, Galerius had prepared to become Augustus in deed as well as in title, but events in the west upset his plans. Constantine, son of Constantius, had been a protégé of Galerius until he obtained leave to serve with his father in Britain. Once assured of the acclaim of the Western legions he gave notice that he would not play a subordinate role to his old mentor. He marched to claim the whole empire, under the protection of the One and Invisible God. The Quadrumvirate had invoked the protection of the old gods and the empire had not been united. Constantine had the intelligence to harness the new moral force for which Demetrius had died. Galerius bowed to events, issued a general edict of toleration for Christians and withdrew from the imperial contest, dying shortly afterwards in Serdica, present-day Sofia. By this time his stock was so low that Licinius, Constantine's colleague in government, would not allow the body to be brought back for interment in the Rotunda. It was sent instead to Galerius' birthplace near Serdica.

The special veneration of Demetrius as patron saint of the city dates from the fifth and sixth centuries when Thessalonica stood like a rock in the paths of successive tides of invasion by the Barbarians, Goths, Avars and Slavs. Whenever the warning sounded, as a new menace was sighted, Thessalonians would make special intercession to the saint and certainly at this period some special providence seems to have protected them.

The most famous intervention by the saint is commemorated in the mosaic in his basilica with its inscription of how he destroyed a barbarian fleet. *The Miracles of St Demetrius,* written in the second half of the seventh century by John, Metropolitan of Thessalonica, relates that in 586 a confederation of Slav tribes came by canoe from the Black Sea to attack the second city of the empire. It was closely besieged by land and sea and the defenders were beginning to despair when, says Metropolitan John, a very great multitude of people clearly saw this champion and true patriot, St Demetrius, wearing a white cloak, first go along the wall, then move about, running with all speed, upon the sea as though on land. A gale suddenly sprang up, the north-easterly still known as the Vardaris, and the Slavs' fragile craft were swamped. The defenders sortied from their walls and the city was saved. Perhaps salvation had something to do with the great girdle of walls bequeathed to the city by Theodosius.

Theodosius the Great (379–395) was the last dynast of the united Roman empire and his walls were on a suitable scale. It is ironic that he is remembered for his bulwark of a city he regarded highly. For, conspicuously among the later emperors, he used barbarian, and particularly German, mercenaries to keep out their fellow Goths — setting a thief to catch a thief. He allowed the barbarians to fight alongside the Romans as allies (*foederati*), under their own chiefs, a complete break with tradition, by which auxiliaries had fought under Roman command.

The pitfalls of the policy soon became apparent, however, as the barbarians raised the price of defending the empire in terms of office and grants of land. This bred an overweening arrogance which aroused bitter resentment among the Greeks and Romans. Matters came to a head in Thessalonica in 390 when Vuterichus, commander of the Goths who Theodosius had left behind in the city while he campaigned in the West, quarrelled with one of the mob's darlings, a young charioteer, over a handsome young slave boy and imprisoned the driver just before a big race in the Hippodrome.

In the ensuing riot, not only was Vuterichus killed, but with him several imperial magistrates and tax-gatherers. Theodosius planned a terrible revenge. He announced games in his honour, thus ensuring maximum attendance. When the crowd were all in their seats a signal was given and Gothic auxiliaries rushed from several points into the Hippodrome, cutting down the people indiscriminately. When the slaughter ceased, upwards of 7000 Thessalonians had perished. Thus did the emperor of whom a contemporary said: 'He loved his fellow citizens and the friends he had known in private life and bestowed on them offices, money and other benefits,' show the dark side of his nature.

In the succeeding centuries, however, the Thessalonians were to be thankful for the patronage of this stern last Caesar of the unidivided empire, for his walls repulsed wave after wave of invaders. They held back the tide of barbarism long enough to permit the flourishing of a civilization which, though it left only fragments behind it, inspires a sense of awe over what it did accomplish.

At the end of the eighth century the Emperor Justinian II gave Thessalonica a respite from attack by routing the Slavs in the Rhodope Mountains on the present Greek-Bulgarian frontier and he gave thanks for his victory amid the gleaming mosaics of St Demetrius basilica, which, already accidentally damaged in a disastrous fire, were soon to suffer wilful damage in one of the most appalling outbreaks of puritanical vandalism in history.

The Iconoclasm stemmed from the apparently simple question of whether to allow the veneration of images, but it became an issue so deeply felt that it ruptured the empire. To allow or not to allow the images of Christ and his saints to be painted was the question, although deeper political motives were present too, and it forced apart East and West.

The dispute had been simmering for a long time, almost from the beginnings of the Church. Many of the earliest converts to Christianity were Jews to whom the worship of images had always been forbidden. Others were pagans who took to the worship of icons with great alacrity, always a matter of great concern to the theologians. One wrote:

They not only ask help of the above images but many, hanging linen clothes on them, place their children in them, as they come out of the font, thus making the icons baptismal godfathers. Some of the priests and clerks scrape the colours off the images, mixing them with the oblation and wine and after the celebration of mass give of this oblation to those who wish to communicate. Others put the Lord's body into the hands of the images from which they caused those who wished to communicate to receive it.

The concern was not only with the proliferation of images but that congregations were worshipping them and not what they represented.

Leo III, the emperor who proclaimed the ban on the veneration of images in 730, used Eastern aversion to the practice as a political tool in his attempts to reassert the waning Byzantine influence in the West. His eastern borders were under attack from the Muslims and he saw an opportunity to secure the support of the Armenians there, who were Iconoclasts. He settled the problem on his eastern flank, temporarily, but opened up a far more serious one in the West. Pope Gregory II in Rome not only challenged his decision and fought off a military attempt to impose it, but five years later started the schism between the two Churches which has still not been healed today, although moves are being made to that end.

One effect of the breach was the transference of the See of Thessalonica from Rome to Constantinople. The Iconoclasm reached a peak after 765 when the Emperor Constantine V launched an anti-monastic campaign comparable to the Reformation in England. Mosaics and frescoes were destroyed and in certain cases the walls befouled with ash. Icons were smashed and burned and sacred vessels misused. Monks were ridiculed in public and forced to marry. Probably at this time the fine mosaic of St Demetrius with four priests, dating from the fifth or sixth century, on the rear wall of the basilica as you enter, was deliberately defaced. Only the heads of the two flanking figures are complete. Other mosaics may have suffered at the same time but they were destroyed in the fire of 1917. The Iconoclasm was the period which saw the first large-scale settlement of Mount Athos.

In 786 a council which had been convened by the Empress-Regent Irene to restore the images was broken up by Iconoclasts, and she moved the assembly to Nicaea. The following year the council granted her wish. Influenced by the nominees of the strong-willed empress, the divines defined the use and nature of images in worship. And their decisions have, with rare lapses, bound Orthodòxy ever since. They differentiated between the divinity of Christ and the painted images of him. The icon was an aid to focus devotion on the Almighty, no more. There was to be no more confusion about pagan-like reverence of images. Furthermore, paintings of the saints, which the Iconoclasts had refused to accept, were considered to be valuable examples for the credulous and usually illiterate congregations.

An associated decision taken at Nicaea which was of incalculable importance in the development of Orthodoxy and its art was to declare the veritable Incarnation of Christ. The puritans had denied that deification and Christ's human form were compatible.

By an irony of fate, just as the Empress Irene lifted the ban on icons the breach with the West was made absolute by the creation of a separate empire. Pope Leo III crowned Charlemagne in Rome as Holy Roman Emperor, justifying his act by the fiction of the Donation of Constantine, by which the first Christian emperor, on his departure for the East, conferred temporal power on the Pope in Italy.

Irene's son, Constantine VI, who was to have married Charlemagne's daughter, thus offering some hope of a survival of united Christendom, was sacrificed to his mother's manic ambitions. Not only was he supplanted in government by his mother's favourite, a eunuch, but he was also flogged and imprisoned. It seemed for a time that his fortunes would be restored, but Irene — never was a woman more inappropriately named — prevailed and exacted a terrible retribution. She had her son's eyes put out and finally deposed him, taking the imperial purple herself, the first woman ruler of the Eastern empire.

Charlemagne's new title to the Roman empire was ambiguously phrased, and the clear implication was that he had inherited Constantine's honours. Irene's pretensions to imperial power were completely ignored in the West although reports circulated that Charlemagne had considered uniting the empire by marrying her. Such an intriguing possibility perhaps never stood a real chance of fulfilment and the humiliated Byzantines turned on her who they blamed for their losses, and banished her, literally to spin out the rest of her life on Lesbos.

The Iconoclasm returned after the death of Irene and it was not until 843 that another woman ruler, Theodora, finally ended it. Freed of its restraints the empire experienced a cultural revival under new rulers, the Macedonian dynasty, and the effects in Thessalonica were described by the writer John Cameniates, a native of the city: 'You might see the impressionable young minds busied with nothing but study of words, from which arts and sciences draw their strength. Am I to describe, on top of what I have recounted, their enthusiasm for musical harmony in hymns or the strains of the singers which charm the heart, of the diligent studies of those who have become ministers of God?'

The first Macedonian emperor, Basil I, was of humble origins. He rose rapidly through the imperial household as favourite of the Emperor Michael III, even marrying the latter's mistress. The favourite was overreaching himself, however, and riding for a fall. The emperor signalled his intentions prematurely by investing another potential successor with the purple boots of imperial status and Basil decided on a pre-emptive blow. He had Michael assassinated after a drunken bout in his villa on the Golden Horn.

After such an inauspicious start to his reign, Basil went on to repair some of the breaches in the perimeter of the empire — one of his predecessors had been ambushed by the Bulgars and his skull thereafter served as a wine cup for their khan, while in the Aegean Saracen pirates raided almost with impunity. His efforts in war were matched by his endowments to the arts and sciences and his missionary zeal, which was directed at the Bulgars as an instrument of policy.

In the previous reign the brothers Constantine (or Cyril) and Methodius, believed to have been the sons of Leo, military commander of Thessalonica, were sent to Moravia (present-day Czechoslovakia) to convert the Slavs. This mission which was reckoned to have brought the Slavs into the civilized world — the saints devised an alphabet and translated the Gospels into Slavonic — was followed up by Basil and so successful was the spread of the Word to the Bulgars that their Church was dubbed 'the eldest daughter of the Church of the East.' But far from neutralizing the barbarian threat on the northern marches, their reception into the Eastern family only whetted the Bulgars' taste for territory.

Under tsars such as Simeon they readjusted the frontier at the emperor's expense and even forced him to pay tribute. Simeon was indeed able to expand his control to within 19 kilometres of Thessalonica, marking it with a stockade, the post-holes of which can still be seen. He was able to do so with impunity as a result of one of the worst reverses suffered by the Greeks in the whole of this confused period. Thessalonica was lost, for the first time in its history, because of incompetence and cowardice.

The city fell not to a Bulgarian conqueror but to pirates, Saracens from Crete, led by a renegade Christian, Leo of Tripolis. On hearing that the Saracen fleet was preparing for a descent, the Byzantine commander Petronas ordered the columns which marked the Thessalonian ancient cemeteries to be uprooted and thrown into the sea as underwater obstacles. He also ordered white marble columns to be cemented in between the courses of Roman bricks in the walls, many of which can still be seen on the western circuit above Vardar Square. But in the midst of the preparations Petronas was supplanted and his plan abandoned — in favour of heightening and strengthening the sea walls. Unfortunately there was not enough time to make the sea walls effective when the Saracens came into sight on 29 July 904, and they very soon broke through the puny seaward defences with the help of transportable towers which they carried in their ships.

John Cameniates has left an eye-witness account of what happened. The citizenry, protected only by demoralized levies and a reluctant band of Slav archers, packed the basilica of St Demetrius, imploring him to show his special favour once again. Patron saints help those who help themselves, however, and as the tidal wave of near-naked, scimitar-wielding pirates swept over the unfinished defences, the Thessalonians broke and ran to the acropolis or tried to escape from the two gates to modern Vardar Square on the west of the city. Thousands were slaughtered but according to John Cameniates at least 20,000 more were herded down to the harbour and embarked for the slave markets of the Middle East. He himself was exchanged for Saracen captives of the Byzantines.

The survivors profited by the experience and strengthened their sea defences with towers, a more sophisticated version of which can be seen at the south-western angle of the walls in the dock area.

It was another Basil, the so-called 'Bulgar Slayer', who finally ended the Slav threat, routing a Bulgar army and sending 15,000 prisoners home to their tsar, blinded. The empire probably reached its zenith in this period; trade prospered and a respite from invasion and internal dissent allowed leisure for the gentler arts.

But the Bulgarian menace had not long receded before a new cloud loomed in the West — that part of the empire which had already become autonomous in all but name. What rested on a name? As it turned out the whole future direction, if not fate of the empire. The fundamental question which split the Eastern and Western Churches was whether Rome should enjoy primacy or whether, as the Orthodox saw it, it should merely be one of the five ruling patriarchates of the Church.

Bickering over precedence had been endemic in the ecclesiastical affairs of the empire but in the mid-eleventh century it became dangerously enmeshed with politics. The Normans made their appearance in the Mediterranean world, drastically altering the balance of power. Byzantium had clung to a rump of the old Western empire, in the heel of Italy and in Sicily, just the area that the Christianized descendants of Rolf the Ganger marked out for their fiefs.

At first the Pope was only too pleased to have Byzantine help in checking Norman nibbling of the 'Donation of Constantine' but the old rivalry of East and West had atrophied into near-total mutual misunderstanding and lack of sympathy and a full-scale ecclesiastical dispute was all that was needed for a final parting of ways. Michael Cerularius, the Patriarch of Constantinople, opened a paper offensive against reforms in the Latin rites and the dispute culminated in the Papal legate marching into Aghia Sofia in Constantinople and placing a bull excommunicating the patriarch on the high altar.

The breach proved irrevocable and soon the Pope was giving his blessing to any Norman design which would despoil or curtail the power of the schismatics across the Adriatic. The Normans' designs were checked, however, by the vigorous new dynasty of the Comneni, whose exploits I relate in the chapter on western Macedonia. In fact the check was so thorough that the Normans did not try to enlarge their territory again in the East for a century. When they did so, in the reign of the last Comnenus, Andronicos I, they chose a target of prime economic and strategic importance to the empire — they struck at Thessalonica. It was a repeat performance of the first sack. Landing at Dyrrhachium (modern Durrazzo in Albania), the Balkan departure point for the Egnation Way; they advanced by forced marches along the Roman road while their fleet made

1 The walls of Theodosius, late 4th century AD, Thessaloniki.

2 Seafront park with statue of Alexander the Great, Thessaloniki.

4 Panaghia Khalkeon (the Church of 'Our Lady of the Coppersmiths'), 13th century, Thessoloniki.

3 *Left* Transfiguration fresco in the Church of Dhodeki Apostoli, early 14th century, Thessaloniki.

5 St Demetrius, mosaic, in Aghios Demetrius, Thessaloniki.

6 Interior of Aghios Demetrius.

7 The Wedding at Cana, fresco, 14th century, in the Church of Aghios Nikolaos Orphanos, Thessoloniki.

8 Objects from the archaeological museum in
Thessaloniki. *Top left* Bronze head of Alexander
Severus. *Top right* The styrrup cup, grave stele.
Bottom right Head of Julius Caesar. *Bottom left*
Apollo, Roman mosaic.

9 Pantocrator, mosaic, in Aghia Sofia, Thessaloniki.

10 The White Tower, built c. 1430, Thessaloniki.

11 The Vision of Ezekial, mosaic, 5th century, in Hosios David, Thessaloniki.

12 Portico of Hosios David, 5th century.

its way round the Greek coast.

The soldiers and the fleet arrived before the city within a few days of each other, a city strong enough in its defences but weakened, if we can trust the chronicler, Nicetas Choniates, by the irresolution, if not cowardice of the governor, a relative of the emperor. The chronicler states that the general was good only at sleeping and was wont to turn the capture of even a Norman soldier with a couple of baggage animals into a triumph. More importantly, the governor allowed wealthier citizens to quit the city with their servants, an unacceptable drain on potential fighting material.

The Normans bombarded Theodosius' walls, particularly on the east, with ballistae, two of which were dubbed by the defenders 'earthquake's daughters'. But again the willpower of the defenders seems to have cracked first — there is some evidence in the chronicle of fifth columnists — and at dawn on 24 August, when the final assault developed, everything was soon over. Norman sappers had tunnelled under the Chamaidrakon bastion of the east wall, propping up the masonry with timber, which they then set alight. After a few hours the tower crashed down and through the dust and rubble charged the new berserkers, savage as Saracens, but knowing that their work was sanctioned by the Holy Church.

Choniates, one feels, gives his imagination full play in his description of the sack; the same things were being written about the fiendish Hun in Belgium, more than seven centuries later. But in view of the rift now existing between the Churches his statement about the desecration of churches is interesting. 'Not even churches were respected as places of asylum; priests clad in sacerdotal vestments met their death upon the holy altar, just like their congregations who in vain cried "Lord have mercy" '.

The Norman occupation lasted only a few months but created a precedent which was to be followed by Franks and Venetians. It drew Thessalonica, for three centuries, into the developing, and in many ways more vital Western orbit, before it sank into the long torpor of Muslim occupation.

In 1204 the opposition of the Western Church to Constantinople reached its logical conclusion when the constant intrigues and expeditions by the West culminated in the sack of the imperial capital itself. In the redistribution of the empire among the Frankish crusaders Boniface of Monferrat received Thessalonica and had the city raised to the status of a principality.

Continuing on into southern Greece to enlarge his fief, Boniface received a message that his wife was besieged on the acropolis of Thessalonica by a combination of the citizenry and Bulgarian allies. He abandoned the siege of Nauplion and hurried north to punish his new subjects. Shortly afterwards he carried the fight to the Bulgars, only to fall in an ambush.

Thessalonica actually passed back under Byzantine rule before the Franks were expelled from the capital in 1261, but they continued to lay claim to it, with the illusory title, 'king of Thessalonica'.

The empire had passed under the rule of the Paleologi, the last dynasty of East Rome, and one in which political decline and a flourishing of the arts is always associated. From being a principate the city was now transformed into a cultural centre which attracted scholars with a bent fot the Classics, and artists and craftsmen who were commissioned to stud the slopes above the harbour with shrines to re-possessed Orthodoxy.

There was a ferment of intellectual and artistic activity but although the Greeks, as a contemporary wrote, 'expressed themselves with more felicity than at any other time', it was a babel when it came to having any effect on the urgent issues of the time.

The cities of the empire and pre-eminently Thessalonica, were ripping themselves apart. The agricultural base on which they depended had been destroyed by invasions from without and civil wars within. It was frequently necessary for farmers to retreat into the city with their flocks but once within the protective walls they were in even greater danger as they saw their livestock die from lack of fodder, which they could no longer afford. The bourgeois took full advantage of their position and with complete disregard for the social and economic consequences imposed impossibly high tariffs. The conditions for a social explosion existed and it needed only the right issue to act as a catalyst. This was provided by the Hesychast dispute which arose from a movement seeking regeneration of the Church through mystical inquiry. The renewed emphasis on the search for an internal route to truth, derisively dismissed as contemplation of the navel, appealed to some as a shutting out of the unpleasant facts, such as the by-now-obvious decline of the empire.

The anti-Hesychasts became identified with the wave of social protest rising in Byzantium, as elsewhere — England for example with the Peasants' Revolt — if only because the aristocracy had so firmly espoused the cause of the mystics.

The latter could be branded as unpatriotic as their single-minded orthodoxy led them to be associated with the notorious remark: 'It is better to see a Turkish turban in Constantinople than a Latin hat'. It would be there soon enough, and even sooner in Thessalonica.

The jacquerie of the second city, the so-called Zealots party, rose in revolt in 1342 and drove out the wealthy. For the next seven years they ruled it as a republic, defying attempts by the nobility to reverse the situation with the help of the Turks. When the nobles insinuated themselves again into the life of Thessalonica and then tried to organize a counter-revolution, they were hurled from the acropolis on to pointed stakes.

The Turks had already gained a foothold in Europe by being courted as allies in this civil strife and they managed to take Thessalonica briefly at the end of the fourteenth century before being forced to disgorge it along with other possessions by Timurlane. They came back in 1430 and this time they stayed for 482 years!

The city had been taken under the protection of the Venetians who apparently had neither the resources nor the will to defend it. At the Trigonion, Turks gained their foothold in the defences, which, un-believably, had been left almost undefended. One of the attackers, sword in teeth, climbed up on to the battlements and finding a wounded Venetian he cut off his head and threw it down to his compatriots as a sort of gage.

Shouting their chilling battle cry they mounted the ladders and swarmed into the acropolis and down into the city.

Thessalonica gave Christendom a taste of the tragedy that was to befall Constantinople 23 years later, but the warning went unheeded. The crusade to save the beleaguered Eastern brethren crumbled in internal discord.

The captured city underwent the usual penalty for resistance after summons to surrender — the sack, so often shown in Christian propaganda. An eye-witness, John Anagnostes, said: 'For the first time, in pitiful scenes, children were separated from their parents, wives from their husbands, friends from their friends, and kinsmen from kith and kin', and were marched out of the city to the Turkish camp to be sold as slaves. Anagnostes put the number at 7000.

According to legend the Turkish Sultan, Murad, took Thessalonica in obedience to a dream in which God presented him with a beautiful and highly perfumed rose. Asking for it, the Sultan was told; 'This rose, Murad, is Thessalonica. Know that you have been destined by heaven to enjoy it. So waste no time but go and take it'.

The rose had in fact lost its perfume; it had suffered from depopulation and dilapidation in the late Byzantine troubles. As to whether its petals bloomed as Turkish rule established itself is a matter of opinion. The invaders re-established much of the city's trade and it took on a cosmopolitan character such as it had known under the Romans. The Greeks were only a part, and at first not the largest part, of the population mix and their churches suffered desecration and conversion into mosques. But the Turks had adopted cultural and governmental traditions from the Byzantines. They ran the city, and indeed much of their other territory in Europe, in largely the same way and built baths (*hammams*), on the Byzantine pattern.

Forced out of their places of worship and penalized as a mere minority among other minorities of infidels — they were even called Rum or Romans, and Greece Rumeli — many Greeks succumbed to the pressure and embraced Islam. Those that did not were heavily taxed, taxes that could be imposed in human as well as monetary terms, for the Greeks could be called on to give male children for service in the Janissary Corps.

The light of resistance was never extinguished in Macedonia in all the centuries of foreign domination. In 1821 the north blazed into open revolt in response to the lead given by the south. But it was quickly extinguished, the Turks being able to rush reinforcements to the region along interior lines, and it proved impossible to keep opposition supported, by sea or land, so far from the main revolt. Thessalonians could see the pillars of smoke drifting from the blazing villages of Halkidiki and were spectators of the slave auctions in the market places as the captives were sold at highly competitive prices.

In the Great Power politics of the nineteenth century, Macedonia was treated as a pawn. The so-called Eastern Question which absorbed the attentions of the European chancelleries really hinged on how the Ottoman empire, the 'Sick Man of Europe', could be shored up to act as a bulwark against Russia. It was certainly not concerned with how the long-suffering minorities inside that empire were to achieve their national aspirations. The Greek, and for that matter the Macedonian, position was summed up by a cartoon which appeared in *Punch*. Greece, shown as a child charmingly dressed in national costume, sits in the anteroom of the Congress of Berlin of 1878, and a statesman of one of the Great Powers is saying to her, 'don't worry, we'll look after you'.

The Greeks themselves had to deal with the problem of national re-unification with very little room allowed for diplomatic manoeuvre. The northern frontier was readjusted in their favour in the Epirus in the 1880s but an uncompromising pursuit of their projected union led them into war with Turkey in 1897, and a bad defeat. In Macedonia the fight stayed underground, until the Balkan Wars of 1912-13 gave Greece allies, in the struggle to dismember Turkey in Europe. The struggle for Macedonian liberation began in 1903 and rapidly developed into a three-cornered one, with the Bulgarians trying to annexe the hinterland and turn it into a Slav speaking area, the Greeks doing their best to prevent it, and the Turks holding the ring and intervening as their own interests seemed best served.

It was a bloody conflict in which no quarter was given. The Bulgarians infiltrated bands of guerrillas, known as *Comitadjis*, into the territory and the Greeks retaliated by arming their nationals and forming bands called *andartes*. Their main paymaster and intelligence-gathering agency was the Greek Consulate in Thessalonica. It channelled funds and helped to smuggle Greek army officers, in plain clothes, into the interior to organize the struggle. One of them was Pavlos Melas, the Macedonian freedom fighter.

In 1912 the Balkan countries managed to sink their differences long enough to concert an attack on Turkey. Greek troops captured Thessalonica on the day after the Feast of St Demetrius, 26 October 1912, and great was the joy as soldiers and civilians embraced in the streets hung with blue and white bunting and gave thanks in churches that had not heard an Orthodox *Kirie eleison* raised in them for half a milennium.

4. Thessaloniki Today

Thessaloniki was a princess of the fourth century BC whose beauty and station received rare tribute — she had a city named after her. We know little about her except that her birth took place under favourable auspices, her father Philip II's conquest of Thessaly, and that as half-sister of Alexander the Great she was a highly eligible match for Cassander, the general who succeeded to the rule of the homeland when the Macedonian empire was split up on the conqueror's death.

Cassander had a good eye for a site, a shallow crescent of flatish land round the top of the Thermaic Gulf which rose to a rocky and easily defended acropolis in the centre. It provided a sheltered anchorage of between six and eight fathoms, protected by rolling hills. It set the final seal on Macedonia's quest for an outlet to the sea, which had been the main motive for moving the capital to Pella.

As the regal Thessaloniki feasted on the rich viands and compliments which attended the dedication of this new symbol of her family's power, the new citizenry were taking up residence in a much less joyful frame of mind. They were conscript settlers who had been moved forcibly from their small cities around the Thermaic Gulf, a precedent established by Philip to colonize the new frontiers of his kingdom. However, these first Thessalonians were not slow to justify Cassander's vision and to capitalize on a natural position which has guaranteed their successors prosperity down the centuries. The city commands the only natural passage from the Mediterranean up through the Balkan chain into central Europe, and this simple geographical fact has conditioned its whole history, bringing tragedy along with commercial blessings.

Reversals of fortune have bred a certain stoic fatalism in the people of this city, which is still the second most important in the Greek-speaking eastern Mediterranean, as it was under Byzantium. Fire, sack and earthquake have time and again wrought havoc with its fabric and the greatest wonder to the visitor is how every fragment left from a rich past has been salvaged and lovingly restored.

Byzantine churches and Roman palaces are set in attractively laid-out squares ablaze with flowers and reached down tree-shaded streets. Beyond a ruin there is likely to be a glimpse of the sea. The sea is never more than half an hour and usually a matter of minutes away for the Thessalonian.

Either strolling, fishing with baited hook from the quay or taking the boat trip around the bay at the weekend, he orientates naturally to it. But he also enjoys the benefits of the countryside. The city is compact, despite having more than doubled in size since the beginning of the century and it unfolds up an escarpment to the heights of the acropolis. There it stops, still enclosed by the towering ramparts of Theodosius the Great. Thessaloniki is a compact city, the older half of which, west of the White Tower, still follows the classical grid pattern of streets. It has an excellent and very cheap municipal bus service that will take you to any point on an east-west axis within half an hour. Save the expensive hire cars for Halkidiki or the interior, you will not need them here. The smart orange buses are recommended for a long journey, say to the fish restaurants, or to save one's legs as the heat builds up and the next church on the itinerary seems a long way off.

The city is best appreciated on foot, however, and this is particularly true of the old upper town, the part of which largely survived the great fire of August 1917 and continues to put up a stubborn resistance to obtrusive development. The acropolis is a maze of narrow alleys and small squares, carrying the scent of flowers, with crumbling Macedonian houses and their more modern colour-washed successors crowding into the shade. Here, where urchins would once run up to strangers shouting *giaour* ('infidel'), only the occasional curved-top fountain with an Islamic inscription and a triple-domed *hammam* just off Kassandrou, remains to remind us that this was the Turkish quarter.

No more than a short walk in a straight line, down on the front along Leofos Megalou Alexandrou and Vasileus Georgiu, stretches the promenade to the fairground in a pattern of flowers, palms and clumps of flowering trees among which paths meander to a children's zoological garden and open-air cafés.

To try to understand this city one can do no better than to go straight to its heart, the Platea Dikastirion, which encloses what is left of the imperial Roman forum, the social and administrative centre of Thessalonica, from where much of the Roman province of Macedonia was governed.

When excavations in 1961 for new law courts uncovered this large rectangle, the development was cancelled and the site was fenced off as a historic monument. This is a numinous place; one can imagine St Paul and, a century and a half later, St Demetrius, conversing with their followers, and preaching here. According to tradition, Demetrius was arrested near here and it is tempting to think of his followers meeting covertly after his death, as close as possible to his now hallowed earthly haunts, in the tiny vaulted chapel which lies among the brick arches and buttresses of the amphitheatre on the right-hand side of the forum as you walk towards the top of the square. Its aura of private sanctity, with fragments of a fresco showing two saints against a background of blue sea, contrasts with the worldliness summed up by the building enveloping it. The amphitheatre was originally a modest structure used in Hellenistic times for contests of verse-reading and singing. The Romans took it over, built it up to the level of the third storey of the modern flats behind, and used it for wild beast shows. The archaeological service has restored several tiers of seats and replaced the stone slabs which, as in the theatre at Thasos, formed a barrier against the pain-maddened beasts.

Dikastirion Square is a gently sloping, tree-lined area, just above the suburban bus station, and together with the crossing of Egnatia Street and Aristotelous beyond it, with its Moorish-style arcades and cafés, forms a harmonious central concourse to the city. A pity then that the archaeological clearance of the forum has been left half completed and the site, except for special permission, remains closed. I could not help feeling that the excavation and landscaping of the site would add greatly to the visitor's as well as to the Thessalonian's appreciation of the city, in addition to helping its budget. The forum in Rome, after all, pays its way.

Thessalonica's forum can be seen, in such detail as has so far been revealed, from the road and what stands out, apart from the amphitheatre, is an underground shopping precinct, with the remains of a mosaic pavement running above it, on a south-east to west axis. The streets around the bottom of Dikastirion are the traditional coppersmiths' quarter and as early texts speak of Demetrius preaching in the arcade of the coppersmiths, they may well have been referring to this precinct, which is practically contiguous with the modern quarter. The arcade consists of brick barrel vaulting which covered small shops and which was supported on marble piers. The long arms of the forum were enclosed by marble stoas of which column bases remain.

Just to the south of Dikastirion Square is the first true Greek cross-in-square church in the city, the Panaghia Khalkeon. Each of the four portions of the roof terminate in barrel vaulting and are crowned in the centre by a dome resting on a drum.

The church, whose brick construction is finished in elaborate external decoration — a style eventually to take over as the principal form of embellishment — dates from 1044. An inscription on the marble lintel of the west door tells us about its foundation, by one Christophorous, a royal dignitary, 'the most famous royal protospatharios and head of Lagouvadia.' He dedicated 'his distinguished church' to the Virgin for cleansing of his own, and his wife Maria's, sins.

The church served as a mosque under the Turkish occupation, during which the southern dome of the narthex was completely destroyed. During restoration work just before the war, original frescoes were found, a rare survival from such an early date. They are difficult to see but include subjects from the Gospels, particularly the Miracles.

To retrace the stages of the mighty struggle between the new political and religious forces in the Roman empire and the old pagan ones, we visited two great monuments, St Demetrius and the Rotunda, and a tiny one, a secret Christian church. We wondered, as we walked up the hill, what we would find of the great basilica, destroyed in the fire of 1917, which left only a shell of the church and a few columns.

This is the fourth church to have stood on this site. The first, a chapel built soon after Constantine's proclamation of the victory of Christianity, was soon replaced, probably about the middle of the fifth century, by the first basilica. It was the donation of Leontius, the Eparch of Illyricum (which covered the Balkan seaboard and Albania), who had successfully sought the saint's healing powers and was cured of his paralysis. The architects, given the task of resurrecting the basilica's successor earlier this century, drew on archaeological evidence and on tradition. Probably the style and dimensions changed little through three successive structures.

Leontius' church survived nearly two centuries before the first of the two disastrous fires on this site, probably about 630, reduced it to rubble. Not everything was destroyed, however, for, as happened after the 1917 blaze, mosaic fragments were found like basilisks, almost untouched by the flames and can be seen today, the oldest decoration of Aghios Demetrius.

We were surprised how much of the physical presence of a shrine, essential to a patron saint, had survived the vicissitudes of two millenia. Most importantly the saint himself has returned. As well as venerating his icons, which Thessalonians did until the church was converted to a mosque in 1493, and again after independence, they now have what is believed to be the skeleton of the saint. It was looted in its bejewelled shrine in 1204 by the Frankish Crusaders, along with so many other treasures of Byzantium, including the famous Quadriga on St Marks in Venice.

The location of the skeleton was always known, the Church of San Lorenzo in Campo outside of Milan — and perhaps as a sign of growing understanding between the Eastern and Western Churches, first the skull was returned to Thessaloniki, in 1978, to be followed later by the rest of the skeleton. Now it rests on the left-hand side of the iconostasis.

The few paces took us across the sanctuary and down a narrow, vaulted passageway leading from the right-hand side of the iconostasis into the crypt. Perhaps we were following the steps of Demetrius' executioners, for most of these brick vaults remain practically unchanged from when they covered the Roman baths. This is probably the most sacred place in the basilica, the martyrdom, and it is appropriate that it is marked by a traditionally reverenced shrine which is delineated by a baptistry, surrounded by marble pillars and resting on a low panelled barrier scored with crosses.

This was the place where prayers traditionally brought miracles and today the faithful throw coins into the martyrdom to accompany vows and wishes, where once they probably used the now filled-in well in front of it. This site can be said to be the oldest Christian votive monument in Thessaloniki.

On the left-hand side of the narrow entry passage is a small room with an apsidal east wall, inset with a fretted marble grill and on one wall of which is preserved a fragment of the mosaic from the original fifth century basilica. It is that popular example of early iconography, the peacock, drinking at a fountain, and is a richly textured piece of work, glowing with sapphire blue, cerulean and gold.

On the wall just outside is an inscription which poses an interesting question about the identity of the basilica's restorer after the first fire — the church was rebuilt in the short space of ten years, between 640 and 650. The inscription reads: 'In the days of Leon you see rejuvenated the church of Demetrius, previously burnt.' Who was Leon? For a long time he was thought to have been Leo III but now we realize that is unlikely, since he was an Iconoclast and would not have wanted an image of himself to be put in the church. It is more likely to have been the eparchos who was in charge of the restoration.

Emerging from the crypt we appreciated what was still essentially his concept, even though another's hand had been at work. This is Demetrius' shrine — other saints and the Panaghia appear but the iconography is a lauding of the city's saint, an equivalent in mosaic of the ancient oath: 'By Demetrius, your saint and the saint of us all, the guardian and patron saint of Thessaloniki.'

Most of the mosaics are, like the original basilica, votive in origin and in many cases the donor is portrayed standing beside the saint. The best way to see them is to return to the south door at the back of the church, where, high up on the walls, are three of the earliest. All dating from the fifth century, in other words from before the first fire, they are in a linear style. There is very little modelling of the forms but a great freshness, both of colour and imagery.

A woman has brought her young son to the saint and their hands are covered by their mantles in the traditional symbol of reverence. The saint is standing in front of a representation of the Proskynetarion (his special shrine), the stand which carried his icon before the high altar, and it seems an intriguing idea that the artist intended a picture within a picture. The saint has adopted the orans position of prayer with arms extended, and his palms are gilded — in fact, he has been portrayed as an icon. This means of portraying sanctity was carried over into portable icons at a later period and often the beaten silver covered almost the whole painting, leaving only the face and hands visible. If you accept this premise that the woman and child are reverencing an icon in the mosaic itself, the artist has produced a very ambitious work for he has also created three-dimensional space by introducing in the background a landscape with rolling hills and cedar trees, with, as a surrealistic touch, a golden amphora perched on a column.

Moving right we see, on the back wall, level with the nave, the saint with four clerics. As in every representation of him in the church he is shown full-face, standing with his hands protectively on the shoulders of two priests, each of whom holds the Gospels in front of him. All three images have been defaced and as the Turks usually plastered over Christian decoration, the most likely culprits are the Iconoclasts. The flanking figures of, on the left, a deacon, with a short beard and dark hair, and on the right an elderly priest holding the Gospels, have largely survived. They have square white haloes betokening that they were still alive during the construction of the mosaic and were possibly sitters for the artist.

The last of this early trio of mosaics is almost hidden behind a pillar near the entrance to the chapels on the north side. It is a fragment showing St

Demetrius with angels. The background is composed of clouds scudding over mountain peaks, an extremely difficult subject to portray in mosaic. The one complete angel actually conveys a sense of flight, his wings beating against the air currents as he descends, blowing a golden trumpet. The lustre of the saint's halo seems to be reflected in his curiously hypnotic eyes.

As you walk towards the sanctuary you see the lamplight glinting from the basilica's artistic focal point, the mosaics on the two large piers flanking the iconostasis. On the right is a representation of the military saint, Sergius (martyred in Rome at the end of the third century), wearing a scarlet tunic covered with the embroidered white mantle patched with a red tavlion, a badge of rank in Byzantium. Around his neck hangs a *maniakon* (a jewelled collar), again denoting high or military rank.

Around the corner of the pier, facing across the sanctuary is the magnificent Kstoi mosaic, showing the saint with two of the men responsible for restoring the church after the first fire. Demetrius is conventionally portrayed with his hands on the shoulders of the other two, but the lay portraits are fine characterizations and one of them holds the key to the shadowy identity of the restorers of the church. On the left is a bishop holding the *philonion* (the Gospels), bound in gold and studded with jewels, with hands reverently covered by his long white robe, and the right-hand figure is an official, wearing cloth of gold and holding a purse and his staff of office. An inscription below states quite clearly why they have been honoured: 'You see the founders of the most glorious church on either side of the martyr Demetrius, who drives out the multitude of the barbarians' fleet and liberates the city.' Yes, but who are they?

The *Book of Miracles* refers to the great seaborne attack by the Slavs (see chapter 3) which historians believed occurred between 617 and 619. The strong, aquiline features of the bishop, accentuated by a bushy, black beard, have been likened to those in a mosaic portrait destroyed in the fire of 1917, a companion piece to a portrait, also destroyed, but clearly identified by that inscription of the crypt which I have already mentioned.

It was the reference to Leon as rebuilder of the church. The ecclesiastical head of the city throughout the period of which we are speaking was a Metropolitan John, who we know organized and helped to rally the defence against the Slavs. It would be natural for him to supervise the rebuilding of the church after a disastrous fire and who else would be associated with him in an honorific but his civilian counterpart, Leon. This, then, could be that Leon.

Facing the donors across the sanctuary is a much later mosaic, probably of the eleventh century, of the Virgin with St Theodore. We are in a very different mood as well as century. The figures are intense, there is a mood not unlike that in Spanish religious painting. The saint is standing in the orans position and the artist has caught a sense of refined asceticism in him, the pale drawn features fringed by a short, dark beard. He wears a scarlet tunic, covered with a tawny cloak patched with a grey tavlion.

The Virgin, wearing a dark red robe (the colour of sacrifice) holds a scroll with the prayer: 'Lord God, hear the voice of my prayer, for I pray for the world.' Above the figures, and unusually in this type of panel, Christ leans forward from a circle of sky, from which rays of light flash down and connect with their haloes, and points to the Virgin.

On the western face of this pier, facing the nave, is a panel of great charm and beauty: Demetrius with two children. In an excellent state of preservation, it glows with fresh, clean colour, predominantly sap green, symbolizing new life. Two children, each an obvious portrait, have been brought to the saint in thanksgiving for recovery from illness or some other benison. They display that solemnity with a hint of mischievousness that you see today in children playing ball against the outside walls of churches in Thessaloniki. Indeed, as they stare down at us they seem to have a live presence.

The best surviving paintings in the basilica are in chapels at the south-east and north-west corners.

Beyond the sanctuary, abutting on the apse, is the chapel of St Euthymios, with a damaged, and darkened fresco of the fourteenth century which is, however, a very good example of the Macedonian School of painting at its height. It shows the saint releasing a prisoner in triangular gyves and, on the right, his funeral bier.

On the north-west side of the church you step into the smoke-blackened chapel which one tradition makes the site of Demetrius' tomb, although a hexagonal outline in the floor of the nave, marking the spot where a silver ciborium stood into the early Middle Ages, is a more plausible choice. Off the chapel and behind a marble tomb of Florentine workmanship designed for a certain Loukas Spanatounis after the Turkish occupation, is a smoke-blackened domed chamber, decorated with strange, surrealist heads of angels. Their pale, intense faces peer from their folded wings like images from the art of nineteenth-century Vienna.

The Pantocrator (Christ's) pale oval face stares out from the darkened curve of the roof and, as a final eerie touch, on the east wall St Demetrius steps out of the way of a scorpion.

Two more paintings are noteworthy and they almost face each other in the south aisle, a few paces from the main entrance. On a pier is a fresco of Metropolitan Palomas, the ascetic leader of the Hesyschasts, whose teachings led to such turbulence in fourteenth-century Byzantium, together with the Palaeologue usurper John VI Cantacuzenos, who played such an important role in the Hesyschast controversy and took monastic vows.

On the south wall of the apse is a fragment of fresco in which the Emperor Justinian II rides to the rescue of a town which is being sacked by barbarians, presumably Slavs. Justinian gave thanks in the basilica for his victories over the Slavs.

Emerging into the sunshine through the vestry door on the north-east side you find yourself in a sunken garden surrounded by the foundations of the earlier basilicas, where children now play. An incongruous touch is provided by a former Turkish bath-house on the slope just behind the basilica. Where Muslims performed their ablutions before entering what became a mosque, today Thessalonians watch lurid B films.

If Aghios Demetrius represented the victory of Christianity, one of the spoils of that victory was the great brick drum of the Rotunda. Constructed as a mausoleum for the arch-enemy of the Christian faith in the East (see previous chapter) it was soon taken over and dedicated to the new faith. Only a short walk separates them. Turn down the diagonal Leonida Iassonidou into Filipou and you see the brick 'o' head. The second largest surviving circular building from the Roman world, surpassed only by the Pantheon itself, it was dedicated at first to the Archangels, giving its name to a quarter of the mediaeval city, but later, more appropriately to the Eastern warrior saint, George.

Now a museum of ecclesiastical history, it is the northerly limit and sole survivor of a great complex of buildings with which Galerius adorned Thessalonica and enhanced his own status, and which ran down the hill to the waterfront. To convert it into a church, an apse was added on the east side, together with an outer encircling wall, eight metres out, into which were let recesses. This outer wall, or ambulatory, has disappeared, but the pattern of piers and corresponding recesses, eight in all, remains intact and is enhanced with an imaginative decorative motif of architectural, possibly stage designs. The eight semi-circular lunettes and curved-topped windows which give light into the shadowy, echoing interior, reveal the dull gleam of the mosaics' ground. The gold, of course, signifies majesty, and it could well have been the fabulous palaces erected by Constantine in the new capital which the artist had in mind when he created the architectural extravaganza we see in the panels: conches, domes, twisted Ionian and Corinthian pillars and amphora-decked cornices.

They present a 'stagey' setting for the figures of saints, in the orans position. The saints, eight martyrs of the Eastern empire and some of them victims of Galerius, occupy the band around the bottom of the dome. To leave no doubt of their identity, or of their sanctity, the dates of their festivals are shown and peacocks, symbols of the immortality of the soul, strut on fake balustrades, under representations of sacred lamps hanging in niches.

Just below the Rotunda stands the surviving arch of a triumphal focal point for the city, the so-called Kamara, where Galerius could either preside over processions in honour of the old gods — niches in the Rotunda are a hint that it may have been used for religious ceremonies — or review troops marching to the East. Two roads, what are now Egnatia and Demetriou Gounari, crossed beneath a domed archway resting on four piers. What we see today are only the north-east and south-west pillars with a linking brick arch, which with a width of 9.70 metres, was something of an engineering feat.

We have to imagine them in square, symbolizing the unity of the empire under the Quadriumvirate and topped off with pediments and a cupola, 21 metres above street level. The arch would, in fact, have given the ancient Thessalonian an iconographic guide to the exact way his overlords' power was distributed. Niches 2,23 metres high, and 0,70 deep, at the top of each pier, held statues of the four emperors. On the south-east side presided

Diocletian and Galerius, back to back with Maximinian and Constantius Chlorus to the north-west, facing towards their fiefs (Italy, Africa, Gaul, Spain and Britain).

The four piers were constructed of marble blocks recycled from older buildings, over which were laid the blocks with the reliefs, which varied in height from 1 to 1.21 metres. They formed a strip cartoon of the Persian victories of Galerius, the victories which had once again given Rome security on its eastern frontiers. It was a security which Galerius was determined to preserve by systemized loyalty.

You can follow the story, starting at the inner face of the north-east pillar, closest to the Rotunda. Galerius, having invaded the mountainous north of Persia, modern Kurdistan, gives battle at a river, shown as a human figure resting against a rock. The Persian leader is about to hurl a javelin but his efforts are unavailing for on the right Victory, in a chariot drawn by four elephants, symbolizing Asia, comes up to award victory to the Romans.

In the band below, a town has fallen and prisoners troop out, some riding camels, under an escort of soldiers armed with spears and shields. Not all Persian towns put up resistance, as is clear in the next stratum, for the emperor is shown, without armour, sitting in a four-horse chariot and being greeted by women, hands resting on each others' shoulders in symbolic submission, and carrying flowers. The bottom frieze, which is badly eroded, shows Roman soldiers leading beasts, possibly oxen.

The 'strip' continues on the south-east side, with, from the top, a cavalry battle, a Roman surprise attack and Persians fleeing across the river Tigris. The topmost band shows the emperor watching his cavalry beat off an enemy attack on a Roman garrison town. Below this, one can make out, despite the poor state of preservation, another Roman cavalry attack. This theme is developed in the penultimate frieze, unfortunately badly damaged, where cavalry are still in pursuit, over an inscription 'the river Tigris' and, again, the figure of the river god. The bottom band has completely disappeared.

The friezes on the opposite side of the pier, facing the long stretch of the Egnatia, are devoted to the theme of 'Clementia Caesaris', or the benevolence of Galerius, a concept which many of his subjects would hardly have shared.

From the top we see him sitting in his camp chair, surrounded by attendants, and receiving the submission of captives, who include women and children. The scene is repeated below, with the order of figures reversed. Below that, in a damaged band, one can just make out a group of female prisoners, one holding flowers and the other a staff. The bottommost frieze shows animal trophies of the Romans, a motif continued on the north-east face of the arch, with camels carrying loot from Persian cities.

The south-west pier is better preserved and here the story line starts on the south-east face, opposite the Thessaloniki fairground, with Galerius gaining support from his fellow Dacians before the opening of the Persian campaign. He stands on a dais between two rows of soldiers who, in auxilia fashion, are wearing mail armour, conical helmets and carrying round shields. They are carrying bannerets with a device of a bearded dragon, probably with some special votive significance for Dacia. On the right Victory holds a cornucopia, signifying impending victory. The story moves round to the north-eastern side in three particularly well preserved friezes. At the top Galerius visits the Armenian city of Eriza, to sacrifice at the temple of the tutelary goddess Anaitis. He is shown approaching in a two-wheeled chariot and a deputation of citizens comes out to greet him with flags and flowers. The temple rises in the background.

Having dedicated his arms, the emperor goes into action against the Persians. Wearing armour decorated with the she-wolf of Rome suckling Romulus and Remus, he rides across the centre of the frieze, fighting hand to hand with the Persian commander. Naturally he wins, the eagle flying over his head in token of this. Two younger officers in the thick of the fray are thought to have been Constantine and Licinius, ironically the very men who were to crop Galerius' honours from his brow.

After battle, triumph, and the conciliation of the defeated — Pietas Augustorum — is shown in the frieze below. Here the unity of the Quadrumvirate is emphasized. Diocletian and Galerius are shown seated with winged victories crowning them, and the coadjutors, Constantius and Maximinian, are standing beside them. Other figures represent the liberation of Mesopotamia and Armenia. The victorious section ends with representations of winged victories standing in conch-shaped niches.

The badly defaced north-western face honours the conqueror of Asia and refers to a second battle and, perhaps, an echo of Alexander's campaigns, the capture of the Persian king's household. This, then, was the record of Galerius' triumphs which the Thessalonians, no doubt, grateful for his patronage of their city — a classical writer spoke of him constructing many public works — erected in his honour.

The arch was linked on one side to the Rotunda by a broad road, lined with stoas and on the other was joined, through a peristyle with the vestibule of the imperial palace, a large complex of buildings which stretched down towards the sea.

Fragments have been excavated over an area of 10,000 square metres, which still gives a good impression of the sheer size of the place. We followed them down the pedestrian precinct of Demetriou Gounari, until it opened out into Platea Navarinou. The palace was laid out along the lines of a Roman camp, with buildings arranged along roads running at right angles to one another. We were able to recapture something of the plan-in-square, as we looked across the ruins from the paved precinct where boys play football and shoppers pass the time of day.

The most impressive building is the Octagon, which survives up to the first storey. Its purpose is unclear although it may have been intended as a mausoleum. Its plan closely resembles the Octagon in Diocletian's palace in Spolito. Both buildings were topped by great cupolas and their geometric patterned floors extended into semi-circular niches. Permission to enter the site has to be gained in writing from the archaeological museum. Only a name plate and a few stones today serve to remind us of the Hippodrome, where the infamous massacre took place. It covered what is now Platea Ipodromiou.

So much of the fascinating mosaic of ancient Thessalonica is now of course underground but occasionally this was done intentionally, as in a tiny, secret church which is tucked into a corner of a sunken garden opposite the church of Aghia Sofia at the top of Pavlou Mela.

The low, barrel-vaulted passage which winds down to the chapel forces anyone of average height to bend double. It opens out into a space where perhaps a dozen people can stand in comfort and which is now adorned with small portable icons. It is not difficult to imagine, as one watches the lamplight flickering on the ornate figures of the saints, members of that early church, Paul's Thessalonians, covertly celebrating Mass away from the prying eyes of their pagan neighbours. In Orthodox churches, at a certain point in the service, a call goes out: 'The doors, the doors, in wisdom let us attend' — a reminder of the days when it was safe to admit only initiates to the sacred rites.

The transfer of the centre of power to Constantinople in no way diminished Thessalonica's status and soon it was to find a Christian patron as munificent as Galerius had been. Under Constantine, Christianity received a cachet as the faith that had been embraced by the emperor, but it had not yet totally ousted paganism. It took Theodosius the Great's conversion to bring Christianity out of the underground and begin to adorn the city with the first of its splendid churches. From the emperor's declaration of the Nicaean Creed as the only acceptable form of official faith the Church could go forward in security.

Its earliest surviving unaltered building, indeed one of the earliest Christian churches, is the Acheiropoietos (pronounced *A-heero-potos*) basilica. It stands well below the present street level in Aghia Sofia, in the centre of town, and in the Byzantine era must have looked no less imposing than Aghios Demetrius. The exterior has a patina of age, necessarily lacking in the other basilica, but inside, the long years of foreign occupation have dealt much more harshly with the church.

The Acheiropoietos is large — its nave is almost 37 metres long and 15.5 metres wide — but now devoid of decoration except in the sofits, or under part of the curved-topped arches. The deep, rich colour of these mosaic fragments is accentuated by the surrounding cool, light-grey marble and white plaster work. In none of the fragments is a human or divine image to be seen, an interesting art historical point for it indicates that the ideas of the Iconoclasm were already present long before it received official sanction.

Writhing tendrils and waving plant forms of the mosaics reflect the acanthus leaves in the Corinthian capitals below. Peacocks drink at the fountain of life and their lyre tails, in deep sapphire, frame the composition, fluted bowls hang in a gold tesselated arc, sprouting exotic deep pink flowers and amphora trail vines heavy with black grapes.

To explain the absence of decoration in Acheiropoietos one has to look no farther than the fifth pillar on the left as one walks up the nave. An

Arabic inscription fringed with laurel leaves, reads: 'The Sultan Murad Khan took Thessalonica in 883' (by the Hagira dating). The inscription marks the conversion of the church to Muslim worship, shortly after the fall of the city. Many churches were to follow suit.

Acheiropoietos dates from the fifth century and was one of the first churches dedicated to the Virgin under the title 'Mother of God', proclaimed by the Council of Ephesus in 431 to end the Nestorian heresy. But there was an earlier building on the site as can be seen on the left-hand side of the sanctuary, where a piece of Roman mosaic flooring in a geometric pattern in black, white and ochre has been exposed.

The empire might be buttressed spiritually by its new monotheism, but Theodosius realized that it also needed physical defences. He built a circuit of walls five miles in length, and today you can follow about half that distance, up and around the acropolis. The near-complete section of the ramparts runs from behind Vardar Square on the south-west, up to the edge of the rocky ridge to the acropolis proper — which affords spectacular views of the city — and down the eastern flank to end just short of the city hospital.

From the water front or the Egnatia it looks a deceptively easy walk and certainly the atmosphere of the old town is best captured on foot. But it is best to tackle the acropolis in two itineraries, making use of the regular bus service for part of the way, unless you feel particularly energetic. The numbers 23 and 24 buses make a circle up and down the acropolis.

Theodosius, or rather his engineer Hormisdas', handiwork is best appreciated on the western flank. Vardar Square, the busy intersection where traffic turns off for Yugoslavia and Bulgaria, or starts its journey west along the Via Egnatia proper, was in the Byzantine period the site of the Golden Gate. From here the Egnatian Way passed along the edge of the city, out through the Letaia Gate and then swung clear of the walls to the north-east in an early example of a ring road. It is this urban section, behind the present-day Odos Irinis, that a still well-preserved section of the wall was specifically meant to guard. But before following the wall beyond Aghios Demetriou it is worth making a diversion to see the Dhodeki Apostoli. It nestles in a small paved square leading off Demetriou, on the right-hand side as you turn down from Langadas and the busy road intersection where the Letaia Gate once stood. Dhodeki Apostoli is probably the most attractive decorated brick church in Thessaloniki and very important architecturally. Externally it represents the most complete and satisfying development of the Greek cross-in-square, with uplifted dome to be found in Macedonia or, now, elsewhere. Internally it has exceptional mosaics of the so-called Revival period of Byzantine art.

The somewhat shabby surroundings in no way detract from the impact of the opulent curved surfaces, seemingly every inch of which are covered by raised patterns of brick. It is a mosaicist's fantasy translated to the exterior in terms of brick and is perhaps best seen as the evening sunlight brings out the deep red and ochre tones and deeply etches the patterns with shadow.

This church, which neither of those meticulous recorders of Greece,

The Palace of Antigonos Gonatas, Vergina.

Philippi, basilica B, as seen from the forum.

Objects including shield cover and leg greaves as they were found in the royal tomb, Vergina.

Leake and Cousinery, saw fit to mention, was probably a seminal influence in Byzantine ecclesiastical architecture in Serbia and Russia. The sophisticated design, with the elevated five domes accentuated by a low horizontal of the roof line, makes just as strong an impact once you are inside. However, the sheer height does make it difficult to see the marvellous mosaics, only discovered a matter of a decade ago. I recommend packing a pair of field glasses in your luggage specifically for just such an occasion.

The mosaics, which have been likened to those in the Karye Kamii in Istanbul, regarded as the touchstone of late Byzantine church decoration, are well preserved and can be seen on the barrel vaulting and pendentives which support the dome.

On the south vault are scenes of the Nativity and Baptism of Christ, which show very clearly the humanizing influence of the Revival. The bathing of the infant Christ, for instance, has the child turning away with a look of trepidation while his mother tests the temperature of the water and gives instructions to a maid servant about filling the basin. Again, the shepherds are true rustics. One of them is wearing a goatskin coat and leggings and they both look up in awe at the Star of Bethlehem. The Magi ride eagerly forward, discussing the wonders they are about to see.

The Entry into Jerusalem, on the west vault, incorporates a lively crowd scene and details of landscape and architecture, while the accompanying Transfiguration is a composition worthy of the patronage of a Constantinople patriarch (Niphon I was the begetter of both church and decoration in the first one-and-a-half decades of the fourteenth century). This was the last great flowering of Byzantine culture under the Palaeologi and this mosaic, in particular, bears the hallmark of metropolitan craftsmanship. It has a marvellous tension, with the disciples visibly trembling in fear among the rocks, the spiky outcrops of which are repeated in the rays of light emanating from Christ. His robe, and the mandorla surrounding him, have the shining quality referred to in Scripture and both his head, and those of the prophets on either side, are given really humanistic quality. Fragments of paintings covering the vertical walls of the church are of good quality but not as important as the mosaics.

The tour of the ramparts starts on crossing Aghios Demetrios. Turning into Odos Diopoulos, the walls rise straight ahead and a right-hand path up Odos Stournara leads into the long street of Oliados, lined with workers' flats. In a small square, about half way up and just off to the left, is another fine cross-in-square brick church, Aghia Katerini. It is slightly smaller than Dhodeki Apostoli, but with its raised brickwork patterns and little domes could have been a pilot for it. It is a true neighbourhood church and is best visited on a Sunday afternoon when it becomes the focus of communal activity. While it is true that some of Greece's Byzantine heritage has now become a museum, most churches are living places of worship and the weekend is the best time to appreciate that role, say during a baptism. We wandered across the square, past a small flower garden, and the separate wrought-iron belfry. We realized from the low chanting coming through the open doors and the figures in Sunday best bound the same way as ourselves that a service was in progress. It turned out to be possibly the most appealing among the Orthodox rites, the reception of another member, in this case a baby girl.

The water in the portable metal font was being tested as carefully as in that mosaic. Meanwhile prayers were being said in the narthex and the godmother had made her vows to the *papas*. The *papas*, now wearing a white damask surplice, breathed on the child three times in token of the giving of the Holy Spirit, and while she was taken to one side to be undressed by aunts, he rolled up his sleeves and gave the water an elbow test. A younger *papas* poured holy oil into the font in the shape of the cross and the relatives formed a circle, young boys holding tapers, as the baby was wrapped in a towel and brought over.

The younger *papas* again made the sign of the cross on the baby's back, and then to an accompaniment of howls, he began to bathe her. This was performed thoroughly, including the hair, and the child was then handed over to her godmother, who held her while the *papas* traced the sign of the cross on her face, hands and feet. Finally he cut three locks of her hair and put them into the font.

The ceremony ended in family conviviality in which any visitor would have been welcome to participate. Flash bulbs popped, sweets wrapped inside china animal figures, and decorated with pink and white bows, were distributed and the *papades*, back in their cassocks, mingled with their parishioners, eating sweets, exchanging jokes and hugging some of the baby's young relatives.

A ten-minute walk through the alleys of the lower acropolis brought us to Profitis Ilia, the third of the exotically decorated brick churches in Thessaloniki. It stands out on its own square on a rise between Olibiados and Kassandrou, from which it is most easily reached, by Odos Profitis Ilia.

The Prophet Elijah — it honours a figure who has a special place in Orthodox hagiography because of his visionary zeal — dates from the fourteenth century and formed the katholikon of a monastery, as did the Dhodeki Apostoli. We had been told by the *papas* at Aghia Katerini to make a point of viewing the church from the south and we saw immediately what he meant. The central dome leans at an angle away from the cross of barrel vaulting on which it stands, rather like the leaning spire of Chesterfield.

The interior gives a surprising sense of space, much more than the other two brick churches, and between the arms of the 'cross' lie small domed chapels. The church was converted into a mosque soon after the capture of the city and the surviving fresco work is fragmentary and in poor condition, although of interest as examples of the Macedonian School.

On the upper part of the east wall of the narthex there is a representation of the Massacre of the Innocents and to the right of it the Temptation of Christ. In the sofits of the windows are fragments of portraits of ascetics. Beside the south door can be seen, dimly, a painting of St David of Salonika sitting in an almond tree and above him are St Ioasef, king of India, and St Barlaam, who is supposed to have converted him to Christianity.

We had made a sufficiently early start still to have enough time left to have lunch on the acropolis and see Hosios David too. This little gem of a church sometimes eludes the visitor, yet it is perfectly easy to find, perched on a tiny belvedere underneath the Vlattadon ridge. To reach it we walked along Kassandrou, took a left turn into Aghia Sofia and followed it up to the beginning of the maze of alleys which thread their way around the acropolis. We took the little lane Odos Timotheou which led us in turn up to the higher slopes, on to in fact Odos Dimitri Poliokitou. Opposite number 79, a flight of steps curved down between small balconied houses. We walked down for a few minutes until we saw a pantiled roof directly below.

The original church of Hosios David, dating probably from the late fifth century, was designed in the form of an inscribed Syrian cross. It was truncated in the Turkish period but what remains is rewarding enough. Hosios David stands on a little belvedere fringed with pines and flowering oleander which form pools of shadow, and is fronted by a south-facing porch with columns, under a deep-eaved, tiled roof. The dome, together with much of the western end of the church disappeared in Turkish times. The elderly guardian, whose house overlooks the church, hurried to open the door, illuminating the rough-cast of the original vaulting, uncovered after centuries of concealment beneath Turkish plaster. But only when he turned on the light were we able to see the subtle colours of the church's real glory, the mosaic of the Vision of Ezekial, which fills the apse.

Contemporary with the building of the church, it is a remarkable evocation in coloured stone of one of the great pieces of mystical writing in the Old Testament. The Prophet Ezekial sits on the right of the composition, dreaming of a regenerated Israel. Dream-like the subject certainly is, but also rendered with a Hellenistic naturalness that had not yet fallen to Iconoclastic ideas. The picture is dominated by a Christ shown, very unusually, as a beardless youth, seated on a rainbow, and holding a scroll. He wears a deep blue robe and pink tunic.

The rainbow arcs across almost the whole mosaic, linking the celestial with the fresh, spring landscape of meadows and trees, bound by the cleansing stream of which the prophet speaks, and filled with recognizable fish. The gradations of colour in the rainbow seem to blend into a warm and delicate glow which is emphasized by the gold tesselation of the rest of the apse. This masterpiece of a mosaic only came to light in 1921.

On our way out, we looked up to the upper right-hand wall of the narthex where a Baptism scene of a later date shows a figure of Christ painted with great delicacy as though partly submerged in the Jordan. On the opposite wall is a Nativity scene with a definitely pre-Revival period Christ. The artist has portrayed, instead of a baby, a miniature man, with broad shoulders and a mature face, and, in the less sophisticated manner, with eyes open even though he is supposed to be slumbering. A sad-looking Virgin in a mandorla sits against a rocky landscape, watched by white donkeys.

Climbing back the way we had come brought us, a few paces up the hill, to a flight of white marble steps, leading up to the walls at their most spectactular point, Odos Eptapirgion, terminating in a belvedere and the huge circular tower of the Trigonion, the defence work at the north-east angle of the walls, which corresponds with the White Tower at the south-east. This point, near where the Turks forced their entry to the city in 1430, is now a pleasant walk, with views out over the eastern bay towards Halkidiki, and with gardens full of orange lillies.

The acropolis proper, the rocky pinnacle of the city, is capped by the Eptapirgion, a seven-towered fortification which was, and remains, a prison and is out of bounds. It formed the point of a self-contained walled salient or bastion, sealed to the south, along the height of the Vlattadon by a wall which ended in the Trigonion.

Walking with this wall on our left, we passed two towers built under the Palaeologi, the last dynasty of Byzantium, in a vain attempt to stave off the fate that was to befall in 1430, and between the towers we noticed a secret postern to allow sudden sorties to beat off any attack on the height of the acropolis. Just beyond the Trigonion was a small gate giving access to the east side of the acropolis and with a Byzantine inscription recording that it was built in 1355 by Anna Palaeologina, widow of Emperor Andronicos III.

We stopped for a meal at this point, at one of the small terrace restaurants just inside the Eptapirgion, beyond the wall. The buses come up Odos Akropoleos and go through the upper of two gates which have been un-blocked for traffic. We caught one back to Aghios Demetriou.

A second itinerary uses as a departure point what is at once an alternative mother church to the basilica of Aghios Demetrios and a very important Byzantine monument, and also takes in the area of the eastern ramparts. It is a simple bus and walking tour which ends up at one of the most charming restaurant areas of the city.

Aghia Sofia ('Holy Wisdom'), which can be glimpsed from the Rotunda, down the long arm of Patriarhou Ioakim, is the closest Thessalonica managed to reproduce its namesake in Constantinople. It is a transitional building between the basilica and the domed church, a provincial experiment using the new Oriental feature of the dome on a daringly large scale.

The dome, which was already fairly common in the East, had been adopted in the capital. The first dome collapsed, however, and perhaps this failure worried the architects in Thessalonica. It is likely, therefore, that they adopted a more conservative approach, mooring their dome on to a solidly constructed near-square, instead of opting for the more radical approach of arching pendentives.

However, although the dome does not rival that of Aghia Sofia in Constantinople, the mosaics inside it do. The band portraying the Ascension is typical of the style of Constantinople and represents the very best of it. The mosaics are lit by natural light from below and the dome is accessible by a walkway which runs round the bottom of it. The light, linear style with which the figures of the Apostles are portrayed can, therefore, be appreciated at close quarters. The figures have been deliberately elongated to counteract the optical effect of foreshortening. They stand in a fantastic landscape of trees and stylized rocks looking up at the Pantocrator seated on a rainbow and supported by two flying angels. His figure lacks anatomical credibility and is evidence that the Byzantine artists of the period simply did not know how to place a seated figure in a curved plane.

The Panaghia (the Virgin Mary), in the apse below, is a century earlier, but with all its imperfections it is a much more arresting figure. Her eyes seem to meet yours as soon as you enter the church and never leave you, no matter in which direction you move. This rather ghostly and commanding figure in a dark robe, begetter of suffering and sacrifice rather than the gentle Virgin of Western tradition, is eloquent testimony of the great upheaval of the Iconoclasm, if you can 'read' the evidence.

This particular figure can, in fact, be dated to the artistic counter-revolution — of no more than 20 years — which separated the two periods of the image ban. This was in the reign of the Empress Irene (797—802) who loved images and tried in her brief reign to reverse the results of a sustained 74-year campaign against them. Her monogram can be seen in the vaulting above the sanctuary.

How far art suffered in this period can be seen in the figures of this Virgin and Child, which have a puppet-like quality, again displaying the lack of confidence in portraying a figure in a curved space. As the Byzantine world felt its way out of the constrictions of the Iconoclasm, its diffidence was displayed in the portrayal of single, often awkward figures like this. And they were often placed straight over the simple crosses which had been the only decoration allowed in apse and sanctuary. The arms of the cross which the Panaghia of Aghia Sofia replaced can just be seen as a faint shadow behind her head and parallel with her shoulders. However, although the cross disappeared, other aspects of the Iconoclasm were retained by apprehensive clergy.

Other than her throne, there is no decoration in the apse, which is a glittering golden concave. Also her robe is of a funeral hue. The puritanical streak in Byzantium, of which this mosaic speaks, was soon to return with renewed vigour and was only ended after having held sway for almost a century.

Leaving Aghia Sofia we walked back up Patriarhou Ioakim to the Arch of Galerius, keeping on past it to where Egnatia merges with the road intersection at the top of the fairground. Here we turned sharp left up the extension of Vassilis Sofias, known as Panepistimiou, after the University of Thessaloniki, which has spread out from the former Turkish Officers' School to cover a large area behind the fairground. At the top we bore left into the entrance of Athinas, until we saw the Turkish Consulate, with its blue and white striped police box, on the corner of Apostolou Pavlou.

Walking up this winding alleyway until we reached a small square, we half circled it and headed back in the direction from which we had come, down Odos Irodotou. A few paces down on the left lay a lovely walled garden with a Macedonian balconied house standing on the left. Facing us through the gate was the odd man out of Thessalonian churches, Aghios Nikolaos Orfanos (accent on the 'a').

With its basilican form — three oblong halls ending in apses — and pitched roof, we could easily have been looking at an early Byzantine church. In fact what we entered was an elaborately painted late building. The church is unique; how it escaped becoming a mosque we do not know. However it happened the paintings were saved from destruction.

The high quality of these paintings, which cover most of the interior, point to wealthy patronage and indeed Orfanos is thought to have been an appendage of the Vlattadon Monastery. In the Middle Ages monasteries in Greece, as elsewhere in the Christian world, were great landowners and repositories of wealth. From an art historical viewpoint the frescoes are extremely important. They are some of the finest early examples of the Byzantine paintings belonging to the fourteenth century but can be further pin-pointed to the Thessalonian variant of it, by a miniature-like clarity of form and by their liveliness — a great deal of care and observation has been given to the landscape and other features of the backgrounds, making each individual fresco a very complete and convincing composition.

They illustrate various themes: the Twelve Feasts of the Church, a cycle of the Passion, the Akathstos Hymn and scenes from the life of St Nicholas. The figures show the full range of human emotions. The narthex acts as a devotional introduction to the church; it is dedicated to St Nicholas and therefore he is the subject of the first story strip we see as we enter. We see his birth; see him sitting at school, and then follow him to his ordination as a priest. Below the early life are scenes from the miracles. The saint comes to the king in a dream telling him not to have a criminal executed. The execution is ordered nevertheless — but the executioner's hand is stayed. In the next frame Nicholas pours oil on troubled waters, which is why every Greek fisherman carries a medallion or an icon of the saint in his boat. Finally, we see him on his death bed and suddenly the model for the gilded and carved lamp standard in the painting is standing in front of us in reality, an amazing survival.

By the time Aghios Nikolaos Orfanos was built, at the beginning of the fourteenth century, the Iconoclastic controversy was, of course, long settled, and the position of the Pantocrator and Panaghia immovably fixed in every church. Except, that is, when an archaic style like the basilica was used. Then, as here, Christ was placed in a triangle — a Resurrected Saviour looking down from above the apse, and supported below by an austere figure of his mother in the orans position. Facing him at the other end of the church is the Assumption, over a fine Nativity scene, a series of five paintings in one panel. The Christ Child seems to regard his adoration with a certain apprehension; the Virgin here is a slender, pensive figure in a dark robe.

On the south wall begins the cycle of the life of Christ. From the Presentation in the Temple (an intimate touch is provided by Joseph offering two pigeons at the altar) we pass to Christ's Baptism — his face is painted with great character — and on to the Raising of Lazarus. Christ is making a gesture of command and a sexton is unwinding Lazarus' grave-cloths with one hand while holding his nose with the other.

Over the west door is portrayed the Entry into Jerusalem, a superb Transfiguration with Christ's heavenly glory indicated by a gleaming white robe and the whole phenomenon proving too much for the Apostles, who are tumbling over the rocks in fear. We pass to a Crucifixion which is very reminiscent of a Cimabue study of about the same time and is eloquent testimony of how Byzantium influenced the early Western masters.

Starting on the north wall we see only fragments of a Deposition, then a Resurrection, with Christ standing on the gates of Hell and Salvation and holding Adam and Eve by the hand while the mouth of the tomb gapes open. Below this is the Dormition of the Virgin, usually over the west door in Byzantine churches, the tormenting of Christ, in which what is already the sacrificial figure of death-like pallor is shown in purple robe. The soldiers, some at least, play derisively on a variety of mediaeval instruments — but two of their number shrink behind their shields, full of apprehension.

A fine Last Supper shows Christ, wearing a gold-embroidered robe, pouring wine for his Disciples. Judas is reaching for the cup and the other Disciples are pointing at him. And so we move on to the Garden of Gethsemene, the arrest and Christ before the High Priests (Ciaphas is rending his clothes while on a table near him is an interrupted game of checkers). The Crucifixion scene has the executioner in the act of climbing the cross, holding the hammer and nails. On the inside walls of the arches on the north side are fine paintings of the Prodromos (St John the Baptist) and Christ.

The painter of the south aisle — there were probably many hands at work in Orfanos — displayed a lively imagination in his subject matter, from the Lives of the Fathers, and particularly the legend of St Jerome in the desert. In the first panel he is drawing a thorn from a lion's paw — surely the original cowardly lion, for he is turning away so that he cannot see his own blood. Next we see two negro thieves of the saint's donkey riding away on camels, and in the last panel the grateful lion leads the donkey back to Jerome. A series of panels of the miracles includes a remarkable Wedding at Cana, with the dignified bride and groom in Byzantine wedding gowns of gold-embroidered white damask and wearing the crowns, variants of which still play a part in the Orthodox ceremony.

Leaving the church and walking back to the head of Irodotou we bore left from the square, along Moreas, until we reached Akropoleos, the street which winds up through the old Turkish quarter to the area indicated by the street's name. When, after only an easy half an hour's walk, we reached the gate which gave traffic access through the acropolis wall, we had come full circle on our two itineraries. A few paces to the left were the gates of the Vlattadon monastery, once one of the richest and most famous in Thessaloniki, and now the seat of a Patriarchal Institute of Patristic Studies, a form of theological college.

Passing through on to a wide, gravelled belvedere, we walked in a grove of pines to the entrance of the katholikon, which looks out over the city. This little church dates from the same high Palaeologian Revival period as the Dhodeki Apostoli. The monastery, of which this is the only surviving original portion, was founded by two Cretan brothers called Vlattaden. Given its dedication, to the Transfiguration of the Saviour, and the date of its construction, in the middle of the fourteenth century, it is thought that it could have had associations with the Hesychasts, the mystic cult which contributed so much to the decline of the Byzantine empire. One of their beliefs was that extreme asceticism made it possible to see the light emitted by Christ during his Transfiguration. Near here the Hesychasts' fervour provoked a dreadful counter-stroke when the nobility, who were so associated in the popular mind with 'navel watching' while starvation and civil war stalked the empire, were hurled from the steep face of the acropolis.

The Vlattadon is a peaceful place today. We arrived just as the worshippers at the Pentecost service were leaving, behind the bishop, each carrying a bunch of leaves from a nut tree. Orthodox dogma prescribes that the faithful do not kneel until this festival when they kneel on the leaves of the nut tree, the nuts symbolizing the hard faith they have, commemorating the old Hebrew feast of the First Fruits. They also read three prophecies from the Old Testament.

As the worshippers chatted in the warm sunshine, a layman walked across to the carillion and rang out a joyous — and vigorous — peal across the upper city, sending the peacocks, which strut near by, fluttering into the trees.

We entered the Vlattadon through the elegant marble doorway, into the dark, cool, interior, pungent with the smell of burnt beeswax. In the tiny vaulted chapel of Saints Peter and Paul, to the right of the sanctuary, paintings of the Macedonian School, contemporary with the foundation of the monastery, can be made out. The Vlattadon also possesses two magnificent early icons which are only accessible on special request.

From the monastery we retraced our steps down Akropoleos to an intersection with a chapel on the corner. Straight ahead, the Odos Aghiou Pavlou or Odos Oxi took a long and leisurely right-hand curve past modern flats and round the flank of a wooded outrider of the acropolis. At first on the right, and then round the bend, on the left, are some of Thessaloniki's best tavernas.

This is the place to come on a warm evening, to sip an aperitif, followed by dinner, on a terrace overhung with pines and odiferous bushes and watch the lights of the city and its shipping twinkling far below. The 24 bus service runs down to the restaurant area and a taxi ride from the lower city costs no more than 40 or 50 drachmae.

We were now outside the walls at one of their most spectacular points and decided to follow them down to the fairground and the sea front and complete our tour with a visit to the archaeological museum.

A few metres below the Trigonion an inscription high up on the wall marks the site of the Hormisdas Tower, with its epitaph to the Persian architect of Theodosius' walls: 'Hormisdas fortified this city with indestructible walls'. No empty boast, as the solid lines of crenellated masonry marching away down the hillside attest. Most of the restoration, of course, is Turkish work, but as with so much else in their culture, the Ottomans were not innovators in military architecture and what you see today is basically late Roman-Byzantine work. As the Turks borrowed from the Byzantines, so the Byzantines had borrowed from the sophisticated Eastern races they dealt with. Hormisdas, for example, may well have distilled the skills learned in studying an impregnable fortress like Hattra in his planning for the defences of Thessaloniki.

The walls corseted Thessaloniki until just before the liberation. Not only were they a sign of military strength, but they also served as a protective enclosure in which trade and culture could flourish. The city was an obvious site for one of the great mediaeval fairs and in fact the Fair of St Demetrius was a commercial magnet for the Balkans, being held around the saint's feast day, 25 October. Merchants would gather at the fair site, then outside the Golden Gate at the west wall, and transact the business which would bring the marks and bezants flowing into the city's coffers.

Today the International Fair, founded between the wars, carries on the tradition. The site with its space-age telecommunications tower, comes alive once a year, in mid-September, as Thessalonians and foreign business delegations throng the complex of glass and chrome pavilions to bargain and simply to enjoy themselves.

Behind the pavilions is a large sports centre, used throughout the year by a variety of clubs. We followed a crowd of early evening revellers out through the turnstiles and across Avenue d'Esperay towards the front. The whole of the triangle between the archaeological museum, the fairground and the White Tower is filled with gardens and groves of pines and flowering shrubs.

This, and indeed the whole of the front, becomes the focal point of the city as the hour of the peripato approaches. Canopied, out-door cafés stretch down to the sea, offering the best *mezedes* (pre-dinner snacks) we found anywhere in the north, and a fine vantage point from which to observe the world of off-duty Thessaloniki.

The equestrian statue of Alexander, gazing out towards the east, commands the quayside and at most times of the day a slow tide of activity seems to eddy round the plinth; fishermen always make for compulsive viewing; the bait sellers enjoy a lively trade and for the children there is always the zoo, housed in thatched huts scattered among the pine trees. The jewel-hued peacocks have the run of the place whereas the two Pindus bears have very constricted quarters to which they certainly have not reconciled themselves.

The White tower (Lefkos Pirgos) is a first-class vantage point from which the visitor can orientate himself when he first arrives in the city. From its battlements he gets a particularly clear idea of the lay-out of the Byzantine city; the full scale of the walls is very apparent and something of the chequer-board street pattern can be seen.

The tower is the physical symbol of Thessaloniki's indestructibility just as St Demetrios is of the supernatural. Dating from about 1430 it could have been built either by the Venetians or the Turks. But certainly its name derives from the coat of whitewash it has worn since the latter made it the site of a celebrated massacre, earning for it the soubriquet, 'Bloody'. The massacre was in 1826, only five years after the awful scenes accompanying the suppression of the nationalistic revolution in Macedonia, in which the Janissaries, the corps d'elite of the Turkish army, had taken a conspicuous part. The Sultan, Mahmud II — one of those who periodically gave a more acceptable image of the Ottoman empire to the Western powers, thus allowing it a longer lease of life — determined to suppress the body, which originally had been raised from Christian slave boys.

In a night of the long knives, or scimitars, the corps' representatives in Thessaloniki were rounded up, herded in batches up the broad spiral staircase in the tower into the low-ceilinged chambers lit by arrow slits and there butchered. It is now used by another youth group, the Sea Scouts, but it is accessible during daylight and entry is free.

The archaeological museum stands a few steps back from the front at the apex of the triangular island site just behind the gardens and below the fairground, where Avenue d'Esperey swings parallel with the sea. This low, porticoed building, set in a sculpture garden where pieces of Roman funerary monuments are displayed, was opened less than 20 years ago and is already too small for the volume of material being uncovered by excavation in Macedonia.

The central gallery, devoted to the treasures of Vergina, is being augmented, possibly superseded, by a new wing. What one already sees is an imaginative display of the artefacts of ancient Macedonia, in magnificent variety, arranged as an introduction to its history, with clear documentation. By the time you enter the hexagonal central chamber where the royal gold gleams you feel very well acquainted with the physical presence of Philip's world.

As you enter the Macedonian gallery you see an iron infantry helmet as worn by Philip's hoplites — the only example of a Macedonian head defence until the king's own helmet was found. This example, dating from the late fourth century, is from Vitsu in the Epirus. In the next case are coins of the Temenidae, Philip and Alexander's dynasty, including one of the horse motifs of Philip which were much copied, even turning up on primitive Romano-British issues. It is interesting comparing Alexandrine coins with the much superior designs of later kings, although under the Romans the Macedonians were still using the conqueror as a motif — with inferior workmanship.

A jewel box a few cases along shows a dance by maenads, one of whom is holding a torch in one hand and a snake in the other — perhaps a link with the snake cult of which Olympias was a high priestess. There are also golden diadems, one set with pendants. Interesting parallels with Vergina, again, are provided by finds from tombs in Katerini, in the shadow of

Mount Olympos, and Kozani in central Macedonia. There are sunburst discs and armour decoration in the shape of lions' heads and a tiny plaque of a Nike a-tiptoe, with her shield raised.

Another shock of recognition is provided by a gold medal minted about the middle of the third century BC when the Olympic Games were held in Macedonia and showing Olympias on one side and Europa riding on the bull on the reverse.

Marble, though dismembered, offers many pleasures in the spacious and sunlit sculpture hall. Fragments though they are, pieces of Greek statuary seem to have a vivacity and luminosity in their own right. For instance, take a group in the first gallery. There is a head, right leg and right hand of Athena of the type known as Athena Medici — this statue was a copy of a lost Phidean work; a superb small head from Olynthos, wearing a stephane or fillet; a grave stele from Potidea showing a husband offering a wine cup to his wife while a servant stands between the couches with a wine-mixer, or *krater*; and a marvellously shaggy head of Serapis, again a Roman copy from a famous Hellenistic work by Bryaxis, of the fourth century BC.

In this hall, also, there is an arresting marble grave stele, reddened by the earth, from Pydna and of the fifth century BC. It shows a mother, seated, mourning for her child, who is standing between her knees and reaching up, trying to grasp her hand. The mother is holding her head in grief.

The second hall is dominated by a huge torso of the second century AD found in Thessaloniki; there is also a portrait bust displaying great character and a grave stele to one Gaius Papillius from the first century BC, the inscription of which is in Latin and Greek.

The hall beyond this has a powerful head and torso of Atlas, from the agora in Thessaloniki but more reminiscent of Highgate Cemetery. Near it is a delightful piece of a Bacchus, vine leaves askew, fallen asleep over his wine jar. The centre of the floor is occupied by a mosaic from a house in Thessaloniki. It features three scenes from the legend of Dionysos and Ariadne, Zeus and Ganymede, and Apollo and Daphne. More pieces of mosaic are framed on the wall — late examples from Pella.

One more piece is worth mentioning — a bronze, to be found in the last gallery just before the top of the stairs. It is a very fine portrait bust of the Roman Emperor Alexander Severus, found in Peiria. Alexander was a deeply religious youth who is supposed to have kept statues of Christ and Abraham in his palace. He ascended the throne after the insanities of Heliogablus — so fascinatingly described by Gibbon — but did not have the strength of character to put the empire back on course and was murdered in Germany by rebellious soldiers.

On the way out, look for a wall case with a pair of exquisite gold and enamel Byzantine bracelets of the tenth century, found locally. They are formed of tiny plaques, showing birds and flowers, in pale blue, greens and scarlet, set in gold rope work.

5. Western Macedonia — I

Fresh from the golden treasure of Macedonia's royalty you will be ready to experience the landscape and the archaeological background which gives it form and life. The search for Philip's kingdom involves a circular tour through western Macedonia, its mountainous heartland. You drive backwards in time, from Thessaloniki, founded by Philip's son-in-law after Alexander's great adventure was already over, to Pella, the new capital, which marked the start of Macedonia's expansion.

Then from the sea and great plain, which her early kings coveted, back to the mythic roots of the Makedonae, the Doric people who came with their flocks to this land and clashed with the savage tribes who inhabited the mountains up ahead. Coming round in a great loop and passing through settlements which the king founded to tame this frontier, you follow him back to the plains — and to his presumed tomb.

The road beckons to the heart of modern Thessaloniki in the form of Egnatia Street — not the original Egnatian Way at this point, but pointing directly to your goal nevertheless. . . . By the way, most of the places we are about to describe can be reached by long-distance buses from Thessaloniki. However, if you are going by car, you take the E20 to Edessa, via Pella. Continuing on the E20 as far as Vevi crossroads, you can either make the detour across the Yugoslav border to Bitola or drive on to Florina. The very attractive route to Kastoria, a secondary road, but quite a good one, offers another detour to the Prespa Lakes. After Kastoria the B road links up with the highway through Kozani and Veria. Naoussa and the Lefkadia tombs are a detour at the half-way stage before Thessaloniki.

On the Egnatia to Pella

Westward then, to Homer's 'Lovely Emathia'; and as a first itinerary we'll take the Egnatia to Pella, Philip's capital. As the car threads through the traffic out of Monastirou and past the marshalling yards and the turn-off to the Indian army cemetery from the First World War, it is worth remembering poor, complaining, Mrs Mary Walker's experience.

Riding in the middle of a caravan of pack-buffaloes and mules, this quintessential mid-Victorian lady, who was accompanying her clergyman husband on a tour of Macedonia, bewailed her travelling conditions — but

as with so many of the breed, kept a searching eye for the enlivening detail
. . . such as vultures.

Here and there you meet with a flock of vultures, or one of them perched on a withered stump, adding to the dreary desolation of the landscape; and as you pass along, large flights of storks rise heavily into the air; stretching their long necks ungracefully forwards. . . .

If she found the heat and dust too irksome, there was just discernible on the horizon 'pale yet firm, the Throne of Jove, capping with eternal snows the gigantic mass of Olympus'.

What took Mrs Walker two hours of refined torture on an unmade road to reach, the bridge of the Axios, or Vardar river, can now be attained in half an hour. The crossing of this, the main water barrier of western Macedonia and the original easterly frontier of the Macedonian kingdom, was then served by a decaying wooden bridge but is now spanned by an aging Bailey bridge, erected by the Royal Engineers at the end of the war. The delays at least seem to be the same.

In Philip's day the Vardar plain was a vast fen where he and his nobles would hunt for fowl. Now it is partly under cotton cultivation and the bright blobs of colour from field workers' kerchiefs on the white-flecked hillside, as the land begins to rise on the right of the road, tells you that you are approaching Pella.

Philip's (actually, Archelaus his ancestor's) palace and the official buildings probably occupied the acropolis, the low hill now covered by the village of Néa Pella. The archaeological site can be identified by the six standing Ionic columns surrounding the peristyle of the House of the Lion Hunt; also by the number of air-conditioned coaches from Thessaloniki turning into the museum car park opposite.

It is probably best to look over the bones of Pella first before crossing the road to see, in the museum, the artefacts of the aristocratic lifestyle it supported. Pella died in 168 BC, together with its empire. The Roman legions commanded by Consul Aemilius Paulus, hot-foot from their victory at Pydna, pursued the remnants of the Macedonian army, minus its king, Perseus, to the capital.

The city, in Livy's words 'rising like an island on its immense earthwork', at the entrance to a large inland lagoon, should have been impregnable. We are told, after all, that 'there was no way to get in except by an easily defended bridge'. But the latter-day Macedonians were not made of the same stuff as their ancestors. In the preparatory skirmishing under the walls of Pydna, the Romans had suddenly advanced and the king, panic-stricken, had had his treasure thrown in the harbour. When Paulus temporarily retreated, Macedonian divers were ordered down to salvage Perseus' baubles. After the battle the king fled to Samothrace, where he surrendered.

Few signs have emerged in the large-scale excavations that have been in progress since 1957 of either burning or systematic destruction. But Pella

Site of Pella

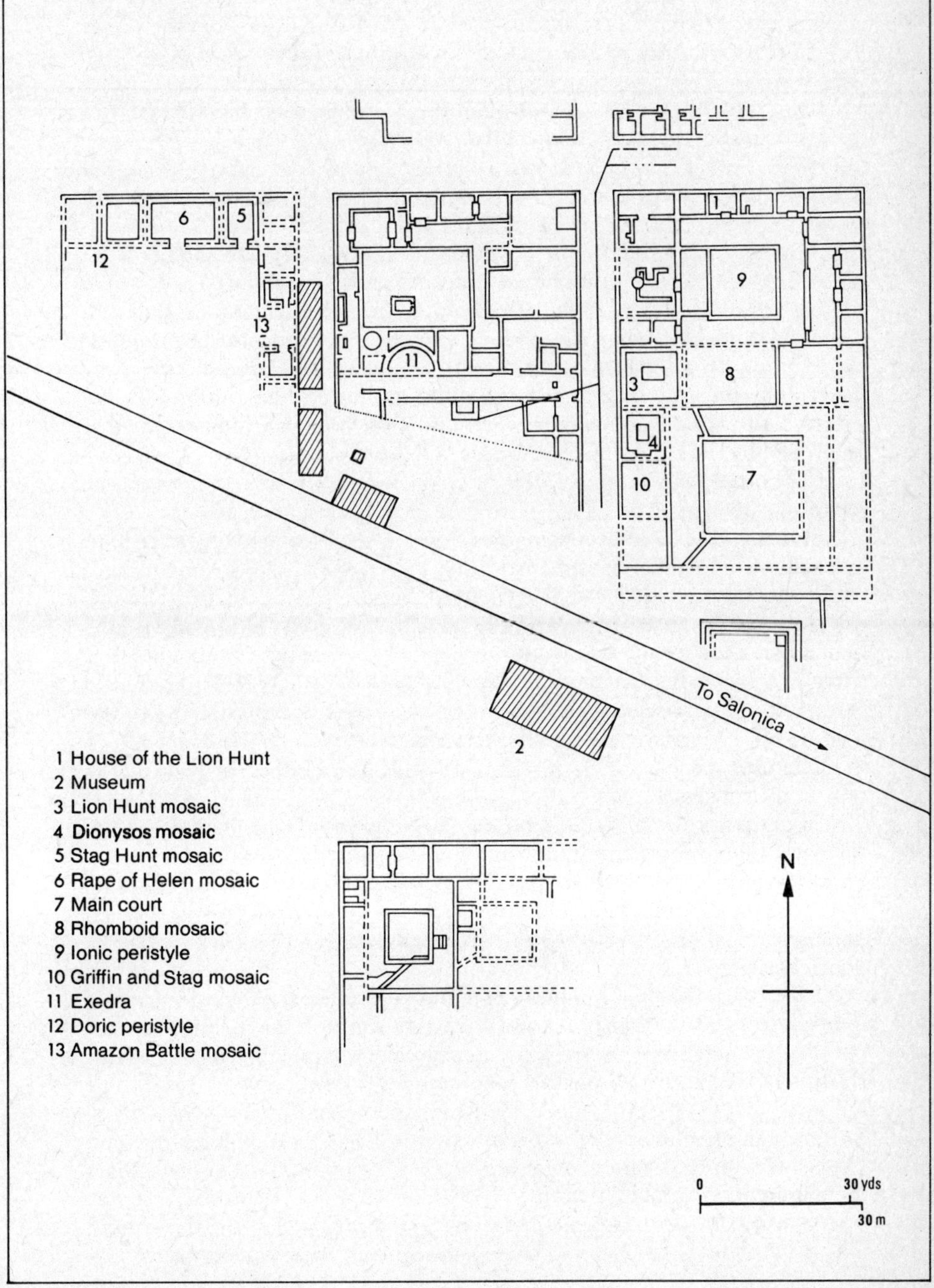

To Salonica →

1 House of the Lion Hunt
2 Museum
3 Lion Hunt mosaic
4 **Dionysos mosaic**
5 Stag Hunt mosaic
6 Rape of Helen mosaic
7 Main court
8 Rhomboid mosaic
9 Ionic peristyle
10 Griffin and Stag mosaic
11 Exedra
12 Doric peristyle
13 Amazon Battle mosaic

N

0   30 yds
           30 m

seems to have become depopulated quite rapidly and we know from classical sources that it provided one of the richest hauls of loot from the despoliation of ancient Greece. It seems likely, therefore, that the Macedonian leaders put dishonour before death and also saved their lives by capitulation, only to grace a Roman triumph. Livy speaks of the awe with which the Romans watched the treasures not only of Pella but of other Macedonian cities processing through the Eternal City behind the chariot of Aemilius Paulus — and taking all day to do so.

Pella's days of greatness began when Archelaus transferred the capital here from Aigai at the end of the fifth century because he needed to be closer to the sea for strategic reasons, and the marshes provided an ideal moat. But Mrs Maria Siganidou, the Ephor of Antiquities for Pella, and her team are still looking for the buildings of state and particularly the palace, which they are quite confident of finding. They took a step, literally, in the right direction during our last visit to Macedonia by unearthing the beginning of a ceremonial road leading towards the acropolis. At the same time they discovered the stylobate of a large building, more than three times the length of any domestic structure yet found at Pella. Its antiquity seemed to be proved by the black-figure vessels found near by, dating from Archelaus' time. Another season or so of excavation will tell whether this exciting promise is realized.

What the archaeologists have uncovered is a city supporting a leisured and cultivated ruling class. Most of the objects which have come to light could only be explained in such terms and the ground plans of mansions like the House of the Lion Hunt certainly seem to confirm it. This mansion, the bench mark for so much of what has been excavated here, is in a block of three — apparently the common domestic plan of the city. It had a central courtyard or peristyle, six columns square, and a porch with the rooms leading off. Across the threshold an ancient Macedonian would have seen the Dionysos mosaic which practically stands as a symbol for Pella and is now in the museum.

It is an invitation to lose inhibitions, to enjoy your host's bounties under the benevolent patronage of the libidinous young god. And, as a design, it is a ravishing evocation of its subject. Dionysos is seen in one of his traditional roles, leading a rout of his followers, but this is not Bacchus the leering, debauched wine-bibber of the Romans, but a sensitive 'free spirit', a deity of youth and vigour.

He sits on the back of a panther caught in the act of leaping, its muscular fore-quarters marvellously rendered considering that the medium is river pebbles. In fact, this is the most sophisticated development of mosaic in this medium. The god lolls on the panther's back, the curve of his almost feminine body reflected in the flowing line of his mount's shoulders. Similarly the feminine bow on his thyrsus, or reveller's staff, floats down to be counterpointed by the arching whiplash of the panther's tail. The impact is heightened by the restrained colour, dark blue and buff, for the background, for the panther's markings, and for the god's wreath and staff with its vine-leaf emblem, and beige and white for the sensuous forms.

Interior of mansion house in Siątista, 18th century.

The Virgin Orans in the apse of Aghios Nikolaos Orphanos, fresco, Thessaloniki.

Sparti in bloom frames caiques in the canal at the neck of Kassandra, Halkidiki.

Near by, on site, is the dark blue and white geometric floor of the anteroom. Beyond was the griffin mosaic (in the museum) which formed another threshold. The griffin has secured its kill, a buck, in mid-leap. It has dug its fangs into the animal's back and to heighten the drama the mosaicist has inserted splashes of blood and reddened the area around the griffin's head, the only colour in a monochrome composition.

On the floor level just above this was found the lion hunt mosaic, also in the museum. The subject irresistibly brings to mind the fresco on the façade of Philip's tomb. There is known to have existed in antiquity, and now lost, a piece of sculpture showing Alexander and his friend Krateros on a lion hunt and it is thought that this might be the only surviving representation of it.

The figure on the left, wearing a *kaysia* (the typical Macedonian hat), rather reminiscent of a trilby, is drawing back, spear poised for a defensive thrust. The lion, its attention drawn by the other hunter, is snarling defiance even as the sword, shaped like a kukri, sweeps down at his head. The figures' eyes would have been formed from semi-precious stones, now missing.

Behind this is the colonnaded court. A street, with a well-preserved drainage system, separated these mansions from a workshop area where terracottas and vases have been found. At a crossroads stood a gymnasium (it has been so called from the strygils or body scrapers found there) and beyond it has been found the remains of a two-storeyed house with part of a staircase and a mosaic showing a struggle between two warriors over the recumbent body of a third.

Opposite is the stag hunt mosaic, the oldest signed mosaic in existence — and in an excellent state of preservation. Two muscular, auburn-haired youths are dispatching a stag, which is being pinioned by one of them, with the help of a dog, while the other prepares the coup de grace with a double-headed axe.

Gnosis, the artist, has displayed his superior skill not only in three-dimensional modelling of the figures — particularly noticeable in the tension of the pectoral muscles and biceps of the axeman as he takes his swing — but in the vivacity. Everything is caught in suspended animation — the short cloaks of the hunters are flying in the wind, the right-hand man is losing his hat and the hound is getting a grip with its teeth, visibly pulling the stag off balance.

The mosaic's border has a pattern of the same strange, twisting plant tendrils which are seen in the tombs at Lefkadia. In this design and the one next to it, the so-called 'Rape of Helen' mosaic, one can see something of the technique used in its construction. A pit was dug, filled with earth, and lined with stones from the local river. On top of this were laid several coats of stucco, composed of sand, pieces of ceramic and lime. Finally the composition was laid out in river pebbles and finishing touches were put with semi-precious stones for the eyes and later, lead for the main joints.

The Rape of Helen covers the floor of an adjacent room in what must have been a truly palatial mansion. Again there is an echo of the royal tombs of Vergina, of the Rape of Persephone fresco. There are the same prancing steeds, drawing a quadriga, or four-horsed chariot, and the struggling female captive.

The story told here is that of the first abduction of the future Helen of Troy, at the age of 12, by Theseus. In best Greek style she was rescued by her brothers only to be handed over in an arranged marriage to Menelaus. The best preserved part of the mosaic is the chariot team, driven by Forbas. The figure of Theseus is almost obliterated but the fragments of Helen's figure give an indication of an imaginative rendering. Her features are distraught and her arms are outstretched towards her friend, Deianeira, who, while gesturing towards Helen, is running away. The large (118 metre square) room, of which the Rape of Helen was the centre piece, looked out, probably through a stoa, on to a peristyle with a fountain. Here was found the exquisite figurine of a sleeping Eros, to be seen in the museum.

Next to this mansion stood another house with an unusual lay-out in that besides the central peristyle, there were two other smaller courtyards, one of which was a sanctuary where the unusual table in the museum was found together with a small bronze of Poseidon.

Retracing one's steps and crossing the Egnatia — extreme care is needed — brings one to the museum, a cool, modern, one-storeyed building as is common in provincial Greece but one which could soon become inadequate for the finds turning up as work proceeds on the 2000 square metre site. All the sculpture here were chance finds, but the objects which really put flesh on the bones of Pella are the result of systematic excavations. The overall impression is domestic — decorated functional objects from those great mansions across, and, indeed, under the road — for some of the most interesting finds have been made just outside the museum. There are large palmettes which decorated cornices, bronze door knockers, a bronze weight of a dog chewing a bone, a bronze brazier, a jewel box shaped like a pagoda and many clay tiles with the names 'Pella' and 'Philip.'

The circular table, mentioned earlier, is probably unique. It is of black slate with bold meander and Greek key patterns, embellished with floreat motifs, in white glass paste inlay. It has a restrained elegance found in many of the terracotta figurines of goddesses which are a common feature of Pella — 150 were found in one tomb alone. Their faces are painted with natural-istic colour and the hair is almost invariably hennaed. Many of the statuettes portray Athene wearing a horned helmet, in her role as protec-tress of births.

In a corner of the first hall is a vindication of Livy's description of Pella's watery setting — hard to imagine now as one looks across the rolling cotton fields shimmering in the noonday glare. It is an anchor with its chain intact and it must have secured a galley that made its way up the river Loudias through the marshes to the Louthia or Loudia lake, the last remnant of which was drained before the war. Livy mentioned a Fakos island, so named for its bean-like shape, which is supposed to have held the royal treasury. Mrs Siganidou thinks that she has identified a feature which could have been it.

Domestic information on ancient Greece is very rare. The only other place where details have emerged of an ordinary Greek city plan is at Olynthos in Halkidiki. An example is the surviving section of what was once an elaborate decor in the andron of a mansion just behind the museum. The stucco, five metres high, and painstakingly reconstructed, shows a cornice and pillars, painted to represent marble. The predominant colours are ochre and pale blue. To see this preserved section in juxta-position with the mosaics is to be given a privileged peep into the living quarters of Philip's courtiers and men of affairs. Also in the museum are a paste frieze of griffins rending a stag (gilded) and a bronze statuette of Poseidon (copy of Lysippus).

This was, after all, the city beautified by the painter Zeuxis, seat of the court which first heard Euripides' *The Bacchae* and *Archelaus* — a tribute to the poet's royal protector whose patronage of the arts was mocked by the Greeks. They said that he spent a lot of money on decorating his palace but nothing on himself, so that many people from all over the world came to Pella to see the palace, but no one to see Archelaus.

Edessa

A short drive through Yiannitsa, an erstwhile Turkish holy place with a mosque containing tombs of the descendants of Macedonia's conquerors and a bronze memorial to the battle which liberated the area from those same conquerors, brings you to one of its most spectacular views, the waterfalls of Edessa. The great double cascade, arches of mountain water and spray, forced under great pressure from the lip of an outcrop of Mount Vermion, into the valley, has always been the guarantor of life to the people of the plains. The benefits can be seen long before you see Edessa, as you pass through acre upon acre of fruit orchards, scenting the air with the fragrance of peaches and the large, deep-pink Macedonian apples.

Mrs Walker, ready enough for refreshments after the heat of the plain, admitted that she had 'scarcely expected the glorious panorama spread before her'. She thought the view from the archbishop's palace, still offering vine-hung viewing platforms up on the cliff,

. . . one of the most beautiful it has ever been my happiness to behold. Far below, masses of walnut trees, chestnuts and mulberry plantations, vineyards and fields of maize spread a rich carpet of luxuriant vegetation.

Far and wide beyond lay the plain of Yenidjeh, softened by a delicate blue haze, and in the extreme distance a thread of silver light; the Gulf of Salonica. To the right relieved against the blue, lilac and grey masses of majestic Pindus, stood out a dark projecting cliff, half hidden in a tangled wilderness of wild vines and creepers, shrubs and trees of every kind; the dashing water appearing at intervals, tumbling and leaping from the rock, until lost in the green maze below.

You cannot, in fact, see the falls from the archbishop's terrace but otherwise our Victorian traveller employed little poetic licence. The brow of the falls still has a wild, somewhat unkempt beauty. Now you can have a café frappé or a meal on the terrace of a restaurant directly at the falls. Here the streams which have gathered force as they course through Edessa, giving it its Slav name of Vodena, the place of waters, come together in two torrents.

The most spectacular view is gained from below, standing on one of the small, railed viewing platforms. Here you can experience the vertiginous lift of seeing hundreds of tons of water taking off from the precipice and thundering past, and below you, into the dripping green tunnel of foliage at the foot of the cliff.

Edessa's importance in antiquity was that it commanded the route into upper Macedonia and remains have been discovered below the cliffs which prove continuous occupation from Hellenistic to Byzantine times. However, it was apparently not Aigai, as was believed until 1977, when Professors Hammond and Andronicos seemed comprehensively to demolish the theory. A sign still points defiantly, however, 'to the archaeological site of Aigai'.

To reach it you drive down the winding hill from modern Edessa, back along the Thessaloniki road, past the signpost to Flamouria, and at the third bridge, where the road takes a sharp right-hand bend, you turn left up a track marked by the sign. Keeping the waterfalls in front of you, you follow the dirt road, left just before a church, and across a small stream — and the wall of ancient Edessa looms in front.

The site, which still has much to yield, as only the area around the main street, inside the wall, has been dug, is one of the most attractive in Greece.

Great courses of dressed tufa blocks have a look about them of sea rocks. And that isn't surprising as this part of the plain was inundated for about 500 years in the early Middle Ages. Purple fig trees provide shade and refreshment as you wander under the beetling ramparts which in classical times made a sweep right up to the base of the cliffs, Edessa's acropolis.

The south gate, which visitors enter, was equipped with towers and a guardhouse. The visiting merchant or farmer could have learnt how long he had until curfew and the closing of the city gates by the sun dials which are set into the posts.

Ahead lies a Hellenistic central avenue, paved in white marble which has been deeply rutted by chariot wheels. The avenue was lined with a covered arcade supported on pillars with varied capitals, perhaps indicative of continual occupation. On either side were spread out blocks of houses and shops. The archaeologists have dated distinct sections of the city. As the visitor walks over 2000-year-old marble paving stones, he can see on either side the remains of Roman shops.

Above, and to the left, he will see the base of a Byzantine wall with a stretch of street still retaining the original paving and crossed by a clay early mediaeval drainage system. In this part of the site have been buried huge storage jars, 1.50 metres high.

The pleasant modern town of Edessa has been built on the ruins of Mrs Walker's ravishingly pretty stop-over, which was levelled by the Waffen SS in 1944. But the same natural features, rushing water and groves of flowering trees, together with what remains of the original town, are being incorporated into the orderly pattern of white concrete and squares which characterize modern Edessa.

The streets have been planted with flowering trees, and the rills and streams neatly bridged. Attempts have been made to restock the seriously depleted fish population in the mountain streams by establishing trout farms in the clear pools of the damned-up river Edessos just outside the town. While we were there, small boys were having the time of their lives, netting and bagging small trout which had escaped from the farm and swum downstream as far as the head of the falls.

Florina and the Lakes

From Edessa the Egnatia winds slowly upwards by passes over the Vermion range, paralleling the Florina-Thessaloniki railway line which runs below through the gorges as far as Arnissa at the head of Lake Vegoritis, one of the largest (19 kilometres long and eight kilometres at its widest point) of Greek lakes.

Arnissa, a sleepy, pastoral town, makes a good picnic stop before the drive to Florina and the frontier. A drive down a rutted track brings one to the shore and a shady spot under a willow from which to enjoy a hamper of wine, taramasalata or goat's milk cheese.

Here we part company with the Egnatia for a while (according to archaeological evidence it swung round the southern side of the lake) and climb more steeply from the scrub-covered gorges on to the arid table land beneath the Voras massif where the Allies had their one success on this front in the First World War, pushing the Bulgars back and capturing Monastir.

At approximately 1000 metres one has a last splendid look out over Lake Vegoritis, from a national park viewing belvedere, before driving on through stone-built villages, outlined against ochre and orange-rust hill-sides — a setting for shepherds and farm boys driving large, angular white and khaki cattle.

After Vevi (the crossroads are beyond) you link up again with the Egnatia, which descends through the Monastir Gap. This is one of the most historic crossroads of Europe. Pause at the southern edge of the great plain which rolls up to the Yugoslav border and beyond, and the strategic importance is very quickly apparent. On either side, the mountains, peaks ribbed with snow, distantly enfold it. The tramp of marching feet seem to be carried on these winds — and military commands, in Latin, Greek, Norman-French, Bulgar and Turkish, perhaps even gutteral accents of statesmen and crowned heads, arguing in a haze of cigar smoke and brandy fumes in some chancellery or European spa.

This plain has meant one thing throughout history and is the reason the Greeks keep a large proportion of their army tied up in these mountains in what some would see as an inexplicably tedious state of watchfulness. It is the strategic corridor to and from the main Balkan chain and central Europe.

Philip of Macedon was the first to realize it, and after completing the hard task of subjugating the local tribe, the Lyncestians, he decided that the gap should be commanded by a colony. He called it Heraclea (after the legendary founder of his house) Lyncestis, a site which has been carefully excavated by the Yugoslav archaeological authorities. It is an hour away, just off the M26, across the Yugoslav border, in the People's Republic of Makedonija. If you have time, it is a recommended diversion. There is also a fairly regular bus services from Florina, although, of course, you need your passport. If you are taking a hire car then you require insurance and a *carta carborante*.

The site is reached after about an hour's drive and is on the left-hand side of the road as you drive into Bitola (the former Monastir) across the plain of that name, one of the few areas left where you will see ploughing with water buffalo. Heraclea was named after the mighty patron god of Philip's house, but it reflects more of peace than war for the Roman conquest brought it, via the Egnatian Way, first commerce and then Christianity.

What has come to light, as at Philippi, is a Roman colonia, and the Yugoslav Archaeological Service has reconstructed some of the main buildings up to the first storey level.

The bath is quite an imaginative venture. You can see in some detail the hypocaust, with its hot-air channels, and the cold (frigidarium) and warm (tepidarium and calderium) rooms.

To the north-east of the bath-house, the remains of a portico was discovered, with some of the votive and portrait statues which once stood there. The purpose of the building it surrounded is unknown but it could have been a bouleuterion ('court house'). It was large — 17.45 by 7.45 metres. The statues are of Nemesis, goddess of justice and destiny (which has led to the tentative attribution) and of Titus Flavius Orestes, a wealthy citizen (the dedication reads 'for his love towards this town').

On the opposite side of the portico are the remains of two early Christian basilicas. The smaller one has reconstructed columns from its chancel screen and all its column shafts from the colonnade marking off the aisle are in place. On the west side the building incorporated an older Roman room with a marble fountain, probably used in baptisms. Nearby is a mosaic floor decorated with game birds, including ducks and pheasants, peacocks and baskets of fruit.

The larger basilica, triple-aisled with a semi-circular apse and a narthex and with a baptistry attached to it, has mosaic pavements in every one of its nine rooms. Below the Christian building remnants of an earlier Roman public building have been found. The pavement in the narthex of the basilica is exceptional. Measuring 21.5 by 4.70 metres, it is a rich evocation of natural life, replete with all manner of fruit and flowers and various kinds of animals. The design features a fight between a lion and a bull, wild goats, stags and a cheetah. The beasts strut and skirmish (the cheetah's muzzle drips blood as it gorges on a deer and a dog tied up to a fig tree bares its fangs menacingly) among the abundance of the earth — palms, cypresses, cherry, apple and olive trees. The mosaic has a border showing wild ducks, swans and herons in one hand and in another the creatures of the deep: dolphins, fish and octopuses.

On the slope above the big basilica a theatre has been uncovered.

We retrace our steps to regain the road to Florina at the Vevi crossroads: it is a short, direct drive of 20 kilometres, and the last town in Greece on this road. Florina also stands in a strategically important position, where the Pisoderian valley gives access from the Vermion massif to the Monastir Gap. Again, Philip secured it with a settlement, probably bringing Hellenized immigrants up from the coastal regions.

More than 2000 years later, that spectacular valley, with its steep, beech-clad sides, was the route taken by another force which appreciated Florina's importance, the Greek Communist insurgents. In February 1949 they made their final attempt to establish a Communist Greek state by force when they attempted to seize Florina as a base. For four days they besieged the lightly held town but retreated when American-staged air drops, and forces coming up from the south, broke their grip. The town was left a mass of ruins.

The new town is pleasant enough, laid out with squares, beyond the roundabout at the Thessaloniki-Yugoslavia turn-off, and at the bottom of Leoforos Megalou Alexandrou, near the bridge which crosses the Crina river and from which the one remaining antique quarter is reached. It also has what is, so far as I know, a unique feature in provincial Macedonia, a civic zoological garden.

Florina also has a good modern museum and when the political situation in the border region permits more extensive archaeological excavation, it has the facilities for displaying the whole range of finds — that could include elephant bones. As it is, it has interesting stele and votive reliefs, including the ubiquitous motif of the horseman and a serpent coiled round a tree, which was a favourite Thracian cult figure and survived into Christian times to become St George and the Dragon.

The barbaric style of these mountain Lyncestians, even as late as Roman times — is reflected in a family grave stele to the clan of one Terentios, of the third century AD. The couch on which he reclines has horse-hoof feet and, in a decorative band, a huntsman pursues a boar, still a favourite quarry in these parts. There is also a relief of the divine Alexander, showing the fairly unsophisticated local workmanship, but contrasted with a torso of Hermes, which was probably a Hellenistic import.

One charming item is a stele with portrait bands of local citizens looking (no pun intended) suitably grave. It reminds one of the little photographers' booths set up in Macedonian market places for family portraits. And talking about markets, Florina has an excellent one, where succulent fresh-water fish can be bought, as well as huge belljohns of wine and brandy, which farmers load on to vans and mules and carry off to warm long autumnal nights.

Florina is also the base for the Prespa Lakes national park, 48,000 acres of water, fen and mountain which marks the frontier of Greece, Yugoslavia and Albania and for their part of which the Greeks have a project. This is intended to allow as many visitors as possible to derive maximum pleasure from what, until recently, was an unfrequented semi-wilderness.

The main problem for the researchers is to reconcile the needs of, say, campers and hikers with the overriding purpose of the park — providing a habitat for the wildlife, and in particular one of Europe's rarest, as well as largest, birds, the pelican.

There are two lakes, Big Prespa and Little Prespa, the latter wholly in Greece, and so the focal point of our visit. The whole of this wild and lonely area has suffered from depopulation for years, particularly at the time of the Greek Civil War of 1946—9, and accommodation is very limited. But where available, it is of the comfortable, unpretentious variety fairly common in Greece.

The best place from which to observe the wildlife is the hamlet of Mikrolimi, a cluster of white-washed fishermens' cottages on the south-east shore of Little Prespa. From here, up to the isthmus, stretch the reed beds from where you may well see an exotic bird rise in a flurry of plummage, neck extended gracefully.

The fisherman who rents you a room will also probably punt you out, provided you have the special pass to approach the bird sanctuary, on to the dark, wind-ruffled water of the lake. For a consideration he may also be prepared to take you across to Aghios Achillios (there is no way you can get past the military post on the isthmus without a suitable pass from the army headquarters at Kastoria).

In the summer months, the lake provides good bathing from a sand beach on the isthmus near Aghios Achillios. There are full beach facilities.

Kastoria

After visiting the lakes it is necessary to retrace our way back to the main road to continue our journey to Kastoria. The road rises through beech woods, intersected with woodmen's trails along which lurch pony trains laden with corded timber, to the top of the Pisodherion pass, at 1498 metres, the historic passage between the Bermoos and Vermion ranges. It is the 'splendid forest with bright distant visions opening to right and left' which made such a pleasant ride to Monastir for Mrs Walker.

Her 'frightfully bad' descent into the valley of the Livadhopotamos is still fairly breathtaking. At the roadside, near the turn-off to the still closed Albanian frontier at Kotitsa, stands a marble bust of the patriot Christos Kota, burnt alive by the Bulgarians and after whom a near-by village was named.

Beyond it a sign points to the village of Melas, formerly Statistan tou Korestian, where another patriot, the most celebrated name from the roll of honour of the Macedonian struggle for independence, was ambushed and killed. Thirty-two year old Pavlou Melas was killed in an ambush on 13 October 1904, by Bulgars with Turkish connivance. The house where it happened has been carefully preserved, with various relics of Melas.

Continuing on the Kastoria road you see Gavros, with its uncharacteristic sienna-coloured houses, on the right, before plunging into a winding valley reminiscent of the Scottish Cheviots. The only signs of life are shepherds and their flocks and it is advisable not to succumb to enthusiasm for a 'good shot' but to restrict photography to long-distance work from the car. The savagery of Macedonian guard dogs is not exaggerated. Several times we were glad to be behind a metal shield when a four-legged fury, hurled itself at us.

You drive through gorges of red oxide, yellow ochre and pink alizarin earth, the road criss-crossing the river by Bailey bridges dating from the Civil War. As you approach Kastoria the deteriorating road surface is reflected in the pull on the steering. You start to climb and then suddenly, from a turn in the trail, you get your first glimpse of Kastoria, the Greek Lakeland, with its town straddling the saddle of a promontary jutting out into the lake.

Kastoria is above all a fur town; it has earned its living from the manufacture and sale of garments and articles made from fur off-cuts since the Middle Ages. Its advantages as a tourist centre have, therefore, been only belatedly realized, and they are considerable, including some of the finest late Byzantine painted churches in Greece, the most exquisitely painted mansions, with excellent boating on the lake.

The lake, the country's second largest and second highest (statistics respectively are: 34,000 square metres in area; 10 metres maximum depth; 650 metres above sea level) gives Kastoria a unique atmosphere and beautiful setting. *Kastoria* means 'citadel', but now instead of protecting it, the lake gives it a peace.

For Mrs Walker it was bright with sunny memories as she recalled her host's 'fresh, airy chamber, with its broad divan covered in spotless linen, the ceiling supported on slender columns, and arabesque decorations, and the cluster of lillies in the niche below, perfuming the soft breeze which stirred the snowy draperies of the long windows overlooking the lake'.

The mansion house of which she was talking may well be one of those now being restored by the Department of Antiquities. Until the turn of the century they paraded all their mercantile glory along the south shore of the promontory, shaded by tall planes and poplars, and some had their own boat-houses.

The merchants have long since acquired an international lifestyle. The mansions were consigned to the rubbish dump of the past. Until comparatively recently the last scion of one of the leading fur families lived alone in one of the mansions, like Miss Haversham, in fantasy; his companions the fabulous creatures inhabiting the frescoes; his music the wind whistling through the rotting shutters like some mockery of Macedonian pipes. He eventually drowned himself in the lake.

Today, the keynote is no longer despair. The past is being carefully preserved in these mansions, the Macedonian equivalents of the Tudor hall house. They are magnificent structures, stone-built up to the first storey and then spreading out, like one of the great plane trees at the lake side, into overhanging balustrades and projections, galleries with carved panels and shutters which have a look of heavy foliage.

They were built on profits derived from as far away as Vienna and Prague, but the craftsmanship which they display was essentially local, carving and painting which combined flights of imagination with locally culled motifs, flowers and fruit which could be seen in any lakeside garden.

They were not the homes of people who accepted the yoke of Ottoman rule easily. Here, and at Siatista, to which I shall refer later, these Balkan businessmen enjoyed their wealth comparatively free from outside inter-ference. They attracted the wealth of northern Europe to their mountain fastness and created there an opulence comparable to the lifestyle of Thes-saloniki. Probably locally trapped pelts played a part in building up the trade. But there is no doubt that Kastoria's pre-eminence was gained, and still is, in the more modest end of the international market.

It relies on two factors: a policy of buying up skins, and particularly off-cuts of skins, which the up-market international furriers discard, and the skills to match and stitch them into garments which have the quality of much more expensive models but which considerably undercut them.

The fur pieces are carefully matched and stitched together and then stretched on boards to dry in the sun. Nowadays fur craftsmanship is not nearly so much of a cottage industry, most of the work being carried out in workshops, but strolling beside the lake you do come across women work-ing on racks of furs, with 'background' provided by a transistor radio slung on a tree branch.

Their ancestors would have sat cross-legged on low divans in work rooms on the first floor of their homes, sheering, snipping and sewing. The techniques have hardly changed and to trace them back into history you only have to jangle the peal of goat bells at the nail-studded wooden door of number 10, Kapitan Lazov, a small alley running back from the south shore of the lake.

It is the folklore museum, a piece of Kastoria's past, lovingly — and I mean just that — tended for the pleasure and edification of the present generation. Jannis Patsofovlos, the curator, is one of those old men who have been given a rare chance to preserve a piece of their experience and bequeath it to the young. Jannis has no English but as he shows you over what is now his home, he nevertheless brings those long-vanished Kastorians back to life.

You enter a stone-flagged hall, with, on the left, the winery and a still-room opposite. The winery has a vat on the side of which a chalk score was kept of how many litres of grapes it contained. As Kastoria is not a grape-growing area, the raw material had to be brought in by boat. The wine was left to mature in a huge cask wrapped in sapling switches and bonded with strips of leather.

A flight of stairs on the right leads to the workshop, restored to its original appearance with low tables in front of the divans laid out with pieces of fur and tools of the craft, shears and flat-sided needles. Hanging up is a 200-year-old merchant's coat, of heavy black broadcloth lined with mink.

At the top of the corresponding staircase across the hall is the winter parlour, the small room warmed by a tiled stove and used when the ice formed on the lake and the wolves came down from Mount Vitsi to scavange. Here Jannis served us with his home-made ouzo and a *mesa* of olives, hard-boiled eggs, fresh white bread and his own tomatoes.

The main quarters are reached from a mezzanine and centre on a large ballroom, used only by the male members of the household. The Greeks kept their women, as far as possible, out of the way of the Turks, but to an observer the general attitude of the two cultures to the so-called weaker sex seems to have differed little. As the dancers whirled and stamped to the rhythms of the bazouki and pipes coming from the minstrels' gallery, they would be watched by the women, crowding into a loft above the parlour next door, who would vie for a turn at the peephole. From their purdah next door, girls of marriageable age would sit and watch while would-be suitors took ouzo or coffee with their father below.

On the second floor are the bedrooms, each with a different design of stove. One room, for instance, is a good example of the pointed-canopy fireplace common in the Ottoman empire. It also has fitted pinewood cupboards containing men's and women's djellabahs, which, for the former at any rate, was standard dress under the Turks. There is also a khaki service uniform worn by Captain Philolas Pihion when he received the surrender of Kastoria from the Turks during the War of Independence in 1913. The date, 11 November, is kept as a public holiday in the town.

The house is kept in immaculate condition as though the family has just gone out for a stroll. One feels the presence of the families who lived here in all the rooms through photographs — family groups, strong single studies of matriarchs and patriarchs, a shot of most of the male population gathered in one of the squares for a festival, and nearly all wearing the fez, and groups of nationalists wearing the fustanella (the Greek kilt), and flourishing swords.

These mansion houses were largely self-contained economic units and while the fur workers made clothing for sale in one room, the women of the household wove the material for their backs in another. They had a special weaving room, a tradition that is carried on in other parts of Macedonia. The room is dominated by a loom and laid out around it are a spinning wheel and instruments for carding and combing wool.

In the courtyard at the back is a lean-to boat-house which 150 years ago would have given direct access onto the lake. The shore line has changed and now the sturdy punt-like craft lies perpetually marooned on its stocks.

Next to it is the house's ouzo distillery, an important part of the domestic economy, not only because it provided the liquor supply, but the medicine chest also. The pharmacy in the still room contains vials of strong ouzo and paprika, considered a sovereign remedy for colds or influenza.

Having shown you the museum, Jannis will take you to see the three mansions which are open for the public so far. At this point I should say that the Tourist Police in Kastoria are particularly helpful with translation and it may even be possible to enlist the aid of an English-speaking policeman to get more from your tour of the town's antiquities.

The Natzi mansion in Vizantion alley is probably the most unusual. The merchant who built it in the eighteenth century traded with Asia and brought home a Chinese servant with an artistic bent, who was set to decorating the main salon. He painted a floral motif but in a distinctive oriental style and using a palette of lacquer red and deep cobalt on a chalk-white background. Nearby are the Basirah and Emmanuel mansions, both of which reflect in their frescoes the nostalgic obsession with the lost capital of Constantinople. As the fall of the Eastern empire receded into history, the Greeks forgot the threadbare reality of Constantinople as it was at its fall, and cherished idealized images of a golden city, strong and many-towered, set on the edge of a sea covered with ships which brought the tribute of the east. These images found their way onto the murals surrounding the parlours, somehow making the Turkish yoke more bearable.

A narrow lakeside road girdles the peninsula, but for part of its length, it is one way. This means that to reach one of the most beautiful and historic spots in Kastoria one has to follow the Orestiados all the way around the rocky south-western corner of the peninsula until it becomes the Leoforos Megalou Alexandrou, the narrow lakeside road which runs up to the mainland.

On foot, one follows the Orestiados in the opposite direction, past restaurants where the Kastorians come to dine on Sundays, and past a children's playground, until it narrows to a dappled tunnel, overhung with luxuriant foliage, and with the lake lapping on the right. Eventually the road widens to form a lakeside landing stage, with restaurants set under great spreading plane trees, at the head of whitewashed water stairs where flotillas of swans drift on the current waiting for scraps. At night the graceful, ghost-like forms and the lights strung between the huge bowls of the trees give the scene a truly operatic feel.

But it is the sacred rather than the profane which attracts visitors to this spot. Just across the road from the restaurants, under a rocky overhang, are the painted portals of the Mavriotissa monastery, the oldest religious site in Kastoria, dating from the sixth century, although the present building is of the eleventh century.

It is really two churches in one building; one dedicated to the Virgin, of the eleventh century, and the other dedicated to St John Theologos. The Church of Panaghia can be dated from the venerable, iron-studded doors of the naos. They are apparently late eleventh century and are contemporary with the refounding of the monastery by the Emperor Alexius Comnenus, subject of one of the most celebrated mediaeval biographies, *The Alexiad*.

His daughter, Anna, provides us with a unique insight into the vital role Kastoria played in the struggle to preserve the Byzantine empire. Through this careful chronicling of her father's achievements we capture the stirring events of 1081. It was at this spot, the Mavriotissa monastery, that the Byzantine army, hard-pressed by the Norman invaders who were later to capture Thessaloniki, temporarily reversed the tide of the war in spectacular fashion.

Kastoria was occupied by a pretender to the throne, Bryennius. His forces were largely composed of Norman mercenaries — Anna calls them Kelts or Latins — and altogether the town presented a formidable obstacle. But Alexius was equal to the problem. Anna says: 'He made a bold, and at the same time a wise decision . . . to make war on two fronts simultaneously, from the mainland and from the lake.' While Alexius kept the Normans in play from the landward his deputy, George Paleologus took his force around to Mavriotissa in skiffs and as the emperor stormed in from one side, his men scaled the cliffs and caught the enemy in rear.

Despite Bryennius' exhortations to fight on, the Normans in true mercenary tradition made their peace, to fight again another day. 'It is right then that each one of us should from now on look to his own safety, some by joining the emperor, others by returning to their native land.'

Two standards were set up, one beside the Church of St George of Omorphoklessia, and the other on the road to Valona in modern Albania. Those wishing to change allegiance to Alexius were to go to St George's, the rest to take the road back to the coast, which was under Norman control. If Anna is to be believed, almost all chose the former and the emperor 'took the road to Byzantium, a glorious victor'. It is very probable that he founded Mavriotissa as a thanks offering for his victory.

Appropriately, the Church of the Panaghia honours the Virgin with a particularly fine Dormition over the entrance to the naos. It is considered to be one of the finest examples of Macedonian painting — the emotion captured in the Virgin's gaunt features bears the imprint of a considerable talent. The fresco, which is well preserved, incorporates the usual image of Christ carrying his Mother's soul, in the form of a baby, up to heaven. St Paul stands at the Virgin's feet and, an unusual feature, among all the aerial activity on the edge of the composition, an angel has cut off the hands of a Jew who has touched her. The naive anti-semitism is reflected also in the shape of two grieving Jewesses in a gynaeceum.

Other panels in the church depict Christ washing the Disciples' feet and, on the right-hand wall, the Betrayal. On the façade of the church is a reasonably well preserved painting of an unusual subject — the geneology of Christ. The Bible's reference to the fruit of Jesse's stem is here taken quite literally — Christ's family tree, portraits linked by sturdy branches, spreads over the weathered plaster in a mirror image of the giant planes a few metres away. Jesse, wearing a pink robe, lies asleep at the root of the tree. In his dreams he sees his line stretching heavenwards through David and King Solomon to its apotheosis in Christ. The design incorporates a splendid archangel, saints and emperors in rich Byzantine robes.

The right-hand angle of the building, forming the Church of St John, has a façade featuring the concept of Death, the great leveller. St Mercurius motions to skeletons in a coffin, who were king and commoner in life.

The painting in the joint narthex of the churches may not be fresco work of the first order — in fact it is typical of the indigenous naiveté found in many church interiors in this region — but it puts over its message with real flair and emphasis. It portrays the Last Judgement and the fate of the sinners must have made the black sheep of the congregation break out in a cold sweat. On the left sit the just, with their crowns, while on the right the damned process down to Hell where a variety of punishments await them. A thief has been hanged upside down with a set of scales around his neck; another man is being dragged along by his beard by a red devil; ethereal angels, like a flight of storks, carry plague-pocked sinners along and drop them among a crowd of shivering sinners. On the right hand side of the narthex redemption is at hand as John the Baptist baptises Christ — but in blood.

In St John's, a smaller, darker church, there is a cycle of the Miracles of Christ, in a very good state of preservation. They include a sensitively painted Transfiguration in delicate greens, greys, pinks and mauves and showing Christ in a mandorla, the aureole which surrounds sacred images in Byzantine inconography; and a representation of the Gadarene Swine. The swine are bristling wild boars which would have been very familiar to the painter, and the headland from which they are leaping resembles the Kastorian peninsula.

Kastoria was occupied for long periods by both the Bulgars and the Serbs and the influence of both is to be seen in the architecture and decoration of its churches. The simple basilica style of the southern Slavs seem to have fitted the pocket and tastes of the Kastorian merchants who founded the churches almost as small private chapels. However, the richness of the fresco painting often belies the uncomplicated structure which contains it.

With its maze of narrow streets threading up and down the steep spine of the peninsula, the town has to operate a one-way system and finding the various churches can be a real problem by car. They are best discovered on foot, but as their keys are kept by the Tourist Police at their office at 25 Grammon Street you may get an English-speaking guide, as I have already indicated.

We will start with the Church of the Taxiarchs, the Archangels Michael and Gabriel, in the Platea Pavlou Melas, which lies off the Platea Omonios, and is marked by a marble bust of the hero. The church is of the three-aisled style known as Monolova and is fourteenth century. Apart from the tomb of Pavlou Melas it has frescoes, with the emphasis on the Church Militant and the best preserved of which are the figures of the Taxiarchs themselves, standing guard on either side of the doors.

A few paces down the hill from Omonio Square and at the top of a flight of steps leading to the town's gymnasium (secondary school), is the eleventh-century Church of the Panaghia Koubedeliki, from the Turkish *kouben*, a dome. It is unique in Kastoria as a Trikhonkos ('three concave') building. The transepts and apse form jutting curves and the edifice is topped off by a central dome hoist on a high drum.

The church was damaged by an Italian bomb in 1940 but fortunately its main feature, a fresco of the Holy Trinity, above the narthex, survived intact. In it the image of God the Father makes one of its very rare appearances in Byzantine art. The image looms over you; the deity sits in a huge golden aureole, while Christ, shown in smaller scale and incorporated into the Father's image, holds a dove. It should be viewed from the left.

In the porch is a series of paintings depicting the life of St George. He is shown on trial before the emperor, in prison, and in the final pictograph, being slowly roasted to death.

The church's paintings date from various times between the thirteenth and sixteenth centuries and some of the latest, and most charming are on the exterior wall of the narthex. Although faded and fragmentary, a fresco of Salome before Herod preserves its sheer panache. She does her dance of the Seven Veils while managing to balance her gory trophy from the Prodromos in a charger on her head.

As on so many of the later Byzantine churches, the exterior brickwork is a decorative form in its own right, a maze of geometrical patterns. Behind the church one can see a section of the town wall built by the Emperor Basil the Bulgar-Slayer, in 1018.

The most powerful of Byzantine emperors also refounded the Church of the Anaryroi after he had defeated its destroyer, the Bulgarian Tsar Samuel, and sent 99 of every 100 of his captives home sightless. Apart from the Mavriotissa, the Anaryroi is the oldest church in Kastoria and was originally dedicated to the Virgin (*anayiroi* means 'without money'). Money certainly figured strongly in its later history, however, for its style and decoration betokens wealthy mercantile, if not princely, patronage bestowed by the donors portrayed in the south aisle. The merchant proudly displays a model of the church while his consort, the epitome of a successful man's wife, stares back at us in her scarlet robes, her long blonde hair tumbling from under a great turban.

One can see evidence of layers of fresco, where the life of St Constantine has been repainted at different periods and in different angles. On the west portico is a finely painted figure of Christ, wearing a blue robe and holding the Gospels.

The guide will throw open both the narthex and south doors to pierce the Stygian gloom and allow you to see not only the paintings clearly but the full extent of the barrel vaulting above the naos.

Just south-east of the Anaryroi, at the end of Elousis, on a crest overlooking the lake, stands the eleventh-century basilica of Aghios Stefanos. Apart from the exceptionally high barrel vaulting covering the naos, the church's main interest lies in its well-preserved gynaeceum. You ascend a stone spiral staircase to the screened gallery which Greek Orthodoxy, following the ritual of Jewish Orthodoxy, set aside for the women members of the congregation. It is dedicated to St Anne, the Virgin's mother, and in an alcove is a painting of the saint with she who was blessed among women, and on one of the arches she is represented as feeding the Virgin as an infant, a very unusual subject.

I certainly advise seeing the last church on this tour on foot, because of the one-way system and also as it can be conveniently included in a walk along the lakeside road which skirts the north shore of the isthmus, the Leoforos Nikes, or Victory Avenue, laid out to celebrate victory in the Civil War.

After seeing the ruined Byzantine tower at the top of the Megalou

Alexandrou, now, together with the piece of wall near the Koubedeliki, the only surviving part of those fortifications which defied Alexis Comnenus, it is worth walking up over the spine at the Platea Davaki and down through the market to the tree-shaded Platea Makedonomekhon.

After whiling away time over a coffee or aperitif at one of the small cafés nestling under the planes at the lakeside, you turn east and stroll down the Leoforos Nikes. On the left fishermen stand in their punts casting their nets into water that can be a cold blue or, as Mrs Walker noticed, an opaque, velvety green, a phenomenon caused at certain times of the year by a growth of algae. The incurably romantic lady wrote of fishermen catching a species she dubbed 'gwelios', some of which weighed as much as 200 pounds. The biggest fish still caught in the lake is in fact the oulianos and it has been known to tip the scales at 90 pounds.

As you walk you come to the Apazari quarter on the right, an area of mansion houses which, with one or two exceptions, has yet to be re-habilitated. In an alley running parallel with the front, and at the top of a narrow flight of steps, lies the most unusual of Kastoria's small basilicas, from a point of view of frescoes. You apply for the keys of the Prodromos to Mr Costas, who lives in the house opposite the church gate. The church is dark and a small torch or even holy candles are needed to see the particular fresco which Tourist Police and custodians alike regard as a tourist 'must'.

The gynaeceum here concentrates not on the joys of motherhood, but on the women's fate if they fall for the sins of the flesh. And what a fertile imagination the painter brought to his stern lesson. The sins are explicit enough: a devil is having relations with a nubile woman; another tempts a couple in bed; another woman (they are all naked) admires herself in a mirror held by a devil. But further along comes retribution — for instance a blonde prostitute suffers a cruel and unusual punishment with a sword.

For a change from dark, musky church interiors one has only to walk on to the end of Leofos Nike, to the modern clubhouse of the Naftikos Association of Kastoria, the organization which co-ordinates leisure use of the lake. To use its facilities you have to belong to an accredited British yachting or rowing club. Presentation of your card will get you free use of a dinghy or skiff. Kastoria is good sailing water, but subject to sudden gusts of wind, which eddy through the mountains, so some expertise with a boat is expected.

Rowing clubs use the lake on summer weekends from 5 p.m. until 10 p.m; Saturdays from 4 p.m. until 8 p.m.; and on Sunday mornings until noon. Enquiries should be made to the president, Mr Nicholas Zoulumis, at Kastoria 22054 (day) or 22876 (evening).

Few visitors will want to leave Kastoria without buying some item in fur. Good value is to be had in purses, bags and slippers, usually made from pony skin, or in 'Russian-style' fur hats or wraps. These range between 200 and 1000 drachmae, but depending on the skin and portion of the animal, the price for coats can rise steeply into the luxury class. The most expensive coats are taken from the animal's back but most garments are made from leg and neck pieces. A jacket from mink's legs can fetch 20,000 drachmae and a blue fox between 12,000 and 15,000 (these pelts are imported from Canada), whereas a jacket from pieces of more mundane fur could sell at about 4000 drachmae. A full-skin fox jacket would sell for about 28,000 drachmae. Canada is now the major source of furs and Australia is the third. One of the low-price importations from 'Down Under' is the kangaroo skin.

6. Western Macedonia — II

Siatista and Veria

Leaving Kastoria by the Dispilion road, which runs along the south-western end of the lake, you leave the junction with the road from Edessa and the military airfield at Argos Orestikon on one hand and turn south-east on the route to Neapolis. This winds between foothills of the Vourmios massif, passing through the attractive small town of Vogatsikon.

Turning left when you pick up the dual carriageway at Neapolis, you follow the signs towards Kozani. After the scrub and twisting highland road it is pleasant to make good time on the carriageway through the valley of the Pramaritsi. Making the journey in the early evening after the heat of the day has broken, you catch refreshing odour from the fertile bottom lands with their fringes of graceful poplars.

Ahead rises a barren, ochre-coloured escarpment which, considering that you are still below the tree line, is an aberration in itself. The landscape seems utterly devoid of timber and watercourses; who on earth would think of settling there? The answer is tax dodgers!

Siatista was founded in the sixteenth century by traders and free spirits who wanted to be free of Turkish impositions like the *haratch* ('poll tax'). In some mountain areas the Turkish writ did not run at all, the power being the *klephts* ('outlaw bands') who play such a potent part in Greek nationalist mythology. But Siatista was unique as a free commune based on trade rather than brigandage. Fur provided the lifeblood here, as in Kastoria; a never-failing luxury market that a little entrepreneurial skill could exploit far and wide. Caravans turned around in Siatista, bringing the marten and sable skins of Russia and eastern Europe and taking back raw cotton, hides, tobacco, carpets — and the luxurious coats made from those imported skins. Siatista was celebrated for one other export and that was its wine, surprisingly enough in view of its barren surroundings and great height (290 metres above sea level).

This produce disappeared due to the great phyloxera scourge after the First World War but the fur industry continues, manufacturing for the same market as Kastoria but on a smaller scale. One factory with a turn-over of three billion drachmae a year and business connections in the United States, employs 250 workers and another 250 on an outwork basis.

In the eighteenth century when Siatista was enjoying its greatest fame as an international caravan centre, its population was between 10,000 and

12,000. (Today it has only 6000 inhabitants.) Its merchants were frequently mentioned in Venetian records, names such as Ionniu, Segouris, Pantazis and Nikolaou. They were the sort of men who were in a position to profit from the opening up of the central European markets after the Austrians gained the upper hand over the Turks in the Balkans at the beginning of the century and forced them to take a more conciliatory attitude in their dealings with Christian neighbours as well as subjects.

The Siatistans' business acumen, which stretched to the caravanserais, where the caravans had to stop on the long treks over the Balkans, brought in great profits. What were those caravans, on which the wealth of upland Macedonia depended, like? An English eighteenth-century traveller has left a description. He says that horses were invariably used in the mountains, although camels, being able to carry twice as much merchandise, sometimes doubled for them in the plains. The loads, each weighing 65 kilos, were carried one either side of the pack horses, which might be in droves of several hundred. The caravans usually travelled for eight hours out of the 24, taking about a month to reach Vienna. One man in five of the drovers tended the horses and there were armed guards and foragers. These guards, who made such an impact on another traveller, looking 'like warriors in their striking costumes and tall black woollen hats' had to pay for the privilege of transporting their goods through Turkish territory, to the tune of five pavas a package.

Certainly it was a profit hard won and much of it went in the kind of display beloved of any bourgeoisie, in great houses, sumptuously decorated. Two of them have been kept up, the Nevantzopoulos house and the Manoussi house. The keys for both, and for the churches of Siatista, are kept at the Nevantzopoulos house, which is on the right-hand side of the main street in the lower town.

The studded wooden outer gate gives access to a small cobbled courtyard with a tree-shaded fountain. The overwhelming impression as one enters the spacious but low-ceilinged rooms is of the great chamber in some hall built by a well-to-do merchant in Tudor England. But instead of the inevitable family portraits in such a setting, here one is faced with a veritable flower show in paint, a bucolic delight in reproducing the beauties of nature — which in this area must always have been in rather short supply.

The colour scheme is ox-blood red and pale citrus lemon yellow. The coffee room, or parlour, on the first floor, is surrounded by a gallery with Arab arches. It is connected to the ballroom above by a wide staircase. Each room has a canopied Turkish fireplace and decorative iron grilles at the windows.

The curator will escort you the short distance, down a winding cobbled alley to the old quarter of Siatista and the Manoussi house, the most majestic single example of the style. John and Athanasius Manoussi were among the most prominent merchants of Siatista and they could also be said to have been among the early patrons of naive art. Some of the frescoes are delightfully Rousseauesque; for instance, fierce, moustachioed hunters cornering a lion which makes a face at them; a parrot with a snake in its beak flying over a Byzantine church, with the date 1787, and hunters stalking what looks like an okapi, and which is gushing blood.

Here in Siatista even as late as the eighteenth century, houses were still being built with loopholed lower storeys. With all their wealth, the merchants could never feel secure, either from the klepht bands, who were not above raising protection money from their own side, or from the Turks. Streets were fitted with gates which could be shut in case of sudden attack and houses were surrounded by high walls with stout gates. Also there was always a postern which gave access to a maze of narrow alleys. If an enemy broke into a house, or the tax collector arrived unannounced, there was always an escape route out the back.

This element of sudden danger, seemingly so at variance with mercantile stability, is also reflected in a small underground room off the main body of the seventeenth-century Church of Aghios Demetrius. It served as a secret school where the local *papades* could ensure the maintenance of Ortho-doxy and therefore a sense of Greek nationality by teaching children their catechism when it was officially prohibited by the Ottoman governor.

Regaining the dual carriageway, you drive through soft, rolling hills, the plain occasionally narrowing to a pass and reminiscent of Pennine scenery. Kozani, ahead, is marked by a certain amount of industrial haze and strip workshop development which increases the closer you get to town. Apart from Ptolemais, just to the north-west and the south-western suburbs of Thessaloniki, it will be the only obtrusive and unsightly industrialization you will see in Macedonia.

Under Turkish rule it was one of the centres which kept alive Hellenism, through its schools and library, which is probably the most richly endowed in provincial Greece and includes mediaeval manuscripts including a vellum copy of one of the earliest maps of Macedonia. At the same time that Kastoria and Siatista were becoming prosperous, a visitor to the town wrote: 'a taste for luxury and an ambition to possess the finer things of life has been introduced. All the well-to-do vie with each other in building and embellishing their houses in splendid style and in living with every luxury and elegance'. Something of that life style can be seen in the folk museum but it declined because Kozani did not enjoy the other two towns' physical isolation. In fact it is the communications centre for the Macedonian hinterland; the junction for Larissa and therefore for the national road to Athens, for Bitola and the Balkans, and for the road we shall take, to Veria and Thessaloniki. It was the obvious pivot for the Greek defence against the Germans and Italians in 1941.

That same conjunction of roads and passes attracted the Turks, too, and their jackals, the Albanians and the Yuruks, so that by the end of the eighteenth-century a citizen could lament: 'We live like sheep among wolves. Our hearts weep for the wretched plight of our community. To what a lamentable and pitiful condition have we sunk, the sad remnants of once famous, but now most wretched Kozani'.

The fact that the town belonged to the Sultana of Turkey was no guarantee of safety as Ali Pasha of Jannina's agents levied protection with impunity. Eventually many of the merchants were driven out and prosperity only really returned with industrial exploitation, and particularly the development of lignite mines, after independence. The town has a pleasant central square, the Platea Nikis, with a distinctive Gothic clock tower, dating from 1855.

By the time you read this a motorway section may have been opened linking Kozani with Veria. The present route is quite adequate, however, and indeed for part of the way very attractive. At first you find yourself crossing a great plain, the former Sarigkiol ('Yellow Marsh'), where you are likely to keep company with farmers on their way to town with their families in wooden one-horse carts. Their wives wear starched white coifs pulled across the lower part of their faces for protection from the sun, but even so the contrast with their lined, nut-brown features is marked.

At Polimilos you begin to climb into the Vermion range, winding up and up, and getting a glimpse of snow-capped Mount Olympos to the right, peeping over the Pierian massif. The tiny village of Zoodokhos Pighi makes an ideal refreshment stop, where you can enjoy a drink at a taverna beside a a splashing fountain while enjoying the view from 1359 metres out over soaring rock faces and dizzy descents.

From here the road climbs to its summit (marked by a roadside shrine at 1371 metres) at Chantova pass and now it winds down the reverse side of what is in effect a vertiginous saddle between the Vermion and Pierian ranges, and points to Veria.

You drive through beech and oak woods, keeping a sharp look-out for the occasional cow, which in this part of the world seem to choose the centre of the roads to take a walk, and soon you reach large apple orchards. The large, sweet Macedonian apples, likely to be offered to you by the pickers, make excellent thirst quenchers until you can order an aperitif at your hotel in Veria.

Veria is a town with two faces. There is the Old Berea of New Testament fame where Paul preached and vestiges of which are preserved in the upper town. And there is the modern town, a ski resort and one of the most pleasant and relaxing environments in Macedonia.

Veria invites leisurely exploration and the way that the old blends successfully with the new becomes apparent as you walk down the hill to the front for the evening peripato. Turn-of-the-century villas with elaborate wrought-iron grills and balconies yield imperceptibly to smart, marble-fronted office and apartment blocks, their clinical lines broken by the frivolity of Syrian hibiscus trees with their pink and mauve blossoms.

The river of people, casually elegant for their evening stroll, finally swirls around the belvedere patio, with its restaurants, coffee bars and flower beds. Far below (Veria is on a plateau at 187 metres) stretch the orchards, intersected with lines of poplars, of the Emathian plain. On the right the Pierian massif rears up and where the lights are beginning to twinkle in the gathering dusk, there in the foothills, the royal tomb of Macedon was found.

Farther along the belvedere and standing in a sculpture garden filled with Roman pieces which give some idea of Veria's importance in antiquity, is the municipal museum. It is an attractive modern building which contains Hellenistic pieces discovered in the area, and painted stele from Vergina.

Veria was under the heel of the Turks from the beginning of the fifteenth century, being maintained as a garrison town to hold the gates of the mountains, circumstances hardly propitious for the growth of religious observance.

And, in fact, the post-Byzantine churches are, without exception, humble basilicas, literally keeping a low profile. We chose to start our visits at the Church of Christ, which stands in a sunken garden on the right-hand side at the bottom of Mitropoleos and the curator for which also keeps the keys for the others. The Christos is particularly well maintained. On the outer north wall, protected by a portico, is a fresco of the Forty Martyrs. The martyrs, wearing only loincloths, are standing in water, and as they drown, their haloes descend to them looking like so many flying saucers. The exterior decoration is completed by a frieze of patriarchs, gravely standing sentinel beside the doors.

The apse is dominated by a Panaghia with two angels and four of the Fathers of the Church. They face the standard Dormition over the west door but the finest painting is reserved for the Life of Christ cycle. There is a particularly lively Baptism with the river given a dizzy perspective and fish leaping out of the water with joy over what is happening. In the Deposition, Mary is depicted kissing Christ with great tenderness.

On the north wall is a group of saints in the Orthodox hierarchy in gorgeous vestments and wearing Byzantine crowns. They include Constantine and his mother Helen, Katerini and Irene. The church has a side chapel of possibly earlier date with, on the north wall, a frieze of saints; Mercurius, Ephthemios, Heralmus (wearing an elaborately embroidered cape with red flowers) and Theodorus.

The Kirikou has the most attractive setting of any of Veria's churches, being well hidden in a courtyard, shaded by old fig trees. It is only a few paces away from Christos, up an alley on the right where the Odos Kontoyiorghaki bends.

Its iconostasis has 11 saints with side panels depicting Christ and the Virgin. The frescoes in the body of the church are flaking and badly in need of the attentions of the ephorate of Byzantine art, which is a pity, as the panel of the Fathers is particularly well painted. The figure of the Panaghia and Christ on the iconostasis as well as the Panaghia in the apse are well preserved although the broken glass in the apse window raises questions about how long they will last if repair is not carried out. The original fourteenth-century door is still in position.

The Church of St John Theologos is earlier, of the twelfth century, and stands just off the road leading into town from Naoussa. It stands in a busy commercial street in its own sunken square. The Panaghia in the apse is surrounded by angels wearing vestments gleaming with gold embroidery. Nearby is a painting of the Resurrection showing disciples in pink-and-gold robes gazing up at Christ who is visible only by his feet emerging from a cloud. A fresco of the Last Supper shows Christ offering bread to his followers who give each other the kiss of peace, traditional in Orthodoxy. In a panel on the left hand wall, a saint is presenting a bejewelled copy of the Gospels to the Panaghia and Child.

On the south wall there is also an intimate Nativity scene with a maid servant testing the bathwater of Christ (an echo, this, of the well-known mosaic in the Aghia Sofia in Thessaloniki). Joseph sits in a corner brooding. Theologos has a bishop's throne of a later period; canopied with carved pillars and a back board painted with flowers.

In the upper town, beside a mosque and minaret, is a reconstructed tribune, of doubtful authenticity, which is claimed as the bema from which Paul preached in AD 59, causing the Jews diligently to search the scriptures, as we know from *The Acts*.

Of much sounder provenance are the fragments of Byzantine walls which you see as you drive in, incorporating a Roman tower, possibly third century, which incorporates in turn grave stele. The wall fragments emerge at the main square from which the Leoforos Mitropoleos descends a steep hill to the belvedere, which stretches along the line of the ancient ramparts, a front of town perhaps not quite comparable with Edessa but used far more sympathetically.

Colonel Leake called Veria one of the most agreeable towns in Rumeli. He spoke of water flowing through every street, supplied by streams which powered mills 'for fulling coarse woollens and carpets, which are made in the surrounding villages or by the Jews of Salonica'.

One of those mills is still in use in Pavrophixal Square, operated by fullers who keep their balance on the slippery wooden slats of the old stone building while they dunk sheepskins in great oaken tubs. The water which rushes under force from the living rock through the back of the mill turns a wheel which operates the vats where the fleeces are pummelled and pounded. It also makes conversation almost impossible.

You emerge from the dripping, dark interior into the sunshine of the square where the waters of Veria's tune changes from a subdued roar to a melodious gurgling beneath the ubiquitous plane trees. In the evening this quarter reverberates to bouzouki coming from small tavernas in the older balconied stuccoed houses.

Tuesday is market day in Veria. The side streets are filled with vendors selling clothing, all types of fresh fruit, cheeses, yoghurts, herbs and a variety of household and electrical goods. But the town has a permanent market, too, situated in the lower part of the upper town, the principal feature of which is a huge old plane tree on which an incredible number of Turks are said to have been hanged in the fight for independence. A pleasant place to have a snack or a coffee is one of the tiny hole-in-the wall cafés lining a narrow alleyway which is completely shaded by the cool tracery of a vast old vine.

The ephorate of Byzantine art has a major task in hand in halting the rot of centuries in Macedonia's churches. In many cases it can only be a matter of snatching fragments from oblivion; the fall of Constantinople was a final blow and half a millenium is a long time for an institution to be muzzled, denigrated and driven underground, its monuments defaced.

One of the things that brings you up short as you wander around churches in northern Greece is the quite casual defacement perpetrated by the Turks; often it was worse when the church had not been taken over as a mosque. For instance, the frescoes on the fasçade of the Mavoratissa are scarred by casual grafitti in Arabic: 'Ahmed was here', if you like.

It works both ways of course. As we have noticed elsewhere, Turkish monuments are often lamentably neglected irrespective of their innate worth, although in Veria the ephorate, under Mr Haris Petsaras, has rescued, among other things, a double Turkish bath. Standing just below the Platea, on the right hand side of the Mitropoleos, it has been restored to its original state, with double domes and entrances, for men and women, pantiles and circular lights of opaque glass let into the roof. The bathrooms themselves will probably be shown as such but the men's bath has been used for storing and renovating frescoes from decayed churches and is expected to have a hall for the display of classical sculpture found in the Veria region.

One magnificent ecclesiastical monument near Veria not only escaped the attentions of the Turks but became a remote refuge for ascetics including a saint, St Dionysos. The monastery of the Prodromos may have treasured its solitude in the past, but it is to be hoped that some steps will be taken to see that it is preserved when the sole *papas* at present serving it dies.

It is majestic in its solitude — it clings like an eyrie to a vast limestone cliff above the gorge of the Aliakmon. It can only be approached by a winding track, so narrow in places that a pair of mules could barely pass abreast. It is approached by taking the first sharp right turn after crossing the barrage of the Aliakmon, 20 minutes' drive from Veria on the Vergina road. We drove along the still unfinished surface of the new national road, turning left up a steep gravel path, which brought us to the monastery track. This winds around the face of the Pierian massif, with, in places, a near-sheer drop on the right, although the track is perfectly safe if negotiated slowly and with care.

From a bend in the track you suddenly glimpse the monastery and immediately afterwards you reach a fork, the bottom branch of which drops down to the gatehouse. In the mountain stillness the only sound is the barking of a guard dog or bleating of goats. If the *papas* is at his devotions or off on a tour of his parish on mule-back (whom his parishioners are is a mystery) you will be greeted either by the old custodian or the *papas's* housekeeper, a White Russian refugee.

The gate house, with a medallion of the Prodromos' head, gives on to a courtyard where peacocks strut. You climb a flight of whitewashed steps and walk along a narrow passageway, with the monastery's katholikon on the right and on the left a stalictite-hung cliff, from which springs of ice-cold, sweet water plunge into rock-hewn troughs. A moist, cool fissure in the rock was used by the monks to preserve food.

The refreshing whisper of running water is everywhere; it courses down gutters through a series of cobbled courtyards which divide the former monastic cell blocks, with their rickety wooden verandahs, it rushes over mossy rock faces in a fine spray, moistening the weeping willow and deep beds of moss which surround an out-door shrine.

The pathway ends at a sheer rock face where a monastic cell has been turned into a shrine — small wonder, for tradition has it that this was the cell of St Dionysos, the sixteenth-century monk who is particularly honoured in a church which has always been closely identified with nationalism.

St Dionysos narrowly escaped death on Mount Athos for converting his monastery of Filotheo from Bulgarian to Greek ritual. He took up residence here at the Prodromos where he reconstructed the nave of the church and re-ordered the monastic way of life.

He also found time for contemplation in this tiny cell. You enter an outer chapel, cut into the rock, which has a particularly well-preserved band of the Apostles below the dome. The painting was probably done with body colour, yellow ochre, black, pale green and pale blue. At the corners of the chapel are the Evangelists with their symbols and above the sanctuary a fresco of the Holy Trinity.

To one side of the chapel is an opening in the rock just wide enough for a man to climb through, which if you do brings you into a tiny cell in which it is impossible to stand up, and which has shelves and niches cut into the wall. In here, St Dionysos mortified the flesh.

From the Prodromos he went to Mount Olympos and founded the Monastery of the Holy Trinity, now named after him, which I shall describe later.

The katholikon which Dionysos had redesigned to his taste is dominated by a later addition, a magnificent iconostastis which though it comes under the heading of folk art is certainly a very superior example of the genre. As one might expect from a region so rich in timber, Macedonia developed, in the sixteenth and seventeenth centuries, its own distinctive type of iconostasis, carved from some valuable hardwood in a three-dimensional frieze of lively natural and Biblical forms.

The best of them, like this one, seem to pulsate with life. This Macedonian Grinling Gibbons has carved a palpably fearful Adam and Eve running from a leafy, exotic Garden of Eden. Farther along we see Abraham frozen in the act of sacrificing Isaac — the carver would not have had to look far for his models of the ram or the thorny thickets — and finally the Israelite spies carrying in the grapes back from the Promised Land.

Along the top of the screen is a frieze of St John's eagles. Below the iconostasis are displayed the monastery's relics, a hand of St Simon Stylites, he of the pillar fame, and a hand of John the Baptist set in silver and encrusted with jewels.

Seli

Macedonia's mountains have defended it as a kingdom and sheltered its rebels under oppression. They even provided the gold to launch it as a world power. Now they are playing their part in developing the region's recreational potential. Skiing is a sport which was a late starter in Greece, despite the mountainous terrain, but it is making up lost time and one of the main centres is at Seli, a tiny hamlet, 26 kilometres from Veria.

Seli is not Zermatt, the pistes are not of top flight competition standard, but they serve a modest little resort, such as this, quite well. Most skiers coming here are Greeks, although with the advantageous rate of exchange, more foreigners are beginning to use the resort, and staying either in the refuge at the foot of the main lift (if they are members of a British ski club), or in the village of Seli or in the modern hotels of Veria.

Seli operates a six-month season, depending on snow, from October to April. The nursery slopes are very gentle but you can attempt the giant slalom, angled at 45 degrees. Details of the ski resort are:

Height of resort — 1740 metres
Giant slalom — 8000 metres
Special slalom — 1000 metres
Ski school; equipment can be hired
Two lifts
Winter sporting events held mid-January to mid-March including the Greek Ski Championships in mid-February.

Naoussa is an auxiliary ski track to Seli, but there are no club-house facilities, the piste is tree covered and the incline is only 65 degrees.

Lefkadia Tombs, Mieza and Naoussa

Leaving Veria, we take the left fork on to the road which heads through the heart of the fruit-growing country. The river Arapitsa, rushing from the gorges of the Vermion foothills above Naoussa and taking springs and rivulets as tributaries as it flows into the plain, created verdant oases here in antiquity which the Macedonians chose for recreation and as a harmonious last resting place for their dead.

Macedonian chamber tombs, all of which had been robbed, were uncovered from time to time in the nineteenth century. One such was the so-called Kinch tomb, named after its Danish discoverer, which is the first sight we get, on the left-hand side of the road, of the Lefkadia necropolis.

Until Professor Andronicos uncovered the royal tomb at Vergina this group of chamber graves provided the best insight into the culture of the Macedonians at the time they strode out on to the world stage. The Kinch tomb has to be left until later as access to the site is gained through the custodian at the Great Tomb or Tomb of Judgement, a few yards farther on and clearly sign-posted.

We turned left along a rutted track winding through peach orchards. In the spring, the Emathian plain glows with pink blossom, but when we passed through it was tinted with early autumnal gold. We crossed the Florina railway line which runs straight through the orchards and then, ahead, a sight met our eyes which in other circumstances might have had us reaching for security passes.

It was as though we had wandered on to a nuclear missile launching site. A structure like a large Nissen hut with a curved concrete roof and fronted by gleaming aluminium hangar doors was sunk into the ground among the fruit trees.

The guide, who speaks no English but has that intuitive gift of communication found in so many of his kind in Greece, lead us down limestone steps and slid back the huge doors. From our vantage point on a viewing platform we were practically eye-to-eye with the triglyphs and metopes, the lively procession of mythological figures painted and modelled, which trip across the façade.

The tomb was discovered accidentally during road building in May 1954 and the combination of weight of earth and action of the bulldozers badly undermined the façade — a real risk which professor Andronicos had to consider — and when we last saw it it was still in a corset of scaffolding.

Just as their funerary monuments tell us so much about the obsessions of the Victorians, so we can reach out and try to touch the Macedonians through their majestic underground temples. They are part barbaric; the bodies of the tomb, massively constructed from blocks of light brown tufa, are menacing and mysterious like a Stonehenge sarsen. But the structures are also graceful and affirmative in the best Hellenistic tradition. The façade on this tomb thrusts itself above the roof level of the burial chamber and antechamber so that, for the mourners and priests, entering its portal must have been like entering a contemporary temple.

The 8.5 metre high façade is two-storeyed; the lower Doric and the upper, which is a blind, in the Ionic order. Four well-preserved paintings, separated by Doric semi-columns, decorate the first storey. From the left we see the dead man, a soldier, who could have accompanied Alexander on his eastern campaigns, for the tomb is contemporary with the conqueror, turning with a gesture of resignation to the inevitability of death.

In his left hand he carries his empty sword sheath, presumably in token that his earthly power is spent, and in his right hand his spear. He wears a scarlet tunic under a cream-coloured leather cuirass. A magenta sash, perhaps of military rank, girdles his waist and a yellow cloak, edged with purple, is draped over his left shoulder.

We pass on to the figure of Hermes, the conductor, who is beckoning the general with his right hand while his winged staff of office, the caduceus, is on his left side. He is wearing a red, short-sleeved tunic with a blue cloak thrown over it. His *keysia* has practically disappeared.

The figures on the other side of the door are suitably withered and with a tragic air. They are the Judges of the Underworld who will weigh the general's deeds and decide whether he is to pass into eternal bliss or to be sent to Hades. Their identities are written for us above; Aikos, on the left, an old man, with hair and dress in disarray, his thin body an unhealthy parchment colour, was Judge of the European souls, and Rhadanthys, next to him, judge of the Asiatics. Certainly Alexander had made sure both had plenty of work to do although the general does not appear to have been a casualty. He is not wearing a helmet, nor is he carrying a shield, the symbols normally associated with a fighting end. Perhaps he was one of the time-expired officers Alexander sent home from Asia.

In a band above this superior fresco work are moulded metopes, divided by blue triglyphs or miniature columns, showing the battle between the Centaurs and Lapiths, the mythological shorthand used by the ancient Greeks to illustrate the strife between higher and lower nature.

The frieze is of carved stucco secured by bronze nails and depicts what would have been a very familiar theme to the general, a battle between Macedonians and Persian barbarians, identifiable by their breeches and Parthian caps. They are shown fighting in pairs, and, inevitably, the Greeks are winning. After being pursued and battered the length of the frieze the poor Persians are finally shown kneeling in abject submission.

The mounted horseman in this last scene could be our general, departing the field of honour at the side of his young leader. We can only guess if this and the other tombs on site contained funerary offerings, possibly including some of the booty from that campaign. The hope of finding such a haul in future excavations is perhaps heightened by the fabulous coup of Vergina.

The dimensions of the tomb are impressive enough; the anteroom measures 640 x 213 centimetres and has a height of 762 centimetres. The burial chamber is 487 x 457 centimetres and with a maximum height of 518 centimetres has the cool elegance of the dead man's andros, the room where he would receive visitors; and after all, he had to receive Hermes here. A podium runs round the room, supporting mock columns with blue Ionic moulding and architrave. The walls are dark red.

Retracing our steps to the main road, we crossed over and, heeding an aged and imprecise sign, followed another track through an orchard, a stream murmuring on our right. The tomb of Lyson and Kallikles is off left in the middle of the first clearing and could easily be mistaken for a well head; no structure is visible above ground.

The guide removed a weighted cover and opened the trap door beneath. What followed would be regarded by some as a descent into Hades itself; I do not advise those who suffer from claustrophobia to make it, and neither need the overweight apply. Broad as I am in shoulder and beam, I just managed to negotiate the hatch and descend the iron ladder which drops vertically into the tomb.

I dropped straight into the burial chamber, the last resting place of brothers Lyson and Kallikles, sons of Aristophanes, an identity clearly proclaimed on the lintel, perhaps so that Hermes would make no mistake. The room was painted with trompe l'oeil to give the impression of looking out through a colonnade, and the three-dimensional feeling had been enhanced by use of perspective. The trickery of the paintbrush, designed to deceive the eye, is continued in the decorative wreaths and trophies on the tympanum, the decorative area below the cornice or, in this case, the vaulted ceiling.

Laurels and pomegranates look as though they are hanging from nails; likewise swords, one with an eagle's head pommel, have been casually slung from pegs by the painter. In fact there is a veritable painted armoury, giving details of the harness worn by those Macedonians who fought the Romans (the tomb has been dated to the time of Perseus, last king of Macedonia). It includes two helmets, one with a trailing horsehair plume and the other an infantry helmet like the one in the Thessaloniki museum, and a shield with the royal sunburst emblem.

Lyson and Kallikles, and their relatives, when their time came, were cremated in the Macedonian tradition on pyres outside the tomb; clear indications of such a ritual were found in excavation. Their ashes were then placed, together with personal jewellry, in niches let into the walls of the burial chamber. These were plastered over and the names of the dead painted over each niche. The six niches on the north wall held the ashes of these two brothers, presumably senior members of the family, together with those of an another brother, Euippos, and those of their wives. This was a well-ordered family mausoleum. The right-hand wall was reserved for the descendants of Kallikles and the left for Lyson's heirs.

It was very pleasant to come up for air, particularly into groves and glades of this bosky place. Our guide was obviously not going to let us overlook perhaps its loveliest and certainly most numinous site. He climbed on to his motor scooter and led off along the Naoussa road to the village of Karpanos.

We took the second turn off and followed him round, over a little stream to a T junction. Turning right at a church and school we set off along a rutted track which leads through apple orchards, inclining right all the time. Just after a bend with a good view of Naoussa, lying on its ridge across the valley, we came to a natural rock amphitheatre standing off to the right, on a shelf above the Arapitsa.

It is a delightful tangle of icy springs bubbling out of the ground and forming streams thick with peppermint and cress; rocky outcrops, caves opening their dark mouths in the volcanic rock — the sort of place primitives peopled with spirits and nymphs. But there were signs of man's hand; weren't those cut niches and steps? As we gradually oriented ourselves we began to discern the outlines of Mieza, the Nymphaion, the school of Aristotle, where he taught his most famous pupil, Alexander the Great. Plutarch tells us that Philip, concerned at the unhealthy influence that Olympias was having on Alexander, sent for Aristotle, 'the most famous and learned of the philosophers of the time', to take the 13-year-old in hand.

Aristotle hailed from Stageira in the eastern highlands of Halkidiki, one of the cities of the peninsula's confederacy which Philip had sacked. But we are told that the king now resettled the site as a sop to the philosopher and, further, gave him and his pupil 'the temple of the Nymphs near Mieza as a place where they could study and converse.' The stone seats and shady walks Plutarch describes have gone, but it isn't difficult to detect the probable lay-out of the school. The typical ancient Greek school was the stoa, often part of a public arcade where pupils could be instructed in the shade and, when the heat permitted, exercise on the adjacent agora.

Mieza, we could see, had used the same lay-out. A long rectangle in form, it used a low rock face, 48 metres long, on to which the stoa abutted, facing south-east, and which was flanked by two rock outcrops, seamed with caves. The post holes and ridge for holding the roof beams of the stoa were clearly visible in the rock, as was the stylobate ('foot'), for holding the Ionic portico which is known to have run all the way around the school.

We ascended the flight of steps to the entrance of the first cave, which has a man-made lintel and was probably kept for offerings to nature. From the portico, steps can be seen leading down towards the river gorge, which is now covered by thick undergrowth, but in ancient times probably constituted those shady walks where master and pupils could debate questions of ethics and politics as well as 'those secret and more esoteric studies which philosophers do not impart to the general run of students' but to which Alexander certainly had access.

Perhaps Aristotle could never have really hoped fully to succeed in his task with such an extraordinary pupil. From Asia, Alexander chided him for publishing philosophical treateses based on discussions they had had at Meiza: 'what advantage shall I have over other men if these theories in which I have been trained are to be made common property?' Alexander concluded by assuring his old teacher that he would rather excel the rest of mankind in his knowledge of what was best than in the extent of his power.

Perhaps he meant it, but Alexander's imperialism and ideas on universalism did not appeal to Aristotle and we know how far he practised what he preached on these preferences. The breach between the two became absolute when Alexander put to death the philosopher's kinsman, Callisthenes, the historian of the Persian expedition, for alleged plotting. We retraced our steps to the main road and, taking the next right-hand turn, made for the hills.

Positioned on a high ridge close to the tombs is the now peaceful town of Naoussa, famous for its fine red wines. It offers a good selection of restaurants with a sweeping panorama of the Lefkadia plain. The wining B road enters the town near a large ornamental garden laid out on the lip of the ridge, over which roars a tributary of the Arapitsa. We lunched under the mature plane trees beside the park and afterwards strolled up to the main square, surrounded by small, clean restaurants with menus of more sophistication than are found in most Greek hill towns, and not expensive.

An unassuming town this, with relatively modern architecture; the contrast with its past could hardly be starker, for Naoussa was one of the standard bearers in the abortive Macedonian revolution against Turkish rule in 1821 and paid dearly for the honour.

We were taken to a spot called Sdoumpani, above the Arapitsa cascade, the site of one of those seminal events necessary in any revolution; I mean the grand sacrifice. Death before dishonour was chosen by certain women of Naoussa and was the final act in a dramatic failure; the Macedonian end of the Greek fight for independence. The women were not immortalized by western Romantic painters as were their sisters in Chios, but they were remembered in song and poetry in the villages of Macedonia and their sacrifice was redeemed ultimately a century later in the Balkan Wars.

Naoussa was a prosperous little walled town in 1822, dependent at least in part on craft work in guns. It had a strong armourers' guild which was able to form the nucleus of a military force when the revolutionaries decided to make a stand in the town, even though they knew the revolt in Halkidiki had failed.

The Turks had threatened to 'strike with no mercy whatsoever' and so they did. An army 10,000 strong, supported by another 10,000 Yuruk and Albanian auxiliaries, attacked the weak garrison, which was further handicapped by a not surprisingly poor morale on the part of the Naoussans.

Finally, on 13 April, the Turks broke in. Some of the rebel leaders fled to the south, but others died where they stood. To this day Naoussa commemorates, in its annual fete, the rapine that followed.

Thirteen young women of the town, knowing full well what fate awaited them if they fell into Turkish hands, joined hands and leapt off the crags of Sdoumpani into the torrent. Their sisters were herded to the slave blocks of Thessaloniki and, fetching good prices in the most desirable category of slave in Islam, White Circassian, were dispersed throughout the Middle East to gratify the lusts of pashas. The heads of the Greek rebel leaders were preserved and sent as trophies to the Sultan in Constantinople.

Mount Olympos and Dium

To the tourist in western Macedonia, Mount Olympos is omnipresent. Depending on the compass point of your approach, it shines behind other peaks and ranges, a pinnacle of snow-capped white limestone, which looms distantly through mist and cloud, seen, lost again, then, particularly if you are approaching it from the north, looming in front of you and blotting out the sky.

Its sheer size and the aura of ancient legends makes Olympos a powerful lodestone. Shrine, recreational centre and symbol of national resistance, Olympos has been all of these to the Greeks and, increasingly, foreigners are making a detour to enjoy its atmosphere.

We took the road that runs from Veria to Vergina, through the cotton fields that cover much of the plain that lies between the Pierian massif and the sea. It swings parallel with the national road at Methone, where Philip was blinded in one eye while besieging the city, of which nothing now remains. The road runs into Katerini, a pleasant if unexceptional town with hotel accommodation for those wanting to break their journey after a long and tiring drive.

We decided to push on to the foot of the mountain. The feed road out of Katerini to the national road is well marked. Of Greece's number one road, which runs from Athens to Thessaloniki, a word of warning should be issued. Although classed as a motorway, it does not qualify as such by most standards. Instead of a road custom-built for speed, with canted surfaces, angled, and with well sign-posted interchanges, you have, in effect, a four-lane carriageway with no shoulder or central reservation, a

13 Lion of Amphipolis, 4th century BC.

14 Capital with acanthus leaf design, Philippi.

15 Coins of Philip II at the British Museum.

16 Torso from the
pediment of the Senate
House, Roman Philippi.

17 Caiques in harbour, present-day Kavala.

18 Statue of Mehemet Ali, founder of the last dynasty of Egypt, outside his birthplace in Kavala.

19 Imaret, Kavala.

20 The mediaeval
fortifications of
Kavala.

21 Geometric mosaic in the House of the Lion Hunt at Pella.

22 Detail of the mosaic in the House of the Lion Hunt.

23 Lake Prespa.

24 The school of Aristotle, showing support holes for the stoa, Mieza, near Naoussa.

25 The Arch of Galerius, Thessaloniki.

26 Column bases, the palace of Antigonos Gonatas, Vergina.

27 Miniature head in ivory, portrait of Philip II, height 3 cm, from the Royal Tomb at Vergina.

road which encourages the vices of Greek drivers without, in our opinion, providing enough safeguards for the unwary. Major drawbacks are the limited access and the lack of provision for making left turns.

That said, the drive to the home of the gods is pleasant, the road being fringed by tall poplars and offering vistas of the sea on your left. We had been advised to stay in the village of Lithokoron and now saw its lights twinkling in the gathering dusk of the foothills over to our right. The turn-off was signalled well in advance and we drove 4 kilometres up a slowly rising road, past an army camp, to our 'base camp' on the lower slopes.

The choice, as it turned out, was a happy one. Lithokoron has the atmosphere of an Alpine village, with new, well-appointed hotels — their deep-eaved roofs and overhanging balconies adding to the illusion. In season (May to September) the tavernas and discos add the touch of Alpine sporting frivolity.

The first sight of the mountain as we stepped on to our balcony next morning was an experience to be savoured. The north face, probably the most spectacular of its many faces, soared above us to the aptly named Throne of Zeus, the summit of Olympos. There are in fact three and they form a semi-circle, rearing their snow-capped crests into the invigorating air to a height of almost two miles.

The Throne of Zeus (2909.3 metres), has another, equally appropriate name, the Stefani, 'classical wreath'. It is a curve of white limestone that drops sheer to the scree, then to the slopes of the Mavrolongos valley, thickly clothed in pine, which is the only practicable route from the east.

A road of good, graded earth with gravelled surface, curves up the side of the valley to a height of 1102 metres. The drops below each bend in the trail get steeper and steeper as you climb. The air is like wine after the stifling heat at sea level and it is tangy with the musk of pine. Besides the conifers the lower slopes of the Mavrolongos are clothed in varied deciduous timber — oaks, beeches, chestnuts and platanos.

The mountain is negotiable by car as far as Prionia, the mountain hut where your assault on the summit changes from four wheels to four legs. Mountaineering on Olympos is organized by an experienced and convivial man, Katafillion 'Gus' Zolotas, who runs the hut, situated at 2100 metres, from which you make the final climb. He saves his guests' strength — and they include many Greek regulars; we know of someone who has made the climb regularly every September for the past 30 years — by sending a mule train down to Prionia to collect them.

The bone-jarring three-hour ride up to the refuge is compensated for by the views, becoming more dramatic with every twist and turn in the trail. You spend the night at Zolotas' refuge (his wife, by the way, speaks good English) and early next morning you climb up to the summit of Mytikas, 'the Needle'. It is a good stiff walk, for which correct hiking gear is recommended, and can be covered in two hours. The best time to go up Mount Olympos is late summer, August to September. Earlier in the season there can be a lot of cloud or heat haze around and below the summits.

On your way back to Lithokoron, it is worthwhile making a diversion to see the ruins of the monastery of Aghios Dionysos, built about 1500, traditionally by St Dionysos, the former Athonite monk. The Olympos massif was a traditional redoubt for the Klephts, those Robin Hoods who kept the flame of resistance to the Turks burning brightly while lining their own pockets. The Turks retaliated by destroying the monastery in 1828, probably in vengeance for the part the men of Olympos had played in the War of Independence. It was to suffer another, and more comprehensive act of desecration 115 years later, when a detachment of the SS came up the trail from Lithokoron and after removing the monks set explosive charges and reduced the building to a shell.

It stands on the lip of a gorge, the wind sighing through the great gaps in its walls, the roofless katholikon and truncated refectory. On a small altar in the chapel of the katholikon, the sacred flame is still kept alive and services occasionally held. In fact, the monastery is still served by a young monk and an appeal has been made for funds for its rebuilding. Meanwhile, what was done here is writ large for tourists of all nationalities: 'This monastery was destroyed by the Germans'.

One of the great sacrificial centres of Macedonia, which was also a testing ground for its military might, lay aptly in the shadow of Mount Olympos. Dium, today, is in some ways as much of a secretive place as it was in the year 1806, when Colonel Leake visited it, recording, with a fine surrealistic touch, that near here he received a messenger with news of Napoleon's victory at Jena. Between the sea and a marsh formed by 'copious springs of water', he found the remains of a stadium and a theatre. 'None of the stonework which may be supposed to have formed the seats and super-structure now exists. . . . Some foundations of the walls of the city to which these monuments belonged are visible . . . but it would be vain to attempt to trace them in such a labyrinth without a guide. . . .'

He could obtain no local help and, after our visit to the site, we were left feeling a certain sympathy with him. Dium is not easy to find. You turn left off the national road, a few metres back in the direction of Katerni, and follow a dirt track across the fields, bearing right past an industrial plant, and in the general direction of groves of poplars, which surround the village of Malathria as they did in Leake's time.

You are likely to meet at this point some of the most savage and persistent guard dogs in Macedonia. Once into the village, signs point out the ancient site and the museum. The latter was shut during our visit for renovations, so we pressed on to the former (normal opening hours).

Leake's 'famous Dium, one of the leading cities of Macedonia and the great bulwark of its maritime empire to the south', was laid bare before the First World War and the excavation being carried out there now under the direction of Dr Pandamalis of the University of Thessaloniki is aimed at amplifying the ground plan of this rather mysterious centre and trying to throw more light on its purpose.

Unfortunately, little elucidation is forthcoming from the guide on the site, even for the older excavations, and the newer digs are still not published as I write. Photography is forbidden. Little now stands above ground level, but even so there are hints of what an important place Dium was. The site forms a rough rectangle, crossed by roads north to south and east to west. As you enter at the southern end of the site, a broad (5 to 5.6 metres wide) road, paved with large, marble slabs, stretches before you. Bearing in mind the sacerdotal role that Dium is supposed to have had, the existence of a large, marble votive frieze, affixed to a wall half-way along on the left-hand side, may suggest a processional way. The frieze, which is Hellenistic, is of alternate sets of Greek body armour and circular shields.

On the right of this way are the ground plans of shops and public baths. The 700-metre-long southern ramparts of the city, built of large, rectangular marbloid blocks, rear up in the background, although when we were there they were not easily accessible. They date from the late fourth century, the period of the consolidation of the Macedonian state when the need would be felt to protect a place connected with cult worship, and inscriptions have been found honouring Olympian Zeus, in whose honour King Archelaus built a temple and the god whose aid, we know, was sought here by Alexander in 334 BC before the Persian campaign. He held a nine-day festival, sacrificing to the god, and after the battle of Granicus he commissioned Lysippus to carve statues of the Companions who had fallen there, to be set up at Dium. They were still there in 147 BC.

Alexander was following a tradition set not only by his ancestor, Archelaus, who had also instituted a drama festival, but also by his father, who gave thanksgiving here for his destruction of Olynthos. Diodorus says:

After the capture of Olynthos, he celebrated the Olympian festival to the gods and offered magnificent sacrifices; and he organized a great festive assembly at which he held splendid competitions and thereafter invited many of the visiting strangers to his banquets. In the course of the carousals he joined in numerous conversations, presenting many of the guests with drinking cups as he proposed the toasts, awarding gifts to a considerable number, and graciously making such handsome promises to them all that he won over a large number to crave friendship with him.

Leake's theatre is over to the west, built on an earthen embankment, near it a small odeon. Evidence has come to light of the catholicity of worship in Dium — the range of deities reminiscent of the pantheon of Samothrace. Traces of sanctuaries have been discovered dedicated to Dionysos (in the theatre itself), Demeter, Aesclypius, Artemis and Isis.

An important Macedonian tomb has been discovered, just to the north of Malathria, which will be opened soon. Dating from about 300 BC , it has its burial couch intact, painted with a representation of a battle between Greeks and barbarians. The vaulted roof has a painted procession of lions, similar to motifs found on Scythian tombs in southern Russia.

7. Philippi and Kavala

Philippi

Philippi, of all ancient sites in Macedonia, has a presence; its stones seem to speak of great events. Here, where the Via Egnatia presented the only route from Europe into Asia, between the Pangeon and Lekanis mountain ranges, the fate of the Roman empire, and in a sense, the destiny of Europe itself, were shaped.

Crenides-Philippi started as a Hellenistic gold-rush town, but almost nothing of that remains. What the visitor sees is a Roman colonia, founded in commemoration of the great battle which took place a few kilometres to the west, and an early Christian settlement — in fact, the first Christian foothold in Europe. Appropriately, the site straddles the road to Drama, which at this point still follows the Egnatian Way. Anyone making the 18-kilometre bus journey from Kavala, with even the scantiest knowledge of what happened in this place, cannot fail to notice the spectacular topography — the pass commanding the route down to the sea at Kavala, the great triangle of mountains which meet here, and in the midst of them the rolling, historic plain itself.

At sunset it is even more impressive, with the arid peaks turning a shadowed purple and the golden light on the plain darkening and reddening. Now the lines of the classical authors, Plutarch, Arrian and Vergil — who may have been a participant in the battle — conjour up the shades of marching legions and flaunting eagle standards. One ghost in particular comes unbidden, that of Julius Caesar, disturbing the dreams of Marcus Brutus: 'Thou shalt see me at Philippi'. He did, of course, in the shape of the dictator's avenging friend, Mark Antony, in the October of 42 BC. What followed was not one battle, but a protracted struggle of manoeuvre and attrition, begun and ended by bloody collisions of the two largest armies ever assembled beneath the eagles.

Each side had had two years since Caesar's assassination to prepare for the struggle and as the Triumvirs, or Caesarian party, controlled the resources of the western half of the Roman world, and the Republicans the eastern half, it is quite possible that the reported figure involved — roughly 80,000 on each side — is accurate.

Cassius and Brutus had command of the sea and the eastern end of the Egnatian Way, with all the resources of Asia Minor and the means to deploy them when and where they wished. They seized Thasos and

Neapolis (Kavala) separated by a gulf no more than 12 kilometres wide, as their bases for a campaign to decide no less than the mastery of the better part of the known world. It was a campaign they started with a defender's advantage, but the Republicans were unable to use their maritime mastery to launch an amphibious attack. The sheet unweildliness of their army meant a long march along the coast of Thrace towards the advanced posts of the Caesarians who had pushed forward along the western stretch of the Egnatia. Brutus and Cassius had attempted to blockade Octavian and Mark Antony in Italy but had failed to stop Antony getting his legions across the Adriatic.

Finding the passes through the Thracian mountains — 'the only known route from Asia to Europe' — firmly held by the better part of eight legions, the Republican army set off into the interior on an arduous flankmarch which added many more kilometres to an operation which had already brought them 1500 stades (approx. 275 km). Guided by Thracian collaborators who themselves 'were astounded at so large an army traversing a route where no water could be obtained and where not even a wild beast could penetrate by reason of the dense foliage', they crossed the Lekanis massif, probably debouching into the plain of Philippi down one of the passes cutting the hills on the right as you drive from Kavala.

They were first at the strategic prize, commanding the edge of 'a beautiful plain extending to the river Strymon, about 350 stades'. It had a slope in favour of the occupiers of Philippi 'but was toilsome to those going up from Amphipolis'. Amphipolis, on the other side of Mount Pangeon, was already in the hands of Mark Antony and he lost no time in matching the Republicans' recent audacious march. 'He advanced with great boldness and encamped in the plain at a distance of only eight stades from the enemy.' Both sides dug in in the approved Roman fashion, constructing embanked marching camps with gates. Appian gives a very detailed description of the Republicans' fortifications.

The plain was admirably suited for fighting and the hill tops for camping, since on one side of them were marshes and ponds stretching as far as the river Strymon, and on the other gorges destitute of roads and impassable. Between these hills, eight stades apart, lay the main pass from Europe to Asia. Across this space they built a fortification from camp to camp, leaving a gate in the middle so that two camps became virtually one. Alongside this fortification flowed a river which is called the Gangites, and behind it was the sea, where they could keep their supplies and shipping in safety.

Part of that vallum can still be traced. The key to the position is a pair of small, conical hills, which can easily be seen from the terrace of the museum, probably the best vantage point for the battlefield. You take your sight-line on a larger hill lying to the south-west. The plain between that and the tumuli was the field of combat, the struggle turning on the possession of the larger of the two, where Cassius' camp was situated. The circumvallation of the camp can today be followed along the remains of an earth embankment through the fields on the edge of the plain. The undula-

Site of Philippi

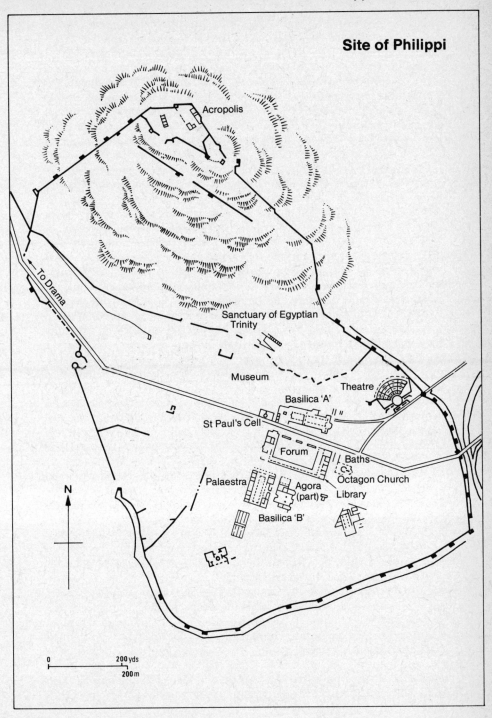

Acropolis

To Drama

Sanctuary of Egyptian Trinity

Museum

Theatre

Basilica 'A'

St Paul's Cell

Forum

Baths

Octagon Church

Palaestra

Agora (part)

Library

Basilica 'B'

N

0   200 yds
    200 m

tions, in which even the position of the gates can be identified, form a protective half circle round the site of the colonia, facing Amphipolis and danger.

From here, Cassius should have been able to see any sudden movement of the enemy. Complacency seems to have prevailed in the Republican camp, however. Cassius and his fellow conspirator had a contented army at their command — if Appian can be believed, each legionary was given 1500 drachmae in addition to his pay — the magazines were full and the auguries seemed to be good. Two eagles had alighted on their standards on the march and were treated as pets by the men. There seemed no reason why they should seek a battle; the fighting season was to all intents finished, and winter was drawing on. Best to let hunger and desertion through inaction decimate the Caesarian ranks.

Antony, their main antagonist as Octavian was still throwing off the effects of fever and was, in any case, an inferior soldier, as his conduct in the battle showed, was indeed very worried. Eastern Macedonia had been picked clean of supplies and the enemy had control of the sea — in fact on the day of the first battle, they scored a great triumph over the Caesarians in the Adriatic. To force the issue Antony despatched a force of sappers to build a causeway through the marshes so that he could threaten the Republican communications with Neapolis and so precipitate a battle.

As a distraction, he drew up his legions in battle array. Ten days after work started the embankment was strong enough for Antony to advance a strong force almost up to the vallum of Cassius' camp. Cassius, taken completely by surprise (the sappers had worked under cover of thick reed beds) attempted a countervallation. The battle started in unco-ordinated assaults, provoked by sheer frustration. Antony's troops charged Cassius' camp with scaling ladders, while on the north flank Brutus' men 'provoked by the insolence of the enemy', fell on Octavian's camp. Octavian had already left, in obedience, he said later, to a dream, and his camp was captured.

Antony captured Cassius' camp after stiff fighting, but at a cost of twice as many dead. The conspirator climbed the acropolis to try to clarify the situation, particularly to see if he could expect reinforcements from Brutus, but the fog of war was too dense to allow him to see Brutus' standards massed in triumph in Octavian's camp. Everything seemed lost for him and now the neurotic instability that marked the conspirator and had caused Caesar to scorn him as 'a lean, white-faced fellow', took over. He fell on his shield-bearer's sword. It was his birthday.

Brutus recaptured Cassius' camp and sent his body to Thasos for burial so that his obsequies should not affect the troops' morale. To reinforce that morale and defend himself against accusations of slothful generalship, Brutus addressed the army. He said that his plan depended on 'hunger engaging the enemy before we do'. They would simply stay behind their vallum, ignoring the other side's provocation and insults. But, as an insurance, Brutus promised his men the plunder of Thessalonica, when they took it. Antony, for his part, was stiffening his soldiers' resolve with bribes of 5000 drachmae a man — and proportionately more for centurions and tribunes — to be raised from the plunder of the Republican camp.

The struggle was stalemated for almost three weeks; November came and with it the lacerating cold rain and mud of a Balkan winter. Antony led his men out every day to offer a battle and brought them back in disgust at night, the challenge rejected. Brutus himself brought on the unwanted final conflict by his own neglect. Appian tells us that a hill, probably the smaller of the tumuli, which lay between the lines, had been garrisoned by Cassius but was abandoned by Brutus. Octavian occupied it with four legions who, protecting themselves with a testudo of wickerwork and hide shields, used it to launch themselves at the enemy earthwork. At the same time he out-flanked Brutus to the south, towards the sea. The Republicans were now the ones on the defensive. Plutarch claims that had Brutus had the news of his fleet's victory in the Adriatic in time it would have made all the difference to his decision on a course of action. In the event he decided to try his fortune in the field and parading his army in front of the camp he threw down the gage. The soldiers 'did not resort to the usual manouevres and tactics of battle, but coming to close combat with naked swords, they slew and were slain'. Finally the gates of the camp were carried, and with them the day. The slaughter was terrible, although again the Caesarians lost twice as many as the Republicans. Brutus fled to the nearby mountains and ended his life like his brother-in-law and co-conspirator, although his conspiracy was not 'in envy of great Caesar' but 'only in general honest thought and common good to all'.

The site of the ancient city offers a lot in a very small compass. Earth-quake rather than sack was the great leveller here, yet enough of the bones of Philippi are left to make the task of decoding a rewarding one.

Philippi drew its life from the traffic of the Via Egnatia; the battle which put the city on the historical map took place here because of it and St Paul followed its course as far inland as Veria, preaching the word. Perhaps the most eloquent stones on the site form the paving of a stretch of the Egnatia which runs along the side of the forum just below the entrance gate on the left-hand side of the modern road. The ancient road certainly could not have been as hazardous for pedestrians as its modern counterpart, which bisects the site, leaving the forum, agora and baths and one basilica on the left, and the theatre, another basilica and the musum on the right. As at Pella, extreme caution is needed with the traffic and you yearn for the ancient way with its flying chariot teams, carts and litters. The section below the gate is deeply rutted by that traffic of 2000 years ago and still has part of its original marble-faced embankment.

Abutting onto the street would have been the rhetoricians' marble tribunes, the city's speakers' corner, where, doubtless, Paul spoke. Beyond lay the forum, large by Roman provincial standards, and the scale of which is indicated by the bases of the porticoes, which enclosed it on three sides. A temple and a library were on the eastern side of the forum and the large sculpted figures in the museum, which came from the principal government building, attest the scale of all the public building in the colonia.

Beyond the south-facing portico and behind the well-preserved drainage system and water conduits were shops, with wells and counters with impressions for weights and measures. The whole of this part of the site is dominated by the pillars of basilica B, a conspicuous early failure in domed building, earlier even than the Aghia Sofia in Thessalonica. Apparently the eastern wall and apse collapsed some time in the sixth century. The western end of the church, inscribed by marauding Bulgars, also fell and the narthex alone remained to serve the original purpose of the site, after a lapse of four centuries. Today two great reddened piers, topped with elegant Theodosian capitals, are enough to show that this was no mean city to the early Christians, those 'saints in Christ Jesus which are at Philippi'.

Just to the south-east can be seen the foundations of an octagonal church, which, in its heyday, must have had a real presence, with an interior stoa of 20 columns on seven of the sides and a marble iconostasis covering the eighth. Today, white wild flowers cluster among the fallen column drums and capitals.

To the west of basilica B are the ruins of a gymnasium, at the foot of which are the lavatories, with marble pans still in place. A little farther on are the remains of the Roman baths, now, sadly, without their mosaics, which were destroyed during the war by the Bulgars.

Across the main road is the Philippi which, if you like, was dedicated to the Dionysic spirit; the setting for theatrical and religious drama. At the top of the steps leading up from the guard's hut is what remains of basilica A, shaken down by an earthquake soon after being built in the sixth century, but still possessing the attractive grey and white marble paved atrium and the tesselated floor of its separate baptistry.

A track leads up to the lower face of the acropolis, to the shrines of the various deities and cults venerated in Philippi; the Egyptian deities, Isis, Serapis and Harpocrates, and the Thracian, Artemis Bendis and Silvanus. These incisions in the rock face are of a deceptive crudity. The inscriptions, which are still partly legible, were dedicated to the rural deities of a still untamed frontier region (the popularity of the Thracian mounted hunter motif, sometimes shown with a serpent coiled around a tree is evidence of the tenacious hold such cults still had until the end of the pagan era). Yet the Philippian cults were served by officially appointed colleges of priests, who, with the magistrates, ran the city.

Following the path from basilica A to the right, round the base of the hill, you come to the theatre — restored but still the only surviving part of Philip's settlement. Its cavea commands a spectacular view over the eastern part of the plain and each August is a popular venue for modern theatre goers when classical drama is presented in the Philippi-Thasos festival of Greek theatre.

Greek festival theatre has none of the rather self-conscious artiness which sometimes accompanies such ventures in the West. The audiences are critical and knowledgeable. They come to experience the living culture of their race. Beforehand, on the lawns, scattered with refreshment kiosks and flowering trees, which cover the levels between the acropolis and the road, they hold small parties. But, as the sun sinks and the acropolis becomes a looming purple shadow, gradually merging with the indigo sky, they troop through the parados (classical entry way), past pillars inscribed to the pagan deities of these mountains, and take their seats in the great fanwork of marble on the hillside.

The play when we were there was *The Phoenicians* by Euripides and it was being given by the National Theatre Company, directed by the Olivier of Greece, Alexis Minotis. The rhythms in the play, both of speech and movement, were quite hypnotic so that even for those with no Greek, they cast a spell. Mr Minotis told us before the performance: 'We do not know how they performed 2000 to 3000 years ago, but we are guided by the language and the metre of the verse for the rhythms, and the expressions give to the words the large value that they have when they deal with larger than life themes.'

Larger than life they are, although concerned with the eternal human frailties. The Greek theatre goer recognizes that the play is bound by two factors, the lyrical and the dramatic; the lyrical being expressed by the chorus and the dramatic by the actors. Minotis explained: 'we do not try to modernize because we consider that these plays are modern to the bone. They are as modern as a column — they express the abstraction of the ancient drama and the convention which is the most important theme in theatre. We are far from naturalism. The ancient Greek drama uses human voices to express eternal themes and phonemena — the mystery of existence and eternity. The ancients were particularly interested in the mystery of existence. Dramatic art stems from one fact — we are born to die.'

Performances start at 9 p.m. and buses run a shuttle service between Kavala and Philippi for the benefit of theatre goers.

Retracing your steps back to basilica A, and then descending some steps to main road level, you come to a small vaulted building, which could have been a crypt or a cistern but which very early in the Christian era was accepted as the prison from which Paul was miraculously released by the earthquake. As *The Acts* tells us:

And when they had laid many stripes upon them [Paul and Silas] they cast them into prison, charging the jailer to keep them safely: who having received such a charge, thrust them into the inner prison, and made their feet fast in the stocks.

And at midnight Paul and Silas prayed, and sang praises unto God: and the prisoners heard them. And suddenly there was a great earthquake, so that the foundations of the prison were shaken: and immediately all the doors were opened and everyone's bands were loosed. And the keeper of the prison awaking out of his sleep, and seeing the prison doors open, drew out his sword, and would have killed himself, supposing that the prisoners had fled. But Paul cried out with a loud voice saying 'Do thyself no harm, for we are here'.

Today there is an English inscription on the wall of this ancient focal point for Christian faith:
'To me to live in Christ and die is gain'
(Philippians 1.21.)

Their imprisonment had a cause that was to become familiar in these early missionary journeys — their preaching hit paganism through its pocket. The Apostles made their first convert in Europe, Lydia, 'the seller of purple', near here. She became the linchpin of a small band of believers which included a servant girl, a soothsayer, probably epileptic, who made money for her master with her prophecies until Paul cured her of her affliction. Immediately the enraged master brought charges of seditious teaching. It was, on the face of it, an inauspicious start to a church for which Paul was to have a special affection.

The approximate site of that first conversion, just down the road from the main site at Philippi, is marked by a fountain and a chapel. But, as often happens in ancient history, tradition here has some firm basis. The Bible talks of Lydia 'going to the riverside, where prayer was wont to be made'. Now the site is the only place near the city where the Egnatia crosses a stream, the Gangites, which provided the 'moat' for Cassius and Brutus' camp.

Near by, before the war, were discovered the bases of a sacred archway which seemed to mark the limit of the 'sacred enclosure' or pomerium of the city, within which religious rites other than those to the accepted deities of the city were banned. Jews, in common with other sects, would have respected this code and it is entirely credible that open-air religious meetings were held beyond the city limits where the chapel now marks the most important of them.

Reversing your steps, you will find the museum standing back from the road on the left. In the entrance hall stands a stele showing a family group. A woman is seated before a table from which a small boy is taking pomegranates and grapes. Philippi's legacy comes to us mainly in marble, and most eloquently in the pieces from the public buildings in the forum, and now in the upper gallery.

There are several larger-than-life figures, like ships' figureheads, which came from a large structure, probably the court house. One group, dating from the second or third century AD, has a pet dog gazing up imploringly at its mistress.

The strong hold that Thracian cults retained locally is commemorated by a votive plaque to Artemis Bendis as huntress, dating from the first century BC. The hunting motif is picked up in sections of tesselated pavement showing a hunting dog attacking a deer and others depicting wild boars and running deer.

The decoration of Philippi's official buildings is suggested by a portrait bust of the Emperor Commodus, he who was so fond of dressing up in a lion skin and parading in the arena as Hercules, and by a lion's head water spout from a fountain in the forum.

Kavala

Paul's first landfall in Europe was Neapolis, the modern Kavala, and it has been the same for countless travellers from the Levant since then. Traffic from northern Europe has, until recently, been transient — a mere overnight acquaintance before passing on to Thasos, or, perhaps, Istanbul. That is a pity because this ancient port has much to offer the visitor.

The second town of Macedonia, it unfolds around a long indent in the lower slopes of Mandra Kari, a range of hills which continue the rocky rampart of the Pangeon massif along the coast to the Lekanis range, the secret approach route used by Brutus and Cassius before Philippi. It presents its fairest face from seaward. As the ferry from Thasos edges into land, the sunlight throws into high relief the acropolis, crowned by its Byzantine kastro, and with the old town clustered around its skirts, and the Turkish aqueduct. Acting as a backdrop and heightening the theatricality of it all are the pearly grey rock faces of the Mandra Kari.

The aqueduct, Kavala's most famous landmark, acts as a gate to the old town, straddling the gorge which runs down from the hills to the waterfront. With its triple tiers, the Kamares is probably the best example of Turkish civil engineering surviving in the old European Ottoman empire. It was yet another example of the Turks adopting part of the Roman or Byzantine genius. Like the *hammams* or military engineering, they could not improve on the idea so it passed into their culture unaltered. The aqueduct was built in the mid-sixteenth century on the orders of the Sultan Soleyman the Magnificent to carry water to the citadel. It worked on the gravity principle, the impetus of the downhill rush of water on one side of the valley being harnessed by gradiants skilfully aligned to 'tease' it into cisterns up in the rock face opposite.

Down on the waterfront the process of delivering the fish from sea to table can be followed through all its stages of raucous bustle, but you have to be up early to see it. The caiques dock at dawn and the fish is humped in crates the few steps across the quay to the fish market where all morning the cacophony of brisk bargaining for small mountains of mullet and scores of squid makes for a kind of street theatre. Nearby are the fish tavernas, nestling in a tree-shaded corner of the harbour, where the catch fetch rather higher prices. To the west, modern Kavala covers the site of Paul's Neapolis, and as it climbs the steep hillside in a north-westerly direction, it follows the route of the Via Egnatia which he travelled. The road winds upward through pine woods, with occasional panoramic views of the dark blue semi-circle of the bay — perhaps scored with the snail-like track of a ferry — and a now lilliputian kastro. The Egnatia crosses a saddle at the top of its climb, formed by the Simvolon ridge which shuts the plain of Philippi off from the sea. Here, traditionally, the footsore Apostles made their first stop on their historic journey and here today stands a fairly undistinguished monastery, dedicated to Paul's companion, Silas. The whole journey has been made the subject of a festival in Kavala on 29 June, St Paul's feast day. Part of the route to Philippi is walked over and tableaux recall the stirring events of *The Acts*.

On the other side of the ridge a section of the old paved road curves down to the plain, below the modern road. Its irregular-shaped stones, set in grass and shadowed by cypress trees, may be Turkish or, conceivably,

Roman, but the course follows the route of the Egnatia and a sign proclaims it as such.

Like Thessaloniki, Kavala's waterfront is part working port and part leisure area, in the form of elegant gardens, laid out on a polder reclaimed since the war. In the early evening you can sit beneath the awning of a smart modern café, sipping an aperitif or café frappé and watch the fishermen preparing for the night's fishing. The prows of the caiques overhang the quayside of the old port where Brutus' galleys tied up, and their rakish white shapes contrast with great, dark pyramids of fishing nets, strung up to dry. As the sun sets the acropolis loses its sharp contours and mellows to a cream-and-gold glow. Overhead swallows dart and dive and the huge Aegean gulls peel off for the cliffs with valedictory calls.

Kavala can easily be covered on foot in a day and an obvious starting point is the old town. At this point it is worth while putting any queries you may have to the tourist office for eastern Macedonia, which occupies a pavilion just off the Platea Eleftherias. They can help with itineraries, bus schedules and hotel vacancies.

Walking back to the fish market and the tavernas, you see a long street, Kountourioutou, leading up to the aqueduct. On the left is the Church of Aghios Nikolaos. Opposite, a steep, cobbled street, Odos Poulidhou, leads up to the old town. Walking up between overhanging balconied houses you come to a fork in the street with a ramp leading up to the left. On the right nestle the domes of the Imaret, the alms house donated by Mehmet Ali and now gently rotting, a memorial to unwelcome guests. Restored, it would make an ideal folk art museum.

The Imaret was a well-appointed hostel for the aged and indigent, a soothing ambience of splashing fountains, soft divans in individual cells and cooing doves. The inmates wiled away their days, smoking, talking and occasionally praying in their own mosque and earned the home the contemptuous epithet *Tembel Henneh* ('the lazy man's home') from the locals. Today, the cells with their shady, pointed arch porticoes and the picturesque small colonnaded courts are storehouses for fruit and vegetables; the mosque is locked and barred. The site is a true asset to the old town; the copper-sheathed domes have taken on the appearance of well-worn leather and many of them are still surmounted by their brass crescents. Over the gateway is a marble plaque, an inscription from the Koran in elegant Arabic script.

Taking the left fork, you climb steeply between balconied houses, colourwashed in yellow and lime and with small, fragrant courtyards. The sea glimmers below you on the right. The street widens at the summit of the acropolis into a small square, surrounded by elaborately shuttered old Turkish houses, and which has a small mosque and Turkish baths on one corner. Straight ahead, the sea appears at the end of a long descent, ending in rocks which are a favourite swimming place for local boys.

You take the alleyway on the right between high garden walls overhung with oleander. A few paces on the left, behind a rusting iron gate, is a cool garden full of odiferous plants, cypresses and palms. In the centre, like a verse from the *Rubiyat* of Omar Khayyam translated into marble, is a sarcophagus, all elaborate foliate patterns and lacy Arabic inscriptions. It is the tomb of Mehmet Ali's mother.

To reach the house of Kavala's most famous son, you descend the long stairway opposite the garden. Turn sharp left at the bottom and you will find yourself in a spacious belvedere overlooking the sea and from which Mehmet Ali, scimitar in hand, looks towards his Levantine conquests from the back of a curveting steed. Ali, born in 1769 in the typical Macedonian mansion house which faces the statue, is supposed to have started his career as a tobacco trader. The Napoleonic Wars, however, saw him serving as a soldier of fortune in Egypt, where he was able to use the political confusion following the expulsion of the French to defeat the Mamelukes and cut out for himself a semi-independent fief.

Despite sending aid to his co-religionist and nominal overlord, the Sultan, during the Greek War of Independence, he was eventually able to confirm his independent status in Egypt and to found a dynasty. That dynasty, which ended with Farouk, maintained the house and garden until the end of the monarchy in Egypt, since when the responsibility has been assumed by the Greeks.

You enter through the type of postern we encountered at Siatista, designed for secrecy and defence. The lower storey displays one difference. Recessed into the wall is a revolving wooden dumb waiter. It connected directly with the harem on the upper floor and ensured that tradesmen and messengers would never have any contact with secluded inmates on the floor above. If the ladies wished to take the air they could summon a servant to yoke up a team in the stables, farther along the entry alley, and, decently enveloped in their black *feridjes* and veils, would go for a spin in a light travelling carriage.

The harem is separated from the selamlik (men's quarters) by a fretted screen and there is accommodation for about half-a-dozen women. This is a modest household considering that Ali's ladies would have had their female slaves with them. They performed their ablutions in a tiny and dark shower room behind the divan-lined sleeping quarters; squatting while the slave disrobed them and sluiced them down with jugs of water drawn from a cistern. It is a world away from the odalisque fantasies of Ingres.

On the desk in the main saloon, patterned by the shadows from the intricately worked wooden shutters, are photographs of the later Egyptian kings, a reminder that Ali's line came to an end only in 1952 with Farouk.

Returning to town along the rim of the acropolis, you complete a circular tour when you re-emerge level with the Imaret. The late morning air is tangy with the smell of baking bread and it is pleasant to sit outside one of the tiny cafés near the Imaret and have a yogurt or a metrio.

To reach the kastro, the Byzantine fortress of Kavala, you retrace your steps up the left-hand alley and keep bearing left until you see the grey, crenellated walls ahead. The entrance is on the east side.

The kastro affords the best view out over the town. Only some storehouses and the former prison survive in what was the bailey but the circuit of walls are intact. The loopholes themselves give you enough of a vantage point, but you can scramble up onto the fire-step from which you can appreciate the complete half-moon of the harbour and the lay-out of the town, one of the most satisfying townscapes in the Mediterranean.

Kavala's excellent modern museum is on the front, a few metres west of the ferry landing. It has the second finest collection of Macedonian tomb finds after Thessaloniki museum. They were all found in a group of tombs at Amphipolis. In the main hall can be seen three gold wreaths of olive leaves (sacred to Athena), with red stone insets, together with gold necklaces — all from a tomb of the third century BC . Other beautiful funerary jewellery are gilded floral wreaths with painted petals. The sort of setting in which they were found, the two-chamber tomb, has been reconstructed near by. Another link with the splendid finds at Vergina are painted Hellenistic stele, one with an epigram.

An unusual piece of Attic ware is a red-figure pelike showing Aphrodite riding a goose over the sea. Near it is an exquisite black-glazed hydria kalpis with two gilded wreaths, dating from the reign of Philip. A gold stater struck under the king is a reminder of why he came to Amphipolis and Mount Pangeon. The only link now with Hellenistic Neapolis is provided by two Ionic columns, part of the temple of Parthenos, from the beginning of the fifth century, and terracotta figurines of deities.

Kavala is a good shopping centre, not only for its markets on the front and near Platea Eleftherias, but also for its varied and reasonably priced shops, mostly found along Odhos Omonias, which runs in a straight line north-west from near the aqueduct. You can buy anything here from a needle and thread to a bottle of cognac or a suit.

A number 4 bus, which can be caught at the Kavala internal bus station near the fish tavernas or outside the cafés on Erithou Stavrou, behind the fishing quay, takes you to the town's beach area, on the far side of the stumpy headland which complements the more thrusting, dramatic acropolis across the bay. The Hotel Lucy, which occupies the headland, has the advantage of two small, sand horseshoe beaches, one private and the other, in the lee of the hotel, public. This little skala has the best of Kavala's nightlife, with cafés and discos on the sea edge, offering a moderately priced evening of dining and dancing.

Beyond the Lucy, the coast is deeply indented with gorse-covered cliffs dropping to sandy coves, in one of which EOT have established a camping site. The road becomes a corniche and below, in one of the best natural sand bays, you glimpse the Tosca bungalow complex. This new carriageway which opens up a highly attractive coastline previously inaccessible because of the Simvolon massif, winds between private villas and long stretches of poplars and cypresses before dropping to the plain of the Strymon to link up with the Thessaloniki-Kavala road. A little past this junction and just before the mouth of the river is reached a sign points right to Amphipolis.

This ancient city, whose loss proved the turning point in the Peloponnesian War and led to the decline of Athens as a power, occupied 'a situation conspicuous both from the sea and the interior country.' This much we know from Thucydides who played a personally disastrous role in the war, although we have cause to be thankful for it.

The lay of the land still gives us instant confirmation of the admiral-historian's statement. The wide, rush-fringed Strymon forms an ox-bow round the base of a prominent hill which dominates the river mouth. A modern village stands on the site of the city which originated as a settlement known as Nine Ways and as such earned a place in Herodotus' *History*.

The Persians evidently regarded this strategic crossing on their line of advance to chastise the Greeks with superstitious awe for they propitiated the spirits of the place with an orgy of sacrifice. First they sacrificed white horses to ease their crossing of the river. Then, discovering that the place was known as Nine Ways, they buried alive nine local youths and nine maidens to propitiate the god of the underworld.

Thucydides spoke of a wall stretching across the base of the hill and linking the curves of the river, as the only defence the city had. Part of this has been excavated and is reached by taking the right-hand road when you reach a fork in your approach to the site. The stretch of carefully dressed white marbloid blocks ending in a gateway, facing the Strymon and clustered with wild red roses, has to be seen in the context of Thucydides' great history. Because it was from this point that the Spartans sortied to decide their battle with the Athenians.

Eight years into the Peloponnesian War, Amphipolis became the battle ground chosen by Sparta to test the Athenian claim to maritime supremacy in the Aegean. The correctness of the Spartiate strategy was soon proved when the colonists in whose loyalty Athens trusted, surrendered the city to Brasides.

Thucydides, dubbed general of Thrace, was given a small fleet of seven triremes to attempt a rescue. He succeeded only in capturing the neighbouring settlement of Eion. Condemned to exile for his failure, he started work on his *History*. His place was taken by the dictator Kleon, who in turn proved himself no general. Having advanced from Eion against Amphipolis, Kleon decided that his position was too vulnerable and retreated again. Brasides fell on the Athenians while they were in column of march, with a manoeuvre calculated to cut their army in two and defeat it in detail, he succeeded and Kleon was killed by a Thracian lancer as he fled. At the moment of victory Brasides himself was slain and his standing with the Amphipoleans can be gauged by the fact that they took his body within the walls for honoured burial and dedicated annual games in his memory.

Amphipolis remained autonomous until its conquest by Philip in 357, who founded another royal mint here to produce his famous gold coins from the ore of Mount Pangeon. The fine tombs discovered here date from the reigns of Philip's successors in the third century. They have built-in marble beds for the dead and one of them is painted with Dionysic animal forms. From these Macedonian tombs have come the fine artefacts in Kavala Museum. A square, simpler grave has a fresco of water birds flying among flower garlands.

Near the summit of the hill occupied by the present-day village are the remains of a Roman villa with a mosaic floor showing the Rape of Europa and near it are fragments of an isodomic-style building with a dedicatory inscription showing that it was probably a temple to Clio.

Amphipolis stood on the Egnatia and there is evidence of its importance in the early Christian era in the shape of fragments of a stoa, with five Ionic and a single Doric pillar and of basilicas and tesselated flooring. This culture was swept away with the Slavic invasions and Amphipolis was left to disintegrate so that, unlike Philippi, later settlers were hardly aware of its existence.

The symbol by which Amphipolis is known today is not to be found on these wind-swept and lonely hilltops overlooking the Strymon, but rather standing guard, appropriately at the crossing of the river where the Persians resorted to their mumbo-jumbo. The Lion of Amphipolis is a splendid beast, portrayed seiant in the conventional Hellenistic way (vide the Lion of Chaeronea) and a monument of disdain and arrogance from his snarling muzzle to his powerful, splayed hind paws. The plinth of what was obviously a large monument was discovered during the Balkan Wars and dredging of the river slowly revealed the pieces of the statue, thought to be a commemorative piece to Alexander's admiral Laomedon, a native of Amphipolis and who commanded his fleet against Tyre. The statue was re-erected in 1936. It is important to note in relation to Amphipolis that the site requires use of a car unless you are prepared for the tedium of a long two-way hike followed by the wait for a Kavala bus.

Looming over the Thessaloniki to Kavala road, to the east of Amphipolis, is a mountain whose dimensions and curiously nipple-shaped peak only become apparent when you are quite close. This is because of the steep folds of the land, which, a few kilometres past the crossing of the Strymon, creases itself into a defile; apparently the one used by the invading Persians in 480 BC. Mount Pangeon was almost as famous in antiquity as Mount Olympos, and unlike the sacred mountain, could claim the dubious distinction of having caused wars.

Paul Collart, the historian of Philippi, points out that the mines of Pangeon were famous from remotest antiquity, in fact, traditionally from the time of Kadmos the Phoenician. The same tradition, of a sort of El Dorado, applies to Thasos, and evidence is coming to light to substantiate it. In fact the exploitation of gold, at least in recorded history, was an initiative by the islanders on the mainland. The Thasians sank mines on Pangeon and particularly at a place called Scapte-Hyle, mentioned by Herodotus, and where Thucydides probably had an estate. They initiated a gold-rush around Philippi at what was then known as Crenides.

Harassed by Thracian tribesmen, the Crenideans made the mistake of calling on the help of Philip of Macedon. Philip was only too happy to oblige and exploited the mines himself, for the aggrandizement of Macedonia was not achieved cheaply. Coinage was already evidence of a state's stability and prestige — Athens used her Laurion silver mines to underwrite her commercial expansion, for instance. Philip, with his imperial dreams followed the example of the Persians and went on to the gold standard.

8. Halkidiki

Halkidiki reaches out into the Aegean like a hand with three fingers extended. The knuckles are the Mount Holomon range, which descends into the peninsulas of, from west to east, Kassandra, now in fact an island, with its narrow neck cut by a canal — Sithonia, and the world-famous monastic state of Mount Athos.

Halkidiki was one of the most important areas of the ancient Greek world, waxing rich on gold deposits and by exploiting its position at the crossroads of commerce. Desolated in more recent times and almost depopulated by the Turks, it was still a prisoner of the past when, in the early 1960s, it was 'discovered' as the new playground of Greece.

The potential — and the possibilities are still by no means exhausted — had always been there for those with eyes to see. A coastline reaching out into the warm Aegean from the landlocked Balkan chain gives the holiday-maker several more degrees of heat; important in a northerly latitude in the Mediterranean. A coastline contrasting spectacular cliffs with sweeping, shallow bays is washed by a sea of dazzling azure, and as clean as its hue.

The three prongs of this maritime trident were at some time in the dawn of the Earth united, and the geological story of Halkidiki has an interest in itself for the rock formations rise and harden as you travel east, rising finally to the shining white pinnacle of Mount Athos itself. Picnicking on Kassandra, on one of the red earth bluffs, fringed with the ubiquitous pines, you can watch the changing patterns of light and shade on the water. In the morning the dark blue-green of the rocks and seaweed stand out in a pale eau-de-nil sea, but as evening draws in and the burnished surface softens, the underwater formations turn to a strange luminous mauve in a soft, still, grey-blue setting.

A snap description of the peninsulas would have Kassandra under the heading 'popular holiday development'; Sithonia labelled as 'unspoiled natural beauty with a certain amount of landscaped development'; and, of course, Athos, 'a monastic republic, the last bastion of Byzantium and well worth visiting for he who has the right spirit'.

Scattered around the first two of these arms is Greece's northern aquatic playground. So off we go, out past Thessaloniki's airport, along a good, new road which in parts is a dual carriageway. We make for Néa Moudania, the small farming town, 70 kilometres from Thessaloniki, beyond which a well sign-posted junction splits the traffic, sending it south for Kassandra and east for Sithonia. Before this the traveller staying at one of the big hotels would have had advanced notice of direction and distance.

With 500 kilometres of coastline, Halkidiki has room to spare for informal as well as organized recreation. From the belt of big hotels and camping sites in Kassandra, for instance, it is only half an hour's drive into mountain scenery, joyous with wild flowers in the spring and covered with the purple haze of heather in autumn.

KASSANDRA

You cannot mistake Kassandra; as you top a rise five kilometres from Néa Moudania you see, dead ahead, the distinctive wasp-waist, already cut by a canal in the time of the geographer Strabo, and beyond it the low, reddish cliffs with their attendant stretches of silvery sand, unrolling into the distance.

This was the Pallene of the ancients, who believed in giants, those monsters last seen creating havoc in the frieze of the Lefkadia tomb lived here. Here, too, the captive Trojan women immolated themselves. As we drove across the canal, with bushes of scented, yellow sparti banked up on either side, our thoughts were far from such things. Below, in a tiny horseshoe-shaped harbour, caiques rode at anchor and in the distance, across the gulf of Torone, we could see the sweep of Sithonia.

The isthmus was known as the Gate of Kassandra and just beyond it, on the bluff overlooking the west coast, once stood its lock, the Corinthian colony of Potidea. There is little left to convey the one-time importance of this city but the lie of the land, a beetling cliff falling away to the sea, helps to fill a landscape in the mind's eye. The crumbling stone towers, probably re-used material, can grow into crowded battlements, and the caiques moving slowly through the canal become triremes bringing besiegers. For Potidea was one of the strategically most important cities in the shifting fortunes of the Greek world. Herodotus gives a lively account of the disaster which befell the Persians when they laid siege to the city after Salamis. One of the garrison plotted to betray the city to the Persians and the method of communication he hit on was a secret message written on a scrap of papyrus which was hidden in the notch of an arrow, then shot over the walls.

The plot was revealed when one arrow hit a Potidean in the shoulder and his companions, breaking off the arrow haft, discovered a message. Frustrated by unavailing months of siege, the Persians finally decided to push on into Pallene. In those days the channel of the isthmus must have been shallow for the invaders saw their opportunity during a particularly low tide. They were half way across when they were caught by the rush of an equally unusual high tide and those who were not drowned were pursued by the Potideans in their boats.

Philip later sacked the city but Cassander established his other city, Kassandria (not to be confused with the modern capital), on the site, giving the name to the whole peninsula.

The road now dips to the tiny fishing village of Néa Fokea, once a dependency of Mount Athos but now offering rooms for rent, one or two tavernas and a small, soft sand beach guarded by a fourteenth-century Byzantine tower.

We pulled in for a drink and saw something which is now a rarity in Greece, although not in Turkey, a dancing bear. His keeper had just taken him down to the sea to cool off. As he lumbered back into the transport, slavering in the heat under an elaborately beaded muzzle, he gave one last pirhouette, followed by a bow. One unusual sight here is the small Church of Aghios Pavlou, which uses a Macedonian tomb as its centre.

There is only one main road on Kassandra, as on Sithonia. About a third of the way down it becomes a loop circling the peninsula. You have a choice, continuing either east or west around the loop — we chose the eastern route. There are some fine bathing beaches and coves a short distance from the road which are good for snorkling.

Beyond Néa Fokea, our route took us across an undulating plateau, farming country, enhanced by clumps of oleanders everywhere. Occasionally we saw the sun sparkle on a cove at the bottom of a chine. Kallithea is a clean, modern village, full of shops, a service area for the big hotels nearby but it does have the remains of a shrine to Ammon Zeus dating from the fifth century BC.

The easterly route runs through country covered with pines and indented with larger coves where some of the hotels are located, often with their own beaches. These hotels offer a total environment to the package trade. Beyond package tour hotels give way to private villas and holiday flats which line the silvery sand and shale beach running almost all the way down to the tip of the peninsula.

Half-way down is the still fairly unaltered village of Polyhronon, which is a recommended stopping place for lunch — it has fish restaurants on the beach — but it is also one of the places about which I issue a word of warning; prices of fish dishes are high and you should always get a price for weight before ordering.

A little farther on is Haniotis, a bright, prosperous town geared to middle-class Greek families on holiday rather than the foreigner on a cut-price holiday. The beach is of particularly soft sand and is shaded by pines.

By contrast, the next village, Pefkahori, is almost entirely given over to rented apartments. The beach is extremely narrow and sparse. Ahead is a bay with an inlet for yachts and although camping is forbidden here, as in various other areas of Halkidiki, there is the large EOT camping site of Paliouri, with full facilities just beyond.

As we rounded the tip of Kassandra (I kept thinking for some reason of Strabo's figures for circumnavigation of the peninsula as 570 stadia — 104,310 metres) the road wound up through fairly rugged red earth arroyos and we caught a brief glimpse of the sea on both hands. The smell of sulphur wafted over to us, identifying the sulphur springs of Louris, where a hydro has been built. The west coast road runs almost at sea level; there is little development but poor bathing, and on the right rises a rocky escarpment where hawks circle. Kalandra is a centre for camping — there is a large centre at Mandi and an EOT site, Kalandra Camping, at Possidi.

Two kilometres further on, a left turn is indicated down to Skala Fourkos, a long horseshoe of soft sand with small tavernas and rented rooms right on the beach. Siviri, six kilometres beyond Fourka, offers the last good bathing on the west coast, apart from Sani Camping, which is reached by its own metalled spur road. At Siviri the road turns inland, and by-passing the capital, the small country town of Kassandria, where simple accommodation is available, it eventually completes the circle at Kalithea.

Olynthos

The journey to the top of Sithonia from the Néa Moudania crossroads takes about half an hour, but allow another couple of hours if you make the diversion to the site of ancient Olynthos, a name immortalized by Demosthenes. The landmark for Olynthos is a line of reddish buttes which rises to the left of the road, five kilometres past the crossroads.

The city occupied a long, sage-green whaleback of an earthwork roughly half-way between ridge and sea. You have to get close before you realize that it is not a natural feature, and the words of Demosthenes come to the fore, that only seven years after its sack by Philip you could walk over the site of Olynthos and never know that a city had stood there.

Today, Olynthos can be approached either through the modern village of that name, the turn for which is clearly marked, or more directly by a dirt road which runs across the fields and an old sign post for which can be seen a few metres past the Néa Olynthos turn. A ten-minute bumpy ride over this brought us directly to the boundary fence of the site and the main gate. The curator has no English but as Demosthenes' words can still be valid if you do not know where to look it is as well to let him guide you to what remains of ancient Olynthos. His local knowledge is considerable as he has watched over this particular site for more than a quarter of a century and has worked with several local directors of archaeology.

Make for the north hill, an extension of the main earthwork, following a path which climbs the west face. On the left you pass the site of the grave pits from Philip's final assault, close to which were found a row of arrowheads inscribed 'Phillipos'. They are now in the Thessaloniki archaeological museum This northern spur is the only part of the pre-war excavations by the American School still visible, and what was discovered around here added greatly to what we know of ancient Greek town planning.

Before you, as you reach the top of the slope, is a grid pattern of streets and house foundations which would have been more substantial but for the Bulgarians, who during the last war removed the lower courses of dressed stones for beach defences. However, the ground plan of some of the houses is enough to indicate the opulence of a city strong enough to defy Philip for several years, and to form a sufficiently powerful obstruction to his plans to warrant its total destruction.

The main mansion, an Olynthian equivalent of the House of the Lion

Hunt at Pella, has several mosaic floors. Closest to the path is a fragmentary study of two lions and a little beyond are designs of Bellerophon killing a wild animal from horseback — legend has it that he invented the bridle — and of a sunburst, rather like the royal emblem of Macedonia. The foundations still preserve fragments of the original plaster decoration.

Walking south along the remains of the city's main streets you reach the plan of a house which possessed its own wine press. Nearby is a 2½ metres deep storage shaft. Any fortress is only as secure as its water supply and it is a fair bet that in Olynthos' case the water proved as unreliable as the citizenry (some of whom formed a fifth column for Philip), for it came in by twin lines of culverts from Mount Holomon and was stored in deep cisterns beneath the agora, at the southern end of the north hill. One of Philip's first acts, after dragging his siege engines into position, would have been to cut the water supply.

Today wild olives and flowering shrubs cloak Demosthenes' famous scene of desolation. In fact, time has thrown a shroud of waving grass over Olynthos, softening the contours of the great foundations of the ramparts. The bones of the city now only protrude as courses of reddish stone at the northern and western ends of the ramparts.

On top of the soft contours of the south-western flank are the remains of a Roman signalling station, probably the same spot from which the Olynthians kept watch, day after day, for a relieving force from Athens which came too late. Their port, Macyperna, of which nothing now remains, lay a few kilometres away across the plain. Below the south-east rampart stretched the groves and vineyards which were Olynthos' life support. Here, too, was the necropolis, and farther out, in the middle of fields, is a fenced-in area with a geometric mosaic floor, all that remains of the so-called villa of Good Fortune. As a suburban house it may have shared the common fate of such in a siege — destroyed to deny it as cover for an attacking enemy.

Returning to the road, you turn left, parallelling the head of the gulf of Torone until you see the distinctive white peaks of the Gerakina magnesite mines away on the left. Just past the turn off for Poligoros a road swings off to the right, through olive groves to Gerakina beach. The 2-kilometre stretch of sand offers the best swimming at the head of the gulf and is sheltered to a certain extent by a grove of mature olive trees. It is the site of one of the most unusual hotels in Halkidiki, the Gerakina Beach. Bungalows are set among the 600 gnarled trees which cast their silver-grey canopy the length of the shallow bay. They are not just decoration but a commercial grove, producing 100,000 olives a season, which give, in turn, ten tonnes of oil. The grounds are fully landscaped and the hotel offers its guests the choice of a taverna with folk dancing and traditional Greek cooking as well as a table d'hôte.

From Gerakina the coast road runs parallel to the sea, through country undulating in early summer under young wheat and barley, ripening to the consistency of gold silk. The regular bus service takes you down to Metamorfosis, a small village overlooking the sea, with tavernas. But the run to

Sithonia starts as you sight a wide, gently curving bay with signs down to Camping Mylos, a site with full facilities, and then the village of Nikitas.

SITHONIA
Nikitas

Nikitas is one of those small fishing villages now feeling the impact of tourism. It has some traditional Macedonian architecture, including the Church of the Assumption of the Panaghia, with frescoes dating from the sixteenth century. On the last Sunday in July, local athletes compete in a very testing swim — 24-kilometres from Nikitas to Kallithea in Kassandra.

At the intersection just past Nikitas you have a choice of embarking on the circular tour of the peninsula by the east coast or of the west — each has its own distinctive character. Taking the right turn past the western route you temporarily lose sight of the sea. Driving through olive groves and a rocky cutting you suddenly come on a long white sand bay, Aghios Ioannis. You can pull the car over onto the hard shoulder and enjoy a pre-lunch swim a few paces from the road.

From here the west road provides splendid views of the peninsula — rocky, pine-covered landscapes and clear blue water — the view round each bend giving the feeling of a painted backdrop. To complete the sense of theatrical unreality, as we drove this route an eagle flew over our heads and settled on a telegraph pole. One of the delights of the north is that quite rare birds are not confined to national parks like Prespa but are to be found quite regularly in close proximity to man. This is also true of birds once quite common in Britain, like jays. Of course, the swarms of the ubiquitous swallow are a constant delight.

Thirteen kilometres from the intersection you pass Kalogrias, a fine shingle and white sand beach, and just past it, the turn for Spathis beach (with a 'no camping' sign) and Elia beach. From here the road meanders between banks of golden sparti, with small coves, approached down dirt tracks, appearing from time to time on the right.

Néa Marmaras

As you pass Lagoundra beach you catch your first glimpse of the mountainous interior of Sithonia and now the sign to Néa Marmaras comes up. This main — in fact the only — town of Sithonia is in the middle of a transformation from a somnolent fishing village to a smart holiday resort. Built on low hills around three small bays, it has hotels, rooms for rent and good fish tavernas overlooking the sea. The essential tiny fishing haven is preserved at either end of town. As you come in, some small tavernas, largely patronized by the locals, are tucked in under the cliff. Then, along the road to Porto Carras, at the southern end of the town, is a good white sand bathing beach. A short stroll from the middle of the village is a small boatyard with caiques on the stocks.

Porto Carras rises ahead like a great twin-headed ziggarut from a Cecil

B. de Mille film set. The great breadth of the bay and the soaring mountain side behind it prevent the design from overwhelming its setting, actually the outskirt of Néa Marmaras.

Porto Carras

A dream of the ship-owner John Carras, who lives in a villa on a neighbouring hilltop, the project was started in the late 1960s on 4500 acres of land between Néa Marmaras and Torone. The idea was to create a self-sufficient estate which would be complimentary to, but independent of, a luxury hotel. With its marina and yacht station facilities this in turn was designed as a magnet for wealthy boating enthusiasts in the Aegean, although they were by no means expected to provide the clientele exclusively.

As things turned out the estate, the commercial venture intended to back up the hotels, was first off the ground. 450 hectares of the hillside overlooking Porto Carras were planted with vines and citrus, almond and olive trees. The wines, the whites especially, have already proved themselves, especially the Porto Carras blanc de blanc, which is considered to be a rival to the best Alsatian wines.

They are produced in the estate's own winery under the direction of a young head vintner, who trained in France. The output averages 1,500,000 bottles of all marques each year. The maturation period is two-and-a-half years. The hotels (the Meliton with 465 rooms and the Sithonia with another 450) have been leased to large foreign hotel groups experienced in market exploitation and it will be interesting to see how they fare in a leisure market. They are well equipped for international conferences, with conference suite, open-air cinema and a championship-standard golf course. A Macedonian village, down by the yacht marina, and still under construction when we were there, is intended as a more informal environment for yachtsmen using the yacht basin, with its berths for 200 boats. Accommodation here is in individual chalets, but there is a further hotel, already open, the Village Inn (85 beds).

Porto Koufos

Beyond the hotels the road climbs steeply through hillsides covered with sauvignon, cabernet and merlot grape vines. This corniche road offers splendid views but until you reach Spalathomissia the beaches are too inaccessible. At Torone, one of the cities of Halkidiki mentioned by Herodotus, an archaeological dig has started which has so far uncovered fragments of walls. Just beyond it a deep horseshoe-shaped sea inlet surrounded by cliffs indicates Porto Koufos (derived from *koufes*, 'deaf'). According to an ancient Greek writer, the harbour got this name because it was so protected from the sea by its cliffs that the sound of breakers could hardly be heard in it.

Today it is a very pleasant lunch stop, with caiques moored just under the taverna balcony. The fishermen here are prepared to consider offers for their services in big game fishing. Tuna and blue shark weighing up to 300 kilos are landed. Fees have to be discussed on an individual basis.

If you are making a day of your visit to Sithonia — and this is the minimum time needed to begin to catch its flavour — then you should make Porto Koufos, or Sarti, 20 kilometres beyond it, your lunch stop. There are no restaurants beyond this point on the spectacular east coast.

The corniche road traversing the point of the peninsula is a particularly attractive run in the spring with wild flowers, clinging to crevices in the white and green marbloid rock faces, and occasional patches of tourquoise sea coming into view. The first beach on the east coast is Kalamitsi, a long stretch of white sand and shingle where camping is permitted. It is separated from another attractive beach, Linaraki — a flat stretch of sand lying in a heather-covered bowl of hills — by only a ridge.

Sarti is approached through clouds of yellow sparti and fields of lavender. It has a long white beach and fish tavernas as well as a few simple rented rooms. A word of warning here for those taking buses. There are few of them and it is best to check on the time of your return.

Armenistis beach is reached by a gravelled path, along which wild daffodils form a trail to the sea. The swimming is some of the best in Sithonia. The road now becomes a corniche once again, with steep rock faces, offering, where traversable, excellent scuba diving.

This is one of seven areas of Greece where spear fishing is officially permitted. Anyone with an acquaintance. of Pliny's *Natural History* will know the reason for the caution. The wrecks of Roman ships laden with the artistic spoils of Greece must still, by the law of averages, have something to yield and past experience of the piracy of archaeological treasures has taught the authorities that they can take no chances.

The north-east corner of Sithonia is a yachting area. The land flattens out opposite Diaporos island and forms inlets and lagoons which make ideal shelter for small boats. On the northerly cape, just where the road swings inland, lies the tiny port of Ormos Panaghias ('Harbour of the Virgin'), an attractive little base for the boats which ply, weather permitting, round Mount Athos. Instead of completing the circle and taking the road back to Néa Moudania, you can make a diversion up the east coast of the main-land mass of Halkidiki and thence into the interior by one of the most eye-catching mountain routes in Greece.

Ierissos

Fourteen kilometres from Aghios Nikolaos (sign-posted from the Nikitas intersection) is the fishing village of Pyrgardikia. It has a wide, white sand beach, dominated by a fourtheenth-century Byzantine tower and there is accommodation in private houses. Another 17 kilometres of winding second-class road takes you to the beginning of the main trans-peninsula metalled road system of Megala Panaghia. First, however, you may want to make a diversion, back down a B road to Ierissos, the northerly of the two ferry ports for landings on Mount Athos. This was the Acanthos of the ancients, a colony of the island of Andros, which enriched itself, as did most of the cities of Halkidiki, by exploitation of mineral wealth and from the slave trade.

The coinage which has come to light and of which there are examples in the museum of Halkidiki in Poligiros, is a testament to that wealth. Fragments of a necropolis that could well have had elaborately painted tombs, are buried among the dunes, and the ancient mole, described by Leake as advancing in a curve into the sea, is still there.

Xerxes' Canal

But the city's wealth, like that of Thasos, availed it nothing when the Great King came. Xerxes was determined to reduce the Greeks to obedience and what better start could he make than force them to cut a canal to shelter his fleet, and landlubberly Asian conscript sailors, from the accursed storms of this area? Vestiges of that famous canal can still be seen, and are sign-posted, at Néa Rodha, which stands on the narrowest point of the Athos peninsula, the depression running between the undulating hills known as Provlaka — from *proalux*, the canal.

By Herodotus' account it was a massive undertaking, planned as much as three years in advance, and one which allowed the Persian triremes to pass undisturbed, two abreast, from the Acanthic to the Singitic gulfs instead of risking the watery grave of their predecessors a few years previously.

Those who were not conscripted into the Persian army were put in the labour gangs, whipped along under the overseeing gaze of a colossal Persian, one Artachaeas. He is supposed to have been just four fingers short of five cubits (2½ metres) and 'had a stronger voice than any other man in the world'. Unfortunately, he died in the middle of the job and Xerxes gave him a magnificent state funeral.

The work went ahead so quickly that Xerxes, 'seeing the great zeal of the Acanthians for his service, and hearing what had been done in the cutting, took them among his devoted friends and sent them as a present Median dress'. As in the case of the gold mines of Thasos, mentioned elsewhere in this book, some doubt has been shed on Herodotus' credibility here, yet the declivity traditionally ascribed to the canal does show traces of classical embanking walls and nearby, about a century ago, was found a hoard of 300 Persian daric coins. The terrain through which the canal ran its one-and-a-half mile course, is fairly low lying — Leake said it was no more than 30.76 metres above sea level. He said: 'At the northern end in particular, there is a large pond, divided from the sea by a narrow ridge of sand. On either side of this pond are foundations of Hellenistic walls.' At the opposite end were artificial mounds, as though part of spoil heaps, in the slopes of which were more foundations containing several large squared masses of stone, and a block of white marble.

The surrounding fields were covered with blocks of stone which Leake thought were probably the remains of the city of Sane. At this southern exit from the canal lies the tiny fishing port of Tripiti, from which an informal ferry service runs across to the unspoilt isle of Amoliani, which I shall describe in the chapter on Mount Athos. Ouranopoulis, eight kilometres down the isthmus, and the last town in Greece under lay control before you get to the Holy Mountain itself, is the alternative ferry port for the mountain. It has a white town beach and ample private accommodation as well as modest hotels. The tree-shaded quayside is usually bustling with Athonite monks on a brief shopping expedition into the outside world. There is a Xenia here as well as a large luxury hotel just outside town.

Returning up the coast road to Stratonion you now head off across country, over the lovely mountain spine of Halkidiki, towards Thessaloniki. It is a route to be enjoyed simply for itself; there are no classical remains — Aristotle's birthplace of Stageira is not worth a stop as nothing really survives, an inferior statue alone marking the great man's connexion. Wild flowers, pine woods and rolling vistas of mountains are adequate compensation.

Spring is the time to see Halkidiki, stippled with colour like some Fauvist palette. It has a richness and variety of wayside flora that we in Britain, for instance, have quite lost since the introduction of intensive farming. Greece has more than 6000 separate species of flower and flowering plant and some of them are extremely rare — a tenth are found nowhere else.

Two factors encourage this proliferation: the mountainous uncultivated terrain, particularly in the north, which is hospitable to mountain plants, and Greece's position at a continental crossroads, with Asia a few hundred kilometres away across the Hellespont and Africa across the divide of the African Sea, from Crete.

Halkidiki would be classed as Alpine foothills for botanical purposes with a flowering period in May-June, although true Alpine plants tend to flower in September. There is one stricture concerning flowers. Their glorious profusion is deceptive. Many species teeter on the brink of the endangered category, so the message is, enjoy them in their wild state; you cannot preserve their beauty once they are picked.

What do you actually see as the car slowly negotiates a switchback of mountain roads? Well, there will be whole fields glowing with carmine poppy heads and pale mauve with wild lavender. Sparti, too, is ubiquitous — great bushes of waxy, soft-winged yellow flowers, on spiky bushes, which make good roadside cover.

But the rock fissure or cliff ledge, and not least the grass verge, offers beauty in small clusters — and sometimes a rarity. Here you will find in profusion the tall, stiff stems, often more than a metre high, of *Digitalis Ferruginea*, a perennial with dense clusters of yellow, bell-shaped flowers (blooms June-September). The wild rose is common, too, with white or blush-pink petals, and so is the *convulvulus*, the local pink variety, not considered a weed here.

Another common, and lovely form of ground cover is the *Vinca Major*, which blossoms between March-June into a five-petalled mauve flower. It could be mistaken for the *Viola Magellensis*, an Alpine flower with large pink petals, or, indeed, for another of the Viola family, the *Delphinantha*, which has the same mauvie-pink petal, but more elongated. Similar to the *Magellensis* is the waxy, yellow *Linum Elegans*, a perennial which flowers June-July and with flowers formed in bunches of from two to seven. Rather similar to this, but with glossier petals, lacking spines, is *Ranunculus Brevifolius*, one of a family of 60 variations of the family *Ranunculus* to be found in Greece.

Very common is a form of Aubretias, *Aubretia Deltoidea*, which takes its name from its D-shaped leaf. It is a perennial with four mauve-pink, kite-shaped petals, and flowers between April-June. A flower which favours rock ledges higher up in the Holomon range is the rather orchid-like *Daphne Oleodes*, with waxy, purplish flowers, growing in thick clusters.

Arnea

What is at stake in Halkidiki is the preservation not only of its wild flowers, but what remains of its traditional way of life. This is perhaps best exemplified in the small town of Arnea, which stands on a ridge below the peak of Holomon. This scatter of neat, colour-washed houses interspersed with some surviving Macedonian wood-framed buildings, is the centre of handicrafts in the north, as well as the campaign for preserving tradition-alism in Halkidiki.

The small, plane-shaded squares glow with the colour of shawls, bags and flockati rugs, which seem to decorate every other shop front. Until a few years ago, the haemorrhage of able-bodied men from the land in search of work in the new coastal developments, particularly of the holiday trade, was threatening to depopulate the hill villages. In some cases this is actually what happened, as in the case of Parthenon, near Porto Carras, where a discothèque owner is now the only inhabitant of a village where the wind whistles through untended olive groves and broken shutters.

As often occurs in times of economic depression the women of Halkidiki rallied round and with government encouragement set up looms in their parlours, the younger ones learning the traditional weaving skills from their elders. In Arnea alone, between 200 and 300 looms keep up a steady clatter that is a paean to unlooked-for prosperity. The Greek Handicrafts Associa-tion in Athens is now the official guarantor of the town's viability. Some of the designs, however, have figured in the revival of local traditions as in costumed weddings and christenings, the ceremonial for which was en-couraged by the Halkidiki Cultural and Handicrafts Association. Self-conscious young people were persuaded to wear Macedonian costume — the headdress of the girls' costumes being modelled on Alexander's helmet.

Local folk festivals, like the one at Nikitas, which I have mentioned, have received a great boost. Apart from fetes (*panighyria*) there are more am-bitious festivals like the one at Poligiros at Carnival time (either the third or fourth weekend of February). Traditionally in Greece this period for easing restraints before the solemn festival of Easter lasts three weeks. The spirit of irreverence here, the equivalent of the old English 'Milord of Misrule', is typified by the women of the town mocking one of the Greek male's most sacred rituals. On the Thursday before the end of Carnival they take over the cafés and tavernas for the day while the men stay at home and do the housework. Also during the period local delicacies are served with free wine in the town square and dancers wind their way through the streets to the music of the Turkish clarinet and the tambour.

Macedonian dances basically follow the traditional Greek patterns of the *syrtos* (slow dance) and *pidiktos* (lively measure). Not surprisingly they are not thought to have changed much since antiquity — particularly the *syrtos*, where the linking of hands and formation of an unbroken circle was a part of religious ritual, as can still be seen on the decoration of ancient vases. Women dancers wear striking black costumes, rather like a Victorian riding habit, but with a calf-length skirt, and teamed with a classical helmet, topped with a large black, horsehair plume. There is a tradition that the women of Macedonia were given the right to wear the helmet after saving the day in one of Alexander's battles in which the men had hung back. From the design it is more likely that it was modelled on a dragoon's uniform from the time of the War of Independence in which the Macedonians played such a brave part.

Poligiros

Poligiros, administrative capital of Halkidiki, lies about 40 kilometres from Arnea, along winding mountain roads. Occupying a shelf below Mount Holomon, it is a pleasant, if unexceptional little town, with a certain amount of hotel accommodation and rented rooms. It also has Halkidiki's fine new archaeological museum, housing finds from the numerous digs in the peninsula over the past few years. The museum (usual opening times; closed Tuesdays) is on the left just before the edge of town on the Paleokastron road.

In the entrance hall and first gallery are interesting terra cotta figurines, quite common in Macedonian excavations although these have a definite Art Nouveau feel about them. Also near the entrance are some superb examples of Attic black-figure ware. A krater of the sixth century displays a charioteer with an acrobat on one face and on the other two hoplites with two young men wearing the himation. Another small piece with first-rate intaglio brush drawings shows a charge with horsemen and foot soldiers carrying shields.

Here, in Poligiros, you can see what is left to us from Olynthos, after the depredations of Philip's phalanxes. There is a lekythos, a tall one-handled urn-shaped vessel, red figure on black, pieces by two of the very few identifiable master vase painters of antiquity, a fragment of Attic red-figure ware by the Amphitrite painter, and a remarkably complete Attic red figure column krater by the so-called Florence painter, showing a warrior leaving his home.

Acanthos, too, is represented, by terra cotta busts from a woman's tomb of about 400 BC, and, a touching discovery from a child's tomb, terra cotta models of animals — a dove, a cockerel and a bee. The third important ancient city for which there is some tangible evidence here in Potidea. In the entrance hall is a graceful marble figure of a woman, her himation tantalizingly slipping from one shoulder. Other noteworthy pieces in the Heröon of Stratoniki, dating from the first century BC.

Petralona

Halkidiki's story goes back a good deal further than the age of Philip and Herodotus, back in fact to the Paleolithic man of 700,000 years ago. Not just any Paleolithic man, but earliest European man. His skeleton was found at a depth of about 30 metres in a cranny of the huge cave which was his habitat, which he must have shared with some of his prey and where he finally crawled to die. He was probably between 30 and 35, a good age by prehistoric standards.

His world, in the great cavern of Petralona, 20 kilometres from Néa Moudania, came to light in 1959 when local villagers exploring for water broke through the roof of what is now called the Mediterranean chamber. By chance they were almost exactly above the spot where the skeleton lay, although it was not found until the next year.

Excavations, which have uncovered valuable clues to our first known European's way of life, have been carried out by Dr Aris Poulianos of the Anthropological Institute of Greece. Shortly after completing his work at Petralona he made, at Ptolemais, near Kozani, another important discovery for the study of prehistory, the complete skeleton of an elephant — far older than the mammoth, a very rare find in northern climes.

To get to Petralona you take the Thessaloniki road from Néa Moudania, and at the Eleohoria crossroads, just past Néa Triglia, bear right. The road to the modern village and cave is well sign-posted and winds up through scrub-covered hill country towards rocky, arid wasteland — in bad winters still the haunt of wolves. A museum of local stone, a cafeteria and a belvedere which looks out over the plain towards the Thermaic Gulf, cluster around the entrance, which is reminiscent of a mine shaft. In fact Petralona has become a major attraction, not only for foreigners, but also for Greeks, and particularly for the young.

Petralona, originally nothing but a massive scoop taken from the earth in a natural convulsion 'before the hills in order stood or earth received its frame', is now a great gothic folly of dripping stalectites, pinnacles of staligmites and screens and fan vaulting composed of petrified limestone. The cavern has become a museum of prehistory, with, at the moment, finds preserved in situ, and the whole scene back lit and bathed in a dark gold and red-ochre glow, against which the limestone formations form livid strands.

You enter the so-called hall of the Anthropological Institute of Greece, from which secure concrete walkways permit a circular tour of the cavern.

On the left models of *Pithicanthropus* or the first recognizable man, have been placed in the rock shelves where fragments of bones from his meals have been found.

He certainly had the use of fire and the remains of what is thought to be the oldest extant fireplace on earth have been discovered near the skeleton. Although the lower jaw of the skull was missing it is possible to say that he had no chin to speak of. This feature, however, was offset by a comparatively large cranium, which indicates fairly well developed reasoning power. Indeed, apart from fragments of his food, the archaeologists have found some of his tools, of quartz, bauxite and reindeer bone.

Our man was what anthropologists call a 'hunter gatherer' and he would have roamed Halkidiki in the Crenian period — part of the Interglacial age — when the climate would have been cold, very much colder than today, yet humid. The cave would have made an ideal shelter, particularly as some of his prey would have sheltered there too. A little farther on into the cavern is a model of a bear, *Ursus Deningeri*, which used it as a den.

After leaving this antechamber you slither through a narrow passageway between the so-called Pillars of Hercules and enter the Great Hall, the oldest part of the cave, resembling the carvings and architectural flights of a Gothic cathedral. On your right you see a shaft in the floor, dropping four metres down to the original cavern floor, dating back perhaps 900,000 years.

Langadas

One other stop is included under Halkidiki, on whose periphery it stands, although the lack of roads from the peninsula into the interior means a long detour through Thessaloniki to reach it. Langadas is an unremarkable village for 362 days of the year. It is what happens there on the other three which is making it increasingly a tourist attraction. For its festival of the Anastenaria (from the Greek verb *anastenazo*, 'to sigh' or 'groan') is probably the last link with the uninhibited rites of Dionisos. Although dedicated to St Constantine and his mother St Helen and dutifully celebrated at their feast — 21 May, and on two consecutive days — it does not have the sanction of the Greek Orthodox Church, which has lately stepped up its official disapproval.

The explanation is fairly obvious and can be found in that ill-defined territory where organized religion and more primitive, atavistic beliefs and rites meet. The reconciliation of religious orthodoxy with such a powerful counter-swell has caused problems for the Church since the very beginning (there are other examples in the ritual scourgings and crucifixions among Mexican Indians, not to speak of the superstitions which fuelled the Iconoclasm).

The aspects of the Anastenaria which cause most concern to the Church, the sacrifice of a garlanded black bull and the ecstatic dancing by initiates on glowing coals while carrying aloft icons, are just those which are now drawing tourists as well as Greeks to the ceremony in their hundreds each year. To those who choose to look more carefully at its ancient roots, the ceremony provides fascinating parallels with the orgiastic worship of the presiding deity of nature and the senses.

The cult of Dionysos did not originate in Greece but in Thrace and its epicentre seems to have been around Mount Pangeon. To Thracians, seeking communion with the god-figure by throwing off all inhibitions was more important than the often sterile formulae adopted by the more civilized Greeks in their worship. Yet, as often happens when the irrisistible force meets the immovable object in these matters, the latter does give way. The Greek colonists founding trading settlements along the coasts of Macedonia and Thrace were familiar with the deity known as Dionysos, or a variant of the name. But they were so fascinated by what they now saw of his worship in this wild, mountainous and forested region, that they transmitted their enthusiasm to the city states of the south.

The ritual was somewhat watered down when embraced by the Greeks; ritual floggings, indulgence in wine and saturnalias, with servants and women taking over the privileges of masters and husbands, replaced the wild rout through mountain glens with devotees, in an ecstatic state of self-hypnosis, dancing and waving pine torches. Do the descendants of those ancient converts to the cult come today to Langadas to capture something of that spirit, so well illustrated by Euripides in *The Bacchae*?:

I am the gentle comb of breezes on the slopes of wines
The autumn flush on clustered joy of grapes
I am the life that's trodden by the dance of joy
My flesh, my death, my re-birth is the song
That rises from men's lips, they know not how.
But also, the wild blood of the predator that's held in leash
The fearful flames that prowl the thicket of the night
I melt as the wilful barriers of the human mind
Gently even in this, except to the tyrant mind
That thinks to damn the flood-tide from the hills
. . . I am Dionysos.

In the play Dionisos says: 'We hold our rites mostly at night, but only because it is cooler.' It certainly is, or was when we were there, in a wholly exceptional late spring of rain and low temperatures. The measure of the Anastenaria's attraction for tourists is that seats for the event now sell at 100 drachmae each. It is held on a large, fenced patch of ground on the outskirts of the village. The preliminaries take place several hours before the fire-walking and may easily be missed by those arriving late in the afternoon for the evening ritual.

Between 11 a.m. and midday on the feastday a three-year-old bull which must be black, ungelded and never have been put to the yoke, is led to the house of the chief of the Anastenarides, the sect which gives the festival its name. In all but their religious practices these people follow the life of the village. It is interesting that they came to Langadas from eastern Thrace in the great exchange of populations after the First World War and although the foci of their devotion are perfectly respectable Orthodox saints, Constantine and Helen, the roots of the ritual come from the heart of the spawning ground for the cult of Dionysos.

These Thracians brought with them icons which enshrined the great tradition of their sect. In 1250 the Church of St Constantine in the village of Kosti caught fire. The icons were heard to moan and some villagers rushed through the flames to rescue them, suffering not so much as a singed hair in the process. From that time to this the rites, probably originating in the Dionysic spring festival, have centred on the fire walking. The sacrifice of a bull, with devotees rending the raw flesh, was a feature of the pagan rite. Its equivalent at Langadas is the sacrifice and butchering of the black bull and the distribution of the meat to the members of the sect.

The animal, wearing a wreath around its neck and with burning candles attached to its horns, is led to a small altar which has been set up in front of the chief Anastenaridi's house and which displays the icons of Constantine and Helen, decked with bells and medallions. The chief sprinkles holy water on the worshippers and then signals for the bull, together with a black kid, also with a candle on its horn, to be taken behind the house to be slaughtered. The goat's hooves are presented to the evening's chief dancer.

Attention now fixes on the icons themselves and on the Anastenarides who will put their faith to the test as night falls. The sect's relations with the Church are distant. Members are infrequent visitors to Mass and often make their confessions to a cross carved on a tree trunk. As the climax of their great feast day of the year approaches, they hold vigil before the sacred icons, known as 'the graces' or 'sires', while slowly drifting into an estatic trance.

Meanwhile, as the day wears on, the crowd gathers in the arena and certainly on the occasion we were there it could have been asked whether they weren't the ones enduring the ordeal. The only distraction from the long, cramped wait was a walk to one of the souvlaki stalls set up around the village or the preparation of the bonfire. Press and film cameramen from many countries immediately trained several thousand pounds worth of equipment on the pile of traditional oak wood. It was now 6 p.m. but another one-and-a-half hours passed in numbing cold before the gates of the arena opened and the Anastenaridi whose family traditionally has the privilege of lighting the fire, strode in.

Unfortunately the pile failed to ignite at the first attempt and a heated debate now ensued with contributions from photographers who were anxious to shoot something . . . anything. A pillar of flame suddenly shot up the middle of the triangular pyre, which seemed to give a Japanese photographer his picture of the evening and afforded warmth to spectators, who climbed out of their seats and joined the press.

Within two hours the arena was pitch dark except for the carpet of irridescent coals glowing on the earth floor. There was a feeling of tense expectancy in the air. The question was passed back and forth, 'where are the Anastenarides?' One journalist said laconically, 'they are in ecstasy'.

We saw the police, drafted in some numbers to the village, moving in a phalanx to line the approach to the arena. It was 10 p.m. Above the hubbub of voices we slowly became aware of a hypnotic rhythm, sounding as though from some wild, bucolic pipes, and underlaid with a steady beat from a drum.

Led by elderly women carrying candles and their elders holding aloft the icons, and accompanied by tabor and reed pipes, the Anastenarides walked into the arena, holding handkerchiefs between them. The beat quickened, and, forming a circle on the periphery of the fire, the dancers began to whirl on to the embers. Holding the handkerchiefs or red sashes between them they crossed the floor with a light, tripping step, at first seeming only to brush the embers, but then to stamp up and down in the middle of them, while swaying from side to side and occasionally giving out groans and sighs.

The ceaseless, scourging wail of the music, the tattoo of bare feet slapping the glowing coals and raising a mist of grey dust, the moaning and the faces of the dancers — masks of sweat with glazed, staring eyes — combined to create an experience that awakened forces far older than the Christian faith. Aristophanes talked of the sleep sent by Sabazios (another name for Dionysos) and of his initiates who went into ecstatic trance after inhaling smoke. Euripides hinted at fire-walking rituals and he was in a position to witness them during his exile at the court of King Archelaus of Macedonia, for whom he wrote *The Bacchae*.

Yet today the descendants of the votaries of Dionysos concentrate all their devotion on Christian saints; in fact they firmly believe that St Helen walks ahead of them through the fire, cooling the embers with water from a silver jug. Who can gainsay them, particularly when later examination proves that they haven't even a blister between them. Prophylaxis through auto-suggestion, or sheer blind faith? How is it done? That is the question that brings the crowds flocking here. . . .

As the dancing reached a climax several of the Anastenarides collapsed and had to be held by those who were not in such a deep trance. Finally they re-formed the procession and made their way back through the village, arm-in-arm and still led by linkswomen. They moved from house to house, blessing the families with the icons. The ceremony is repeated in less elaborate form on the two following days.

Buses run out to Langadas from a small bus station in Odissios, just off Metaxas Square in Thessaloniki at 20-minute intervals, and take tourists back to the city after the dancing.

9. Mount Athos

Athos, the Holy Mountain, conjours up an image to many of a delightful anachronism; smiling old monks with long white beards, keeping open house on a remote mountain, where women are actually forbidden to set foot. It seems to ring familiarly but its nature is not so well understood.

The Holy Community forms the last bastion of Byzantine culture and its monasteries are storehouses of art treasures accummulated over 11 centuries of patronage to this, one of the holiest of places in the Orthodox world. It is unique in that it is a self-governing state, its autonomy guaranteed successively by Byzantine emperors and modern Greek governments.

The tourist usually sees Aghion Oros from the deck of a boat, but the dedicated man may want to spend the full permitted four days in residence on the mountain. I shall describe both ways of experiencing Athos. Residence on the Holy Mountain requires an authorization which is not as complicated a procedure as it has sometimes been presented. As I write, however, there is talk of tightening up the rules of entry; perhaps reducing the length of stay for all but genuine pilgrims and restricting access by foreigners, most of whom certainly cannot be placed in that category.

Ironically, the world-wide move towards puritanism or orthodoxy in religion has affected Athos just at a time when it has begun to recover from the years of decline, when a dwindling number of monks and decaying monasteries raised serious doubts on whether the community could survive. The Holy Mountain seemed to be dying and rumours were flying of irrational schemes to save this bastion of Byzantine art. Slowly, however, the tide of settlement on Athos turned, with younger men coming forward. They were thoroughly imbued with the religious fervour on which the community of the Holy Mountain had originally been founded.

The form of admission to Athos is designed to discourage the merely curious, and the sensation seeker. A would-be visitor first applies to his embassy or consulate, which is supposed to give a rough vetting. It is wise not to state, ingenuously, that your reason is simple tourism. Otherwise, there should be no trouble in obtaining permission, provided there has not been a flood of applications, as often happens in high summer. Your application is passed on to the Ministry of Northern Greece, in Platea Diikitiriou, Thessaloniki, tel. 270-092, which issues the necessary recommendation for a residence permit.

Armed with this, you make your way to either Ouranopolis or to Ierissos, the ports on either side of the isthmus of Athos, which I have mentioned separately. Both make pleasant night stops to enable you to catch the early boats without resorting to a break-neck dawn drive.

Papers and passport — this must be taken with you — are checked on the quayside, and I emphasize that this is no exercise in paper shuffling. A party of Germans who tried to board our boat without proper documentation was turned back.

The two-hour boat trip is perhaps the most spectacular part of the visit. Much of Athos is girt with spectacular cliff scapes and many of the monasteries — there are 20 in all on the promontory — seem to pass in revue as the tiny, double-deck ferry ploughs through the ultramarine water down the west coast. You see the barrack-like Bulgarian house of Zografou ('the Painter'), up on the cliff and then, near sea level, its astonishing architectural near-relative, St Panteleimon. This great house with its green-painted onion domes is known as Roussikon ('the Russian') and is still keeping the flame alive for the lost northern patriarchate of Orthodoxy.

A stop is made at each monastery's landing stage to drop some of the necessities of life and to pick up monks who are either making their way to another monastery or taking a look at the outside world. The tiny port of Daphne boasts a customs post, the main task of which is to ensure that cine-cameras are not taken on to the mountain, and, on the outward journey, to make spot checks on baggage. The Athonite Holy Superintendancy has become rather nervous since, it is reported, portable icons started to disappear from time to time.

We boarded an ancient KTAE bus which twice a day makes the vertiginous trip up the trail to Athos's capital, Karys, where the formality of checking papers is gone through. The monks habitually cross themselves on journeys and on this one the insurance could be considered especially necessary. The over-loaded bus occasionally crunched to a halt as nothing but changing gear and willpower would get it round some precipitous bend.

Karys is a small town standing on a plateau amid woods and scrubland. A deeply rutted earthen main street winds between a scatter of shops, maintained by lay brethren, one or two cafés and a post office. Its main claim to fame is the Basilica of the Protaton ('Foremost'), dating from the tenth century, where possibly the finest surviving paintings by the fourteenth century master of the Macedonian School, Manuel Panselinos, are preserved.

The attribution is not definite, but what can be said about the frescoes is that they sum up what we mean when we speak of the Macedonian School. In the painting of the Virgin appearing to St Pachomios, for instance, there is a characterization and a sense of the dramatic not seen in contemporary painting in Constantinople. The artist uses foreshortening and angular composition together with strong colour.

Behind the Protaton a flight of white marble steps lead up to the Holy Superintendancy, where a long wait ensues before permission is granted to venture out on to the mountain. Our papers were taken by a small, gnarled man wearing a pill-box hat with the double-headed eagle insignia of the community. He also collected a stamp fee from each of us and then disappeared into the long chamber across the hall, occupied by the Epistasia, the Secretariat of the Holy Community. A murmur of voices, the occasional glimpse of a black robe hem, and then he returned holding a sheaf of Diamontirions, the attractive passport, marked with the double-headed eagle and embellished with images of angels floating above the Holy Mountain, without which you cannot be admitted to a monastery. It is a recommendation to the individual *achondaris* (guest master) to extend hospitality to the visitor. Although hospitality is enjoined on the monks and in practice the visitor would be unlikely to receive a rebuff, attitudes to guests do vary between monasteries — a subject I shall return to.

The party which had landed at Daphne now split up and made for the monasteries which had been selected for the night stop. The monasteries fall under one of two heads, coenobitic or idiorrhythmic. The word 'coenobite' derives from the Greek for 'communal life' and the houses of this persuasion adhere to the popular concept of monastic life; the monks work, eat and pray together.

In idiorrhythmic houses, on the other hand (the word denotes 'un-orthodoxy' or 'eccentricity') the brethren still pray communally but their working day, food and other aspects of their lives are organized on an individual basis. The division extends to the monasteries' dependencies, the *sketea*, which are miniature monasteries; other subdivisions are the *kellia*, literally cells of three or more monks; the even smaller *kalyvae;* and the *hesychasteria*, tiny lean-tos or even caves, where true ascetics can concentrate on spiritual matters without any distraction. Food, such as it is, is lowered to them and only when it is untouched can the brethren from the monasteries tell that the hermit's earthly struggle is ended.

The future of Athos would seem to lie with the coenobitic persuasion. There are 13 monasteries of that persuasion compared with only seven idiorrythmic, but more importantly the constitution allows the conversion of the former to the latter, but specifically precludes a change in the opposite direction.

Bearing in mind the four-day time limit, it is worthwhile planning your visit to include coenobitic and idiorrythmic houses which lie within easy walking distance of each other and which offer an insight into the life of Mount Athos as well as a chance to see some of its richest treasures.

Karys is almost dead-centre of the promontory and you will find that the monasteries on the east coast make an accessible grouping. Stavronikita, for example, is only about an hour-and-a-half's walk away, and can be combined, in a delightful walk along coastal paths, with Iviron and either Filotheou or Karakallou.

Stavronikita

Stavronikita is a small monastery (its guest house has only 20 beds —

Stavronikita is a small monastery (its guess house has only 20 beds — but it has to be remembered that its accommodation is also for Greek pilgrims) but it is one of the most attractive and as a Greek friend told me: 'its men are the best in spirit'. Its origins are obscure and it was ruined in pirate raids in the early Middle Ages. Reconstituted in the sixteenth century on the orders of the Patriarch of Constantinople, it brought the number of full monasteries on Athos up to today's total of 20. Recently it led a movement among idiorrythmic houses back to the coenobitic system. Approached from the west, the monastery resembles a fortified Tuscan hill village, with its crenellated tower and loopholed walls, with overhanging balconies. Inside, its stone-shingled buildings are grouped around a court-yard which is crossed by an old aqueduct.

Several of the monks speak English and in fact they include a former British national, Father Nicholas. The treasures include a rare mosaic icon, St Nicholas Streidas. One of the many miraculous icons on the mountain, it gained its name from the oyster reputedly clinging to the saint's forehead when it was fished out of the sea. When the shell was struck off, blood gushed from the icon. The library contains 54 mediaeval illuminated parchment membranes.

An hour or more should be allowed for the walk on to Iveron. The scenery is much as Leake described it: 'The road descends the hills obliquely by a rugged path through vineyards and amidst a great diversity of hilly ground covered with woods'. The rugged paths are no exaggeration in certain cases — our party stumbled into the dead end of an overgrown orchard and finding our way back to the main track added an extra hour-and-a-half to the journey. Distances can be deceptive and although the mule tracks connecting the monasteries are well within the capacity of an averagely fit person, it is as well to consider factors such as the midday heat and the total lack of refreshment. Stout but comfortable walking shoes or boots, a thermos flask and a supply of non-perishable foods are advisable items to pack.

Iveron

Iveron, supposedly founded by four Georgian noblemen (hence the name, 'of the Iberians', or Georgians) is third in the Athonite hierarchy and an idiorrythmic house. It is a large and attractive monastery with the second largest katholikon on the mountain and a notable treasury. While the monks in no way transgressed the rules of courtesy it was rapidly made clear to us that we would be advised to make our night stop at a coenobitic house. Filotheou was suggested; 'they are more progressive monks', was the excuse given.

The community here affected an exaggerated formality in dealing with each other — putting on a public face perhaps, and you could not help wondering whether it covered a gap in communal life inseparable from the idiorrythmic system.

Before we left we were given a tour of the monastery's treasures: the library, thought to be the most valuable among the monasteries of south-eastern Europe, and its own miracle-performing icon, that of the Virgin of Portaitissa ('of the Gate') housed in its own chapel. One of its miracles was supposed to be the curing of a seventeenth-century tsar's daughter, in return for which Iviron was granted the lands of the monastery of St Nicholas in Moscow. The age-blackened icon, almost completely encased in silver-gilt and studded with semi-precious stones and enamels, was deeply reverenced by our guide who sank at its feet, uttering, 'Our Holy Virgin, Mother of God'. We crossed the courtyard to the splendid katholikon, first erected in the eleventh century and restored in 1513. Its main features are a geometric patterned marble floor, preserving the inscription 'I erected these columns and they shall not be shaken by time. George the Iberian, monk and founder'. Hanging above it is a great silver-gilt chandelier, dating from after the restoration.

Apart from its 2000 manuscripts and 15,000 printed books, the library contains Byzantine documents, including chrysobuls of Constantine VII Porphyrogenitos (946-958), Romanos II (960) and Basil II, the 'Bulgar Slayer'.

Filotheou

The trail to Filotheou ran beside the sea and time passed pleasantly enough in the landscape of odiferous trees and bushes — which attracted multi-hued butterflies — until we realized that we had under-estimated the distance and night was drawing in. Fortunately the lorry which takes bundles of timber — the Holy Mountain's chief source of revenue — from the monasteries down to Daphne — hove into sight and delivered us at Filotheou's gatehouse, together with assorted dry goods.

The guest-master spoke American-accented English: 'You three guys will be in this room', he said. I had teamed up with an Italian newspaper delivery van driver and a German doctor. The rooms, reached by an outside staircase, were clean and comfortable. Not the least of the pleasures of the 'retreat' here is re-discovering the soft glow of oil lamps, which give a lustre to the Byzantine frescoes lining the refectory, where we joined novices and pilgrims at the long trestle tables. The food was quite adequate: a hash of various beans in oil, tomatoes and olives, washed down with white wine from the monastery's own vineyards.

Services on Mount Athos are arranged in accordance with a monastic day which breaks down into three 8-hour periods, devoted to prayer, work and sleep. At Filotheou the Liturgy began at 3:30 a.m., the monks being summoned by the rhythmic banging of the *semantron* (the long wooden hand gong). We did not hear it, having been given a dispensation to lie-in until 5 a.m. We were roused by the guest-master and after performing our ablutions in the cold-water washroom, we made our way gingerly down the staircase and, guided by the low chanting coming from the katholikon, crossed the darkened courtyard.

We were not allowed beyond the narthex and the ritual of the service, unchanged over so many centuries, came to us only dimly, as if through a proscenium. The candles on the altar flickered on a mediaeval crucifix. The only other light came from an occasional shower of sparks as the censor was swung by one of the shadowy figures, gliding in and out of the sanctuary, and the reflection from one of the gold-embroidered copes of the celebrants.

As dawn came up we breakfasted on a purée of chestnuts, herb tea and black olives and bread; then, making our way through young pilgrims gathering for a Bible class on the balcony of the guest house, we shouldered our packs and set off our different ways. No charge is made for hospitality on the Holy Mountain, but obviously it is a gracious gesture to make a contribution on leaving to the monastery's hospitality chest.

My companions variously intended to climb Mount Athos, spending a night in the refuge hut near the summit, or walking on to the tip of the promontory, staying at one or two more monasteries. Climbing the Holy Mountain itself was in vogue for visitors in Leake's day, although he was told (in October) that the climbing season was past. He lamented: 'When the autumnal tempests have begun in this stormiest quarter of a sea in all parts fickle and subject to gales, weeks may pass by before such a day occurs as would secure a perfect view of distant objects from the summit'. He might well bewail his luck for the view from the summit (2033 metres) gives a panorama of almost the whole of the northern Agean. According to Aeschylus, it formed one of the beacons which signalled Agammemnon's return to Cleitemnestra. Its white limestone pinnacle, which Strabo likened to a woman's breast, can be climbed in a day, using the dependent house of Kerassia, which has overnight accommodation, as a base.

Instead of accepting the invitation to mountaineer, I took the 'easy' way, joining a group of Italian dental students in the hair-raising lorry trip down the mule tracks to Karyes. Even the return bus journey to the harbour seemed more bearable by comparison. The wait for the one return ferry of the day (departure at midday) was enlivened by a scene at the quayside as a caique pulled away, leaving a young monk behind. He crossed himself and, skirts tucked into his belt, took a flying leap into the stern sheets, to the cheers of on-lookers.

Grand Lavra

I can do no better at this point than list the other monasteries, with their treasures, and rate the hospitality likely to be encountered. Grand Lavra, the original monastic foundation on Athos and now the biggest, also enjoys a reputation for open-handed hospitality. 'Lavra of the Black Habit', 'Lavra of Lord Athanasios', and, popularly, 'Great Lavra' are other designations.

The eremetical life was already established on Athos, when, in 885 the Emperor Basil I issued a chrysobul establishing the mountain as a refuge exclusively for hermits and monks. A tradition existed that the Virgin, in the company of St John the Evangelist, was on her way to visit Lazarus in Cyprus when her ship was blown off course in a storm to Athos. Landing close to the present site of Iviron, she was so taken with the beauty and peace of the promontory that she begged it as a gift from her son. A voice was heard granting the request: 'Let this place be your inheritance and your garden, a paradise and a haven of salvation for those seeking to be saved'. Among the latter were many refugees from persecutions of the Iconoclasm and the Muslim invasions in the East. The shepherds and laity who had previously had the run of the mountain were driven out after Basil's edict. Henceforth, 'the Virgin's garden' was to be enjoyed by her devotees alone.

Then, in 963, St Athanasios founded Great Lavra with the financial aid of his friend, the Emperor Nicephorus Phocas and his monastic system was soon sufficiently strongly entrenched to beat off a challenge made to its authority by the hermits, who appealed for adjudication to Constantinople. The resulting *Typikon* ('charter'), which was granted still binds those monks' successors today.

Great Lavra shelters 380 monks, 56 of whom live in the monastery and the rest of whom are scattered among its dependencies. It is an idiorrythmic house. Its buildings resemble a charming Macedonian village, standing on a headland above a fortified harbour, at the bottom right-hand corner of the promontory. A defensive tower at one corner of the monastery was funded by the Emperor John Tsimiski, successor to Nicephorus, and whose name is commemmorated in one of the most pleasant Thessalonian boulevards.

The katholikon, dating from the beginning of the eleventh century, is in the form of a triconchal Greek cross and is a gallery of the work of Theophanes the Cretan. The paintings, dated 1536-60, include portraits of Nicephorus Phocas and his nephew John Tsimiski. The church, which also has a pair of bronze doors with panels in high relief, rather like the 'Gates of Paradise' on the Florence Baptistry, contains a fragment of the True Cross. The tomb of St Athanasios is to be found here, while his iron cross and staff are preserved in a chapel dedicated to him near the treasury.

Lavra's treasury is the richest on Athos. It contains the crown allegedly worn by Nicephorus Phocas, the gold, jewel-studded cover of a Gospel book, traditionally associated with the emperor, the miracle-working icon of our Lady of Koukouzelissa, with a brooding mother figure and a very Macedonian child, a very expressive mosaic icon portraying St John the Theologian and dating from the thirteenth century, priestly vestments and plate.

The library, which shares the treasury building, has 2046 manuscripts, 407 of them on illuminated vellum.

Vatopedi

Vatopedi, at the opposite end of the east coast from Lavra, is the only Athonite monastery which keeps modern time. It follows the Gregorian calender in contrast to its neighbours which still cling to the old Julian calender. Idiorrythmic, it claims a founding tradition that the son of a late

Roman emperor was washed ashore here from a wreck, so an edict was issued for the foundation of a monastery, to be called Vatopaedion (an allusion to the bramble bush he clung to). In actual fact the house was founded within a few years of Great Lavra. Rather barrack-like in appearance, its stern face is matched by the austerity of its monks, who number some of the most zealous of the new blood among them.

The monastery's most precious relic is housed in a chapel of its own. It is the girdle supposed to have been worn by the Virgin Mary and known to have been kept in the monastery of Vlachernae and in Aghia Sofia in Constantinople before its fall to the Turks. It was given to Vatopedi by King Lazarus I of Serbia. The treasury is rich with bequests: mosaic icons, a jasper goblet given by the Emperor Manuel Comnenus, gold-embroidered vestments and silver-gilt plate. The katholikon has fragments of the True Cross, a diptych of Christ and the Virgin, 'the Ninia of Theodora', and what is claimed to be the reed on which Christ was offered the sponge of vinegar on the cross.

Vatopedi is well equipped with modern conveniences and is linked by a motor caique service with Ierissos although the choppy seas prevailing on this coast mean that it is uncertain and irregular. Mules can be booked here to take you to Karyes.

Chelandari

This Serbian monastery, fourth in the Athonite hierarchy, is in the process of changing over from idiorrythmic to coenobitic practice. It is worth making the effort to discover this house, well off the beaten track as it is, nestling amid thick woods at the neck of the peninsula. For it has an unbroken connexion, going back nearly 800 years, with the Serbs, like the Russians, representing another lost patriarchate of Orthodoxy. It preserves much of their traditions and some of their treasure. All the monks are southern Slavs.

The walk there from Vatopedi takes about three hours, going by the coastal route and the monastery of Esphigmenou — undistinguished and bearing scars of military occupation, complementing the section of Napoleon's campaign tent preserved in the treasury.

Chelandari, or Khiliandarion as it is alternatively known, displays hospitality 'with the heart'. The title is supposed to derive from *chilioi* and *andres* (meaning '1000 men') from the number of monks it was originally intended for. Now it houses about 70. It was founded, 1197, by a Serbian prince, Stephen I Namanya, whose son renounced the world and became an Athonite monk himself. His father eventually joined him. They laid the foundations of the prsent house.

The tall buildings, of mellowed brick with whitewashed and balconied upper storeys, cluster around, but do not crowd, the moss and grass-softened contours of the courtyard. The strongest shapes are the two venerable cypress trees near the katholikon. The church was built in 1320 and is frescoed with images including the Serbian tsars and rulers, some of whom paid state visits to the monastery in its greatest days, in the thirteenth and fourteenth centuries, a period when Serbia ruled much of Macedonia, as part of a great Balkan empire which has left embarrassing echoes in more recent times.

Small chapels of the monastery, lying outside the walls, also have fine frescoes of the period, which have recently been rediscovered. The treasury is in a modern building near the katholikon and is probably second only to Lavra in opulence. It includes a cup, given by the Serbian imperialist Stephen IV Dusan, who visited the monastery and gave it a chrysobul signed 'tsar and emperor of the Serbs and the Greeks'.

The monastery's collection of icons is one of the most precious relics of Byzantine art that we have and includes a Pantocrator of the thirteenth century; a mosaic icon, the Theotokos Hodegetria, a haunting Virgin and Child of the same date; five cameos, two representing Christ, two of the Panaghia and the other showing St Demetrius; two crosses containing parts of the True Cross and presented to the monastery by its founding patron; a Byzantine cross set with crystals in which the images of Christ and the Virgin are supposed to appear; and part of the Crown of Thorns.

Monasteries of the South-West Coast

Perhaps the most attractive group of monasteries on Athos lies on the south-west coast. It comprises two of the most spectacular sites, Simonpetra and Dionysiou, and two charming smaller monasteries, Gregoriou and St Paul. The whole itinerary would take up about half of your allotted stay on Athos. Simonpetra is two hours hard walk to the south of Daphne. It clings like an eyrie to a cliff face, more than 300 metres above the Singitic Gulf, and its sheer presence tempts the visitor into using superlatives to do it justice. On three sides the drop is sheer and the monastery is actually connected to the cliff by a viaduct. There is a legend about its construction which gives an idea of just how difficult it must have been. One Christmas night, St Simon, a hermit who lived on Athos in the fourteenth century, saw a light burning on the ridge now occupied by Simonpetra. He took this as a divine commandment and began to lay the monastery's foundations.

His band of helpers were terrified by the height at which they were expected to work and began to leave the job. Simon sent his servant, Isiah, to them with some aquavit to revive their flagging spirits but the man slipped and fell over the precipice. To everyone's amazement he landed on his feet with not a drop spilled. The story sounds suspiciously like the favourite Greek trick of balancing a glass of water, upturned and sealed with a napkin, on the head during a dance. It is a charming tale and enlivens (as if it needed it) the moment when you step onto the balcony and look down the dizzy cascade of rock at your feet.

The monastery was prosperous to start with, but was then beset with a succession of disasters, mostly fires, the last of which in 1891, completely destroyed it. Rebuilt largely with the financial help of the last tsar of Russia, Nicholas II, it has now regained a large measure of prosperity. It is coenobitic and the first foreign language of the monks is French.

The coenobitic house of Gregoriou lies in a natural rocky amphitheatre above a picturesque little harbour. It traces its origins to two founders, Gregory of Sinai and Gregory of Syria, the first of whom brought the earliest monks and the latter who built the first monastery. It is first mentioned in the fourteenth century and suffered severely from Saracen raids and fire, particularly from a devastating conflagration in the eighteenth century. It was rebuilt partly with alms raised on orders of the Sultan. In the katholikon are three portable icons, one of St Nicholas, dating from the sixteenth century and set in silver, and two of the Virgin, surnamed the Galakprotropoussa and Pantanessa.

One-and-a-half hours along the coastal track from Gregoriou is a Simonpetra in miniature, the coenobitic house of Dionysiou. It is built out over the lip of an 80-metre high rock and is reached by a steep flight of steps from its landing stage. I should say here that caiques do link coastal monasteries and inquiries about taking this softer option should be made to the guest master of the appropriate house.

Dionysiou was founded at the end of the fourteenth century by St Dionysos of Korseos, near Kastoria, aided by the Emperor Alexius III Comnenos. The katholikon, with its five deep-red domes, contrasts with the huddle of grey stone buildings surrounding the courtyard and faced on the sea-side with white painted, overhanging balconies. It is decorated with frescoes by the celebrated painter Tzorzis, who followed the style of Theophanes, exempler of the school. The church was restored, after the usual scourge of Athos, fire, by a Voivode of Moldavia, one Peter, and Tzorzis dutifully represented him with his children in the right-hand aisle.

The Macedonian carved wooden iconostastis has a highly unusual feature — it is covered with beaten gold and displays five icons, representing the Great Deesis ('Christ on the Cross') between the Virgin and St John, acting as intercessors, and painted about 1540 by the Cretan Euphrosynos. On the left of the narthex is a chapel dedicated to the Panaghia of the Akathistos, in which hangs an icon, one of those attributed to St Luke, and executed in wax and mastic. This striking piece, dark and simple in concept, is set in a deep frame of beaten silver. It is supposed to have been carried around the walls of Constaninople to encourage the garrison during the siege by the Slavs in 626.

The frescoes in the refectory were done about 1600 by the Cretan painters Daniel and Mercurios. They include full-size representations of the Fall of Lucifer, the Heavenly Stair, the Miracles and the Life of the Baptist. The door is carved with mythical beasts.

The treasury contains the Cross of Helena Paleologina, a gold-embroidered, sixteenth-century *epitaphios*, the shroud used in the mock-burial at the Orthodox Easter, an ivory plaque of the Crucifixion, dating from the tenth century and a reliquary in gold and enamel, in the form of a cross-in-square church, made from the bones of the Patriarch Niphon of Constantinople. It was Niphon who ordered the construction of the cross-in-square Dodheki Apostoli in Thessaloniki. The library is well worth visiting, with its collection of illuminated parchments.

The guest-master here spent many years in the United States. He and his fellow monks are particularly helpful.

Aghios Pavlov, a coenobite house, has a superb setting in a rocky defile near the foot of Mount Athos. A mountain torrent tumbles beneath it. It took its founder, Paul Xeropotaminos' Christian name (tenth century) and in the Middle Ages benefited, like Chelandari, from the munificence at Serbian princes.

The daughter of one of these princes, Mara, wife of Sultan Murad II and mother of Mohammed II, was a benefactress of the monastery. She was given a fragment of one of the gifts of the Magi, looted from a church at the sack of Constantinople, and determined to present it to St Paul's. When she landed on Athos she heard a voice from heaven saying that only one queen was allowed here and that was the Queen of Heaven. Mara immediately returned to her ship. There is a chapel of St George with paintings of the Cretan School dating from 1550.

Monasteries of the North West Coast

A further group of monasteries lie together on the north-western coast-line; those that you see on the inward journey to Daphne. The first monastery to come into view at the water's edge is Docheiariou, a coebobitic house founded in the tenth century by a disciple of St Athanasios. You are most likely to reach it by water, passing through the pitched roof watergate. The katholikon was built during the sixteenth century and is decorated with paintings by the same Tzorzis who frescoed Dionysiou. Its treasurey contains a miracle-working icon, the Panaghia Gorgoypecos ('sharp of hearing'), a piece of the True Cross and the skull of St Dionysos of Mount Olympos.

Xenophontos stands well, also at the waterline. Coenobitic, it was founded in the tenth century by St Xenophon and grew in prosperity when the Byzantine admiral Stephen, commander of the Emperor Nicephoros Botaneiates' fleet, took the cowl in the next century and received lavish imperial endowments for the house he had entered. It was the first monastery on Athos to return to coenobitic practice after a long period when most of the Athonite houses had become idiorrythmic because they could not maintain a communal lifestyle. There is a katholikon, the largest of the Greek houses on Athos, and dating from the beginning of the nineteenth century. But just beyond the entrance to the monastery still stands the original church, decorated in the sixteenth century with paintings by the Cretan Antonios.

St Panteleimon is popularly known as Roussikon ('the Russian') – and it looks it. A great coenobitic house, laid out here in the reign of Catherine the Great, it became the focus of the pan-Slav crusade of the nineteenth century on Mount Athos. The Holy Mountain was flooded with Russian, monks as deliberate policy by St Petersburg. St Panteleimon alone had 1000 and more were scattered throughout other houses. The take-over attempt by the Russian patriarchate failed and the mountain retained its predominantly Greek characteristics.

Until 1968, when it suffered in a disastrous fire, the monastery maintained a suite of guest rooms hung with photographs of the imperial Russian family. Sknce then guests have been moved into some of the previously disused buildings near the boathouse. The katholikon is built in distinctive Russian style with green and gold onion domes. Its interior is painted in a recognizably Novgorodian style and, according to a decree of 1875, services must be conducted in Russian as well as in Greek. The treasury contains a mosaic icon of St Alexander Nevsky, the warrior saint of Russia, and imperial Russian sacerdotal vestments.

Most visitors will see Mount Athos from a tour boat. The tour can be booked at several points; either from agencies in Thessaloniki, or through hotels there or on Halkidiki. Coaches pick you up at your hotel and take you onto the tiny fishing port of Ormos Panaghias. You run the risk of being turned back short of it, however, if weather conditions make the trip too risky.

The small ferry sails down the western side of the Athos peninsula, water that is notoriously turbulent. At the best of times you are likely to encounter a swell. A three-hour round trip takes as its half-way marker the southern tip of the peninsula at Karoulia, reached in about two hours.

On the return leg the helmsman follows the coastline as closely as weather and decorum allow, to permit the best possible view of the monasteries and photography which does not need a telephoto lense.

The return journey breaks for lunch on the delightful small island of Amoliani, which is separated from the Athonite isthmus by a narrow channel of deep blue water. Tavernas cluster on terraces around the tiny landing stage and serve fresh fish and kalimaris, washed down with chilled retsina. The stop-over allows time for both a leisurely lunch and a stroll or a swim before re-embarking for Ormos Panaghias. The coaches await you and take you back to Thessaloniki in time for dinner.

We make one observation about this trip. It is not for those with young and possibly fractious children; nor is it for the elderly in poor health. You make a very early start (the tour operators will tell you at what time you should be waiting outside your hotel for the coach — usually 6.30 a.m.). You then sit for several hours under a broiling sun, possibly in choppy sea conditions.

28 Gold larnax which contained the presumed bones of Philip II, Royal Tomb, Vergina.

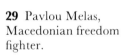

29 Pavlou Melas, Macedonian freedom fighter.

30 Exterior of mansion house in Kastoria.

31 The Sin of Vanity, fresco, from the gynaeceum, Church of St John, Kastoria.

32 Ballroom of Kastorian mansion house, no. 10 Kapitan Lazou.

33 Monastery of Vatopedi, Mount Athos.

34 Dancers whirl in ecstasy on glowing coals in the Anastenaria festival, Langadas.

35 Frescoes in the refectory of the Dionysion Monastery, Mount Athos.

36 Beach cove, Halkidiki.

37 Caiques being built, Thasos.

38 Christian basilica and pagan shrine juxtaposed, Aliki, Thasos.

39 Old marble harbour, Thasos.

40 The agora, Thasos.

41 Going home in the evening, the foothills of Mount Iypsarion in the background, Thasos.

10. Thasos

It is an hour's ferry ride from Kavala to Macedonia's only island, Thasos, an almost circular slab of marbloid rock 9½ kilometres from the closest place on the mainland. At some point in the dawn of time a gigantic volcanic upheaval pushed a cone of limestone, 1045 metres skyward and this peak, Mount Iypsarion, today gives Thasos its shape, steeply sloping into the sea on the east and spilling out into the wide skirts of coastal plain on the western side. The island is 86 square kilometres, 24 kilometres north to south and 19 kilometres across.

The ancients dubbed the island 'the golden'. They were not indulging in hyperbole, although they could have been. It is clothed today, as then, in luxuriant pine and deciduous forest and although the wine, famous in antiquity, is no longer made there, the equally celebrated marble is still quarried.

As the ferry ploughed across the Gulf of Kavala we were reminded that this was the very route by which Cassius' men brought his body, under cover of darkness, for secret burial in the island so that his obsequies would not dismay his army. It was a place which seemed naturally to attract great historic forces, and that, in the nature of things, meant trouble. Thasos was threatened by its own wealth — Athens tried first to buy its alliance, then to destroy its power and Philip harnessed it to his grand design for the Greek world. Obviously a place of some character. . . . We looked across at the looming mountainsides, rising in places sheer from the water, with growing interest.

We rounded the north-eastern cape and saw the town of Thasos, also known as Limen ('the harbour') unfolding against a natural amphitheatre of thickly wooded ridges. The jutting mass of the acropolis on our left was a reminder that modern Thasos occupies the site of its ancient namesake. It is a pleasant town with small hotels scattered along a broad sea front which acts as an apron stage, where the Thasians stroll and dine out, and which youngsters use as a race track for their cycles.

Thasos town lives with its history; for instance the blunt-bowed ferries which provide the island's life-line tie up at the front, but in classical times shipping would have made for the natural semi-circular haven a few metres using some of the original marble blocks and displaying the bases of the pharoses, it shelters fishing caiques where once beak-prowed trading vessels or galleys berthed. Fringed by aged plane trees, it is a picturesque setting for some of the best fish tavernas on the island. Just beyond, and below the acropolis, are the stocks of a boatyard where caiques are still built.

Thasos' town beach is just beyond the marble harbour — a long strip of fine sand shaded by the feathering branches of tamarisk trees and backed by cafés. The island's other beaches and villages can be reached by using the excellent bus services, the time-tables being posted inside the station (*stasis*), which is on the front near the ferry landing.

Taking the Potamia road from town and turning left up the hill at the Silenus gate, brings you, after 20 minutes, to the Makryammos Bungalows Hotel. It has perhaps the best beach on the island, a horseshoe of silver sand with good safe bathing. Privacy is ensured by the steep pine-covered slopes which run down from the rear of the acropolis to the sea. Bathing is open to non-residents, by the way. Islanders are now keeping their fingers crossed that projected explorations for undersea oil deposits off Thrace will not affect such clean swimming facilities.

Hire cars are expensive and getting very much more so with the fuel crises, but they are available through Auto Service Thasos (tel. 21535) — which offers a range of well-maintained cars — or from the Thasos tourist agency on the front, which will also book you accommodation (tel. 22546).

When on an island, why not use the obvious element — water — to get to your destination? Each morning at 10 a.m. a motor boat picks up at the jetty beside the ferry terminal, for Scala Potamia, probably the best beach on the east side of the island. It brings its passengers back in the evening.

Many visitors, perhaps most, will want to explore at their leisure and if so they can take picnic hampers made up from the excellent food shops in Thasos. There is a profusion of Macedonian fruit to choose from, local cheeses and salami. Many shops specialize in local honey, either pine or flower, as well as packets and sachets of herbs.

The first visitors to Thasos of whom we have a record came from those arid, sun-scorched islands far to the south which are so familiar to today's tourist. They were the Parians, who came in the seventh century BC in pursuit of a legend as potent for its time as El Dorado; the mines of Thasos. The Phoenicians were supposed to have struck gold there, colonizing it under their leader Thasus.

The Parians exploited not only the rich resources of their new home but became economic imperialists, opening up mines on the mainland and consolidating their gains with settlements like Crenides (Philippi). The basis for the wealthy city-state which they created was apparently quite obvious to Herodotus and his contemporaries, although some doubt has been cast on their credibility in more modern times. In Book VI of his *History* the father of the subject said that the Thasians

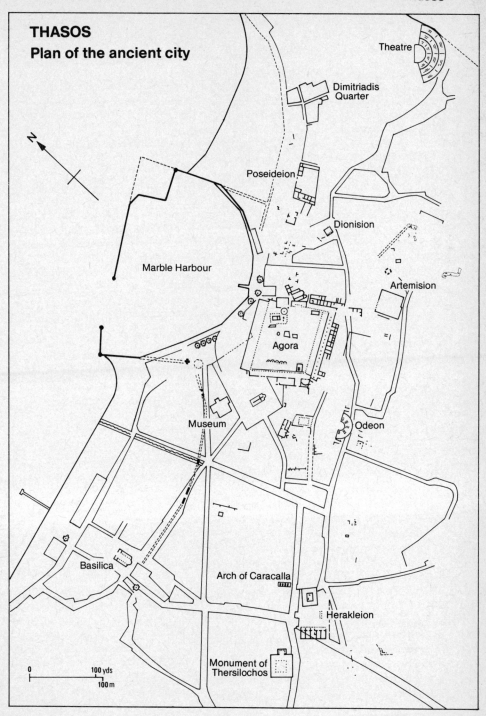

THASOS
Plan of the ancient city

N

Theatre

Dimitriadis
Quarter

Poseideion

Dionision

Marble Harbour

Artemision

Agora

Museum

Odeon

Basilica

Arch of Caracalla

Herakleion

Monument of
Thersilochos

0   100 yds
          100 m

were masters of the gold mines at Scapté-Hyle [Pangeon], the yearly produce of which amounted in all to 80 talents. Their mines in Thasos yielded less, but still were so far prolific that, besides being entirely free from land tax, they had a surplus income, derived from the two sources of their territory on the main and their mines, in common years of 200, and in the best years of 300 talents.

I myself have seen the mines in question: by far the most curious of them are those which the Phoenicians discovered at the time they went with Thasus and colonized the island, which afterwards took its name from him. The Phoenician workings are in Thasos itself, between Kinira and a place called Enira, over against Samothrace: a huge mountain has been turned upsidedown in the search for ore. Such then is the source of their wealth.

The instructions could not have been clearer. However, modern geologists have been very sceptical of the legend, claiming that the rocks were not auriferous. But even with these pessimistic reports the archaeologists of the French School on the island believed there might be something to the legend and pushed on. In 1978 the school's cartographer, Tony Kozelj discovered one of the mines on the slopes of the acropolis and continued his exploration.

He took time off from the excavations near the agora to climb over the slopes of Mount Iypsarion, checking man-made shafts and holes for clues — broken clay lamps or shards of pottery. He also questioned elderly peasants in the Kinira area and it was from one of them, after many months of painstaking but fruitless investigation, that he got the vital lead.

A 70-year-old shepherd remembered that, as a boy of ten, he had lost one of his flock in what seemed to be a crevice in the mountainside. He cut a sapling, propped it in the hole, and climbed down, hand-over-hand. He found the sheep, but he found something else too; what appeared to be the entrance to a grotto. Exploring further, he found himself in the entrance to a long hewn gallery, seemingly disappearing into the heart of the mountain.

He went no farther, but his excellent memory led Tony Kozelj to the spot — 570 metres up, a three-hour hard climb. Kozelj and other members of the French School made their way through the two-metre high entrance (the tree was still there and had rooted), down a steeply sloping shaft for about 50 metres. They found small niches cut in the walls and the remains of clay miners' lamps. Everywhere were the marks of picks and mattocks.

The shaft narrowed and the roof level dropped the farther they advanced. They were reminded of Pliny's description of gold mining which 'surpassed the labours of the giants'. He said that by the aid of galleries driven to a long distance, mountains were excavated by the light of torches, the duration of which formed the set times for work, the workmen never seeing the light of day for several months. These mines, he said 'are known as *arrugiae* and not infrequently clefts are formed on a sudden, the earth sinks in, and the workmen are crushed beneath; so that it would really appear less rash to go in search of pearls and purples at the bottom of the sea, so much more dangerous to ourselves have we made the earth than the water!'

Four hours' walking, part of the time bent double, and then scrambling, brought them to a halt before narrow and now impassable galleries where it would have been dangerous to venture. More research needs to be done but one discovery made by the archaeologists seems vindication enough — they have found traces of auriferous rock in the mine.

Kinira will never be accessible to the visitor, but the other mine discovered on Thasos might well be. Details of the discovery have been published by the French School. Its entrance is just below the grotto of Pan, which I shall be describing later in this chapter, and would therefore be quite accessible to anyone making the tour of the acropolis. In fact it has an entrance and an exit, or air outlet — it could serve equally as either. The mine is not far from the secret stairway, and if a threat developed any gold recently discovered could be spirited away by this route.

With the acquisition of wealth went the need for security, which when they acquired it, the Thasians found was ephemeral. Herodotus said: 'The Thasians . . . resolved that, as their income was very great, they would apply their wealth to building ships of war, and surrounding their city with a stronger wall.' Most of that circuit wall, subsequently twice rebuilt in classical times, still stands. In a remarkable state of preservation and 4 kilometres in circumference, these massive, squared-off courses in the ashlar — Isodonic pattern of the early classical period, were the symbol of the island's pride and independence and whenever they fell, it fell too.

The first occasion was when Darius heard that the Thasians were preparing to revolt, just as he was about to chastise their presumptuous fellow Greeks. The Thasians were probably lucky that they received merely a command to dismantle the new walls and to bring their ships to Abdera, where the Great King was assembling his fleet. 'Obedient to the orders of the king' the Thasians complied. Indeed, when Darius' successor, Xerxes, continued the policy of bringing Greece to heel, the islanders tried to outdo each other in their appeasement of the Persians. When they heard that the Persian army had reached their colonies on the mainland opposite, the Thasians prepared a great banquet for Xerxes which cost the equivalent of one year's revenues. One of their most prominent citizens, Antipatros, son of Orgeus, personally contributed 400 talents of silver to the cost. News of the battle of Salamis brought a rapid about-face in Thasian policy, when, as with many of the Greek city-states, it was deemed safe to identify with the Greek cause.

Again, during the war of the Delian League in 465 BC, the island tried to shift from a commitment, this time in the Greek camp, to neutrality. Athens had made itself the leading maritime power in the Aegean and saw its chance to oust Thasos from its lucrative mining and trading interests. Taking Athenian protection meant a second summons to demolish all fortifications.

As we followed the lines of those ancient ramparts up the side of the acropolis we reflected that if so much had survived two acts of demolition what must the original structure have been like? They were reinforced with 12 watch towers and had nine gates and we made our starting point the Chariot Gate, the closest point to the sea at which the defences could be entered. Our route would take us up over the acropolis, and moving south and west, back down the landward side of the enceinte into town.

We took our bearings on the marble harbour and the whitewashed, two-storeyed Turkish customs house on the far side of it. The start of the walk is the lane which passes behind the customs house and which is lined with neat, balconied fishermen's houses. We had been told to keep looking on the left-hand side as the gate could be missed. We did not expect to find it sunk in someone's garden, however; an old woman came out and gestured us to come on to her garden balcony so that we could get a better photograph.

Both pillars, three metres high, are standing but the one in the garden absorbs the visitor's attention. The now pitted and darkened marble surface is incised with a bas-relief of Artemis in her chariot, doubtless ready for a moonlight drive, with Hermes holding her horses' heads. She could just as easily have represented a wealthy and liberated young Thasienne, approaching the town gates for an outing; hair pulled into a pony-tail and wearing a himation, open at the front for greater ease of movement.

The gate gave access in a piece of wall which defended the two harbours.

A few yards farther on, opposite the foundations of a domestic housing area of the ancient city, we came to a second set of carved, marble gate pillars, the so-called Gate of Hermes and the Graces. The god, nude apart from a short cloak, seems to be moving out of the frieze, right, towards the city, but turns to three female figures who are tripping after him.

The track started to rise slowly to the right, our footfalls over the worn stones and grey-green gneiss deadened by pine needles and our nostrils savouring the smell of pine trees which grew denser as we climbed. To the left the land dropped away to the boat yard, near the site of the ancient harbour, one arm of which we could see submerged, ending in a circular pharos platform.

On the headland we rested at the site of a Byzantine basilica, cross-inscribed fragments of tombstones lying scattered everywhere, and which was built on the site of a pagan shrine with a catholic dedication to Zeus, Athena, Artemis and the Nymphs.

One last glimpse of the local boys diving off the rocks into the deep cobalt blue water surging around the foot of the headland, and we were following the lines of the ramparts ever upwards, our only companions bees and beautiful butterflies, flitting through the tangle of odiferous bushes at our feet. The acropolis is the home of butterflies; lemon yellow with black barring and edges to wingtips, brown, grey and silver-white, with alternative barring and patches, and a species blue/yellow at the wing roots, with black edging.

To our right now lay the theatre where a season of classical Greek plays is performed every August. Built into a natural glade in the hillside, its cavea (seating plan), very little of which now survives, fans out almost up to the line of the ramparts. The oaks and pines tend to crowd in, giving it a rather gloomy feeling at certain times of the day. But in antiquity it must have been a fitting stage for the works of Euripides or of the Thasian hegemon, regarded by Aristotle as the originator of parody in comic writing.

From here we started the climb to the summit of the acropolis, the contours of the land steepening all the time so that the sea was now a distant and occasionally seen burst of incandescent blue as the sun strengthened.

We came out on the eastern lip of the rock, a full 137 metres above sea level, on the ramparts of the Genoese fort. At the beginning of the fifteenth century the weakened Byzantine empire ceded various Aegean islands, including Thasos, to the Genoese in an attempt to keep them out of the hands of the Turks. The Gattilusi family became effective suzereins and built this kastro, with keep and outworks, reinforcing the already precipitous face of the rock. A partially obscured notice says that you climb the walls at your own risk and you may feel that the view is grand enough from what was the bailey of the castle without climbing up on to the platform, below which the drop is almost sheer to the lower slopes. The Genoese obscured the remains of a shrine to the Pythian Apollo, but re-used marble from it can be seen in the fort's walls.

One of the most complete Genoese remains is the fortress chapel. It has the usual semi-circular apse and fragments of fresco showing figure and floral subjects on a ground of red stucco. We found a guardhouse with a postern gate — tightly angled to provide either enfilade or to allow the garrison to make a surprise sally — and turning sharp right to regain the path, looked up and saw a gleam of white in the wall. It was a bas-relief of a funeral feast, of the late fifth or early fourth century BC. The dead man lies on a couch, propped up on an elbow (a common symbol in ancient Greece) and raising his cup in a valediction. His wife sits opposite him on a stool. A horse is being led in on the left and an apparently naked youth is on the right.

The terrain opened out as we made our way through olive groves to the second summit, and the stylobate and fragments of column which are all that is left of the Sanctuary of Athena Poliouchos ('Mother of the City'). This temple, which acted as a magnificent crown to the city and could be seen from far out at sea, striking glints from the sun, occupied a large terrace 51 metres from east to west and 20 metres from north to south. It had the usual cella ('central shrine'), but unprotected by an outer colonnade, and was approached through a pronaos ('forecourt'), and opisthodome ('porch'). On the north and east the terrace had to be artificially raised, where the rocky outcrop became sheer. We sat in the shade of a tree which clung to the very edge of the abyss, and enjoyed the superb view of Thasos town and harbour.

Between the sanctuary and the final summit we crossed a col and diverged a little to see one of the most charming spots on the island, the sanctuary of Pan. Facing us at the end of an olive-shaded glade was a low, flat rock face with a niche cut into it. Using the footholds cut below it we climbed up and saw a charming dedicatory carving, a world away in spirit from the august marble building which used to tower over it.

Pan plays his pipes to an audience of goats and deer — and may be playing still for those who visit this place in the dawn or at dusk. For someone had left on the rockshelf in front of the grotto an offering of black grapes and red roses.

A few paces and we had attained the summit of the acropolis with some of the finest accessible views on the island, including Samothrace. South-westward rose the secondary acropolis, a spur of the one on which we stood and which masked the finest sand beach on the island, Makryammos. To the south, dominating all, rose the white limestone peak of Mount Iypsarion, its spurs dropping sharply in the east in forest-covered cliffs, and becoming quite spectacular sheer rock faces in certain spots. We would see all this and much more at close quarters.

First, however, to complete our tour of the ramparts. We now negotiated the one part of the walk which demanded strong nerves, the descent of the secret staircase from the Gate of Parmenon, named after a carved inscription on it 'Parmenon made me'. The gate is set in the thickness of the ramparts at the beginning of one of its best preserved stretches — down to the Gate of Heracles.

The staircase is nothing but rock steps cut into the sheer southern face of the acropolis; a vertiginous exercise but the only direct way down in antiquity, as now. Today there is an iron handrail all the way down the twisting descent. Two huge eyes, a good luck talisman, gazed at us from one of the rock faces as we started down. We prepared to close ours and grasp the handrail tightly.

We came out on the boulder-strewn lower slopes and walked back to town inside the ramparts. The Silenus Gate lies where the line of walls crosses the junction of the road to Makryammos and all the eastern arm of the island's circular road. The gate's identification symbol is a lively two-metre high bas relief of Silenus. He is nude apart from a pair of calf-length boots and although his priapus has been defaced at some period he has his tail and in his right hand carries a cantharus of wine.

We had spoken to workmen excavating a domestic quarter at the Gate of Silenus the previous year and they told us of work planned for the continuation of the fortifications in the field across the road. Now we were able to see the operation in progress, the cleaning and restoration of a particularly well preserved section of the wall, the so-called wall of Heracles, pierced by the Gate of Heracles. As the presiding deity of the island Heracles was honoured with a shrine, the remains of which are just below the Silenus Gate on the road into town.

A ceremonial route probably linked the shrine and the gate named after him and this is one area where excavations are in progress. In fact, it would not be too much of an exaggeration to say that the whole of Thasos town is one large archaeological dig. Either older excavations are being resumed and developed or exploration is starting in some new quarter and direction. The visitor to Thasos will always find something fresh happening in archaeology, possibly under his hotel balcony, and the archaeologists themselves are ready to explain their work.

The Wall of Heracles is being cleaned, earthen banks and shrubs cleared away and the finely laid courses of white marble restored to their true glory. Unfortunately that cannot include the bas-relief from the gate, which was removed to the museum in Istanbul before the First World War. It depicted a favourite motif on Thasian coins, Heracles the Archer. The god knelt, his head covered with the lion's skin (a favourite pose on coins of Alexander the Great) he is drawing his bow at an unseen foe.

Piece by piece, the great mosaic of archaeological discoveries in Thasos is fitting together to give a more comprehensible picture of life in this rich polis. Prof. Maffre and his team have been concentrating on the ceremonial way which various inscriptions and foundations of shrines have indicated ran up to the lower slopes of the acropolis, linking its temples with the city's heart, the agora. When we were there they had just uncovered the way's junction with the main road which bisected the city laterally, running through the Passage of Theores and entering the agora from the landside.

The steep marble setts have raised ridges every few paces, to stop the sacrificial animals from slipping and right on the junction stood what appears to have been a bath house. From this point the agora is entered at its south-eastern corner.

Today the agora is a large sunken grass square, 100 metres in area, pocked with column fragments, marble tribunes and altars and covered with traces and indents in the grass. Some help is obviously needed if there is to be a feel for the pride of buildings which once stood here.

And what a spot it must have been. At the Passage of Theores the calls of the shopkeepers, combined with the shouts and bellowing of merchants and pack animals trying to reach the comparatively open space of the arcades beyond, must have been bedlam. The passage consisted of marble walls ending in pilasters and once embellished with magnificent bas-reliefs, now in the Louvre, which depicted Apollo and the Nymphs. The importance of the passage was established, however, by the inscription found on its walls, the so-called 'theores' — lists of festivals and of those who would officiate in them and represent the city at various other shrines and oracles in the Greek world.

The entrance to the agora was through a long portico and colonnade which ran round three sides. Seeking welcome shelter under a great tiled roof, embellished with palmettes, the ancient Thasian would have seen, behind the portico, a large gallery with a central row of supporting pillars. At its extreme eastern end was the oldest named monument in Thasos, that to Glaucos, who was one of those first settlers from Paros. The inscription to Glaucos is in the museum.

From our visitor's vantage point, the long south-eastern section of the portico would stretch away for 92 metres, supported on 31 Doric columns, three of which are now standing. It completed the eastern sweep of the agora with a further 33 columns, donated by two brothers Euphrilles and Micas. At the angle of the portico, where it turned west, stood a big altar, 2.74 metres by 1.30 metres, and below it 5 exedras (semi-circular extensions of the portico), in which stood statues of various public benefactors of the agora with a further 33 columns, donated by two brothers, Euphrilles and Dionosodoros and Hestiaios. One of the statues found in this area — it was lying in an apsidal room which opened on to the long gallery — was a statue of the Emperor Hadrian, which can also be seen in the museum.

Near the waterfront are the remains of a propylaea ('gateway') and steps which would have given access to the city — the only access along the waterfront until you reached the Chariot Gate. One totally unexpected hazard for the archaeologists has proved to be the high level of the water table. The subterranean water level has risen with the ground over the centuries (about a metre).

Retracing your steps to the propylaea you see the stylobate of the north-west portico stretching across the agora, even with only a couple of columns re-erected, an impressive architectural monument. Its breadth can be measured from the distance of the column bases to the back of the stylobate — 12 metres — spanned by single beams, with no intervening supports. Only the forests of Macedonia could have furnished such enormous pieces of timber.

Thasos had a catholic taste in deities and cult figures and the market place was an obvious site for their public observation; the sanctuary of Zeus for instance was 'Zeus of the Agora' and stood in the lower left-hand corner as you look out from the site of the north-west portico. It consisted of a small temple opening on the east to an altar and attached to it was a circular enclosure. Only the foundations remain.

If the trader or his customer preferred to heed the exhortation 'now let us praise famous men' he would walk to the centre of the agora where a shrine was dedicated to just that proposition. It is known as the Sanctuary of Theogenes because an inscription identifying the famous athlete was found there.

A ring let into a marble foundation course, where sacrificial animals were tethered, is all that remains of the shrine. But the traveller Pausanius relates the glories which led to its erection. 'I have already spoken of the greatest successes of Theogenes in the Olympic Games. He also won three times at Delphi, thrice at boxing, nine times at the Nemean Games, 10 at the Isthmian.' He is said to have won 1400 sporting crowns.

Nearby is the foundation of another altar dedicated to the two grandsons of Augustus Caesar, Gaius and Lucius, whose death at an early age while they were being groomed to succeed him, was regarded with great suspicion. Two bases which held their statues can be seen but all that remains is the head of Gaius, which is in the museum.

On the north-east of the agora stood the sanctuaries to Poseidon, Dionysos and Artemis. The first two formed a sacred precinct, of which very little remains, although the site is only partly excavated. We know that the Thasians paid semi-divine honours not only to their famous athletes but also to the Muses of the dramatic arts.

It is appropriate that the shrine dedicated to Dionysos, the epitome of full self-expression, should nestle below the theatre and it is there and in the museum where the spirit of his shrine is best preserved.

The sanctuary was approached by a flight of steps and through a porch with four columns. Facing the worshipper was an enclosure in the shape of the Greek phi arch, against which stood a semi-circular exedra, reflecting the shape of the cavea in the theatre. On it stood statues of Dionysos, the Muses of Comedy and Tragedy and figures representing the dithyramb, the song of Dionysos, and of Nicterinos, the nocturnal song.

The beautiful head of the god of the unfettered spirit was found near this exedra. It can be seen in the museum and is the most sublime piece of Hellenistic sculpture found on Thasos; 0.60 metres high, and turned slightly to the right, it has the androgynous features associated with the god, but rendered with a real humanity, often absent in the subject

The museum contains other statuary from the sanctuary. There is the (headless) statue of the Comic Muse, 1.70 metres high, represented as a young woman (although the dedication on the base is to an actor, Philemon). It originally held a mask in the left hand.

The Poseideon, near by, was a trapesoidal building looking over the port. On one of the column bases near the entrance was found an inscription giving the dedication: 'From Xenophanes, son of Myllos to Poseidon'. Six apartments which opened onto the court of the sanctuary were apparently used by a dining club devoted to the god, for their banquets.

A beautiful piece of sculpture found there, and which is one of the finest pieces in the museum, indicates the worship of one of the female deities. This small (0.385 metre) Hellenistic piece, designed for an interior shrine, shows Aphrodite, or perhaps Amphitrite, sitting side-saddle on a dolphin and naked to the waist. The folds of her fallen himation are repeated behind the head as the curveture of her graceful form is picked up in the arch of the dolphin's back. The design recalls the Aphrodite of Cnidus, one of Praxitiles' masterpieces.

The area of the Artemision, mentioned by Hippocrates in his *Epidemics* (the father of medicine visited the island and left a gruesome, if fascinating account of its inhabitants' ills) is attracting fresh interest from the archaeologists, as it forms part of the general quarter of the sacrificial way.

The vestiges that are left to us of ancient Thasos indicate building conceived on the grand scale, and much of the sculpture in the museum, which lies in a garden filled with palms and pine trees, just west of the agora, matches it.

Outside is a huge seated eagle and a Roman torso in armour which displays a Medusa's head on the breastplate. Facing you as you enter is a towering and unfinished kouros of a young Apollo, 3.50 metres high and dating from the beginning of the sixth century. It is in the stiff archaic style which came to the Parian sculptors of the Cyclades from Egypt and the kouros carries a stylized sacrificial ram.

The museum provides a fairly comprehensive tour through styles of Greek sculpture and it is interesting to compare, for instance, a head and wings of Pegasus, with an Assyrian feel, from the Sanctuary of Heracles, and, roughly contemporary with the kouros, and, from the same sanctuary, a horse's head of only 30 years later. The earlier work is highly stylized while the latter has all the life of a running Bucephalus, nostrils flaring and eyes flashing.

A fine piece in the right-hand gallery is a funerary statue with the semi-circular design of a Michelangelo pièta, showing the body of a young girl with her head slightly turned, supported under her arms by a sorrowing attendant. There is also a recumbent figure of a young man with a finely modelled torso, resting on one arm, and near by a series of portrait busts from the agora. They are of Julius Caesar, a negro slave, Lucius Caesar and a presumed portrait of Plato, a reproduction of a bust made originally for the Academy in Athens.

Thasos is girdled by a coast road, which enables you to drive round it in about three hours. But, for leisurely exploration, the island is best treated as two tours, one down the spectacular east coast and the other down the gentler, more cultivated west coast.

For the eastern leg, we left Thasos town past the Heracleion and kept straight on at the Silenus Gate. The road winds slowly upward through viridian green pinewoods, set in rich red ochre earth, flecked and scored with dazzling white outcrops of marbloid rock. Eight kilometres over a steep saddle, we reached the village of Panaghia. The time to arrive there, as in all Greek villages, is early evening. Siesta is over, the heat of the day has broken and the herdsmen are bringing their flocks in from pasture.

Panaghia slowly bestirs itself about 6 o'clock; the small square comes alive with the mumur of humanity and the clipping of hooves and tinkling of bells. Those individualists, goats, wander here and there, nosing into odd corners, attempting to chew bric-a-brac on souvenir stalls and the people follow the flocks down crazy-paved alleys and streets from the upper town like a Verdi chorus. Farmers noisily conduct deals by the fountain, youths show off new motor cycles to friends and *papades* stroll among their flock, stopping now and then to extend a ring finger to be kissed.

This gentle, unaffected scene can be best appreciated when sipping an ouzo under the huge plane tree which spreads over the square. The tree is supposed to be exactly as old as the beginning of the movement for Greek independence, an event which exacted a high price where it failed, as in Macedonia — and Thasos. Massacre and pillage followed and venerable churches would either be sacked or pillaged and abandoned. But as we climbed the back alley of the village, between neat cottages with vine trellises and arbours we came to a church which had been restored, thanks to the munificence of a returned son — a not uncommon event in Greece. A plaque on the outer wall reads: 'the great benefactor Botiaios Ellinas, resident of the United States, borned [*sic*] in 1895 in village of Virgin Mary of Thasos.'

As we walked back to the car in the night-scented mountain air we had to remind ourselves that we were no more than a quarter of an hour from the sea and it hardly needs saying that an ideal day trip is a visit to one of the nearby beaches, say Scala Potamia, returning in the early evening for an aperitif on a mountainside terrace.

From Panaghia the road dropped gradually, though still passing through spectacular scenery, to the village of Potamia, Just beyond, a left fork dipped down to a 4-kilometre horshoe of fine white shingle and sand with a gentle slope into turquoise sea. We had reached Scala Potamia, probably the second-best swimming on the island. This is one of our recommended alternatives as a place to stay; there are five good D class hotels, catering for families, at least two of which have self-catering facilities and laundry rooms. There are also three fish restaurants on the beach, which have the franchise for small sailing dinghies and peddaloes. The bay is open and the water can be choppy, but the beach, where camping is allowed, is quite safe for children under supervision.

We strolled to the south mole where old fishermen were mending their nets in the shadow of a former monastery boathouse, now used for storing fishing tackle. Thasos still supports a small fishing community which sends caique 'mother boats' out at dusk, each trailing seven or eight 'chicks', cobbles with triple kerosene lamps slung in the stern. After dusk they slowly trawl up and down a section of the sea, nets spread in their wake to catch the fish bobbing up to the lights. From the shore they resemble a procession of fireflies.

The Potamia fishermen have their own delightful little chapel near the bus stop at the skala. This Church of Aghios Nikolaos, patron saint of seafarers, has a stone-shingled roof and a tiny apse. It has a floral fresco decoration and at some time an Ionic pillar from a pagan sanctuary has been incorporated into the nave. The icon of St Nicholas has a charming 'crest' of a carved seagull.

From Potamia the road forms a corniche, the uninhabited islet of Kinira lying offshore. Where the land drops most steeply, near the village still called Kinira, we were very near to the area of gold mine workings, as described by Herodotus. Today it is given over to honey cultivation and rows of hives line the roadside, interspersed with tents for collecting the honey.

Smoke gun in hand to stun and drive away the bees, the beekeeper takes the frames containing the honeycombs from the hive. Skimming the surface of the comb with a heated knife to cut the wax he then puts it in a barrel which is spun with a crank. The honey is drawn from the tray by centrifugal force and drains into the bottom of the barrel through a spigot.

At one point the woman in charge of this operation — bees buzzed round her head and she wore no form of protection — cut a slice off the honeycomb and let us sample it.

Farther on the road dropped to an undulating plain dotted with olive groves, a fish restaurant appearing on a small beach to our left. We rounded the shoulder of Cape Babouras, the south-eastern edge of Thasos, and ahead on a small, low headland lay Aliki, the site of the ancient marble quarries. From here the boat loads of Thasian marble went away south to build the sanctuaries and public buildings of the city states and later for the huge public building works of the Romans.

It was and is coarse-grained and the Parian settlers who first worked it probably found it a less satisfying material than their own native limestone. Parian was a by-word for fine texture and luminosity in marble and as such the Cycladic stone was used principally for statuary. But such beauty was not easily won; it was ripped from seams at the end of long dark tunnels in the interior of the island. In Thasos, on the other hand, the great building slabs and column drums were mostly hewn on an open-cast basis, and lowered direct to the ships moored at the foot of the cliffs. There, one huge column drum, 9 metres long, still lies in the shallow water lapping across a partly worked stratum.

Aliki combines perfectly hedonism and scholarship — fine swimming and a meal at a beachside taverna can be enjoyed literally at the foot of the oldest Doric site on the island. The beach, on the east side of the pro-montory, is reaching by scrambling down the hillside from the road and from the same vantage point can be seen the pillars of a sanctuary, on the western shore. The beach is reached quite easily but the sanctuary itself is fenced off and unless you are prepared to wade through the shallows, the only entrance is through a gate behind the taverna (key obtainable at cottage at bottom of hill).

The headland was apparently a sacred place from the arrival of the Parians onward. There were two shrines, known for convenience as the north and south, apparently dedicated to sea deities, for graffiti have been found on the steps of the north shrine hinting at voyages under way. There are also vows made in return for the safety of the marble-carrying ships *Serapis, Heracles, Poseidon, Artemis* and *Aesclepios*. One inscription is a thanks offering to the 'Two Saviours', the Dioscuri, who were the patrons of seafarers.

Crews of marble boats bringing offerings for a safe voyage would enter either shrine through one of two entrances in a wall which was fronted by a porch with five Doric columns between two pillars in antis, and above which was an architrave, which carried triglyphs and metopes of sophisticated workmanship. The larger of the two interior rooms seems to have been a sacrificial chamber.

At a more primitive level, the protection of the local spirits was invoked in grottoes which honeycomb the headland. There is one in the cliff just behind the south sanctuary and another, larger one, 25 metres away, where votive figurines were found. A third grotto can be seen in the cliff face opposite the taverna.

Above the pagan sanctuary, on the very tip of the promontory, are the remains of a Christian one; two churches of which the ground plan and columns remain. Apparently the site was abandoned in early Byzantine times, perhaps as early as the sixth century and probably because of pirate raids.

The remains of the classical quarry fall away on the south-east side of the headland. Erosion has honed the marble cliff to the consistency of a glacier, a smooth river of cold limestone in which the pick marks and matrices of slabs and pillars left by the ancients can be seen clearly. The marble strata run right off the bottom of the site under the sucking deep-blue tide rip, which turns light turquoise where one of the old cuttings remains.

Beyond Aliki the barren bottom of the island affords spectacular cliff scenery, particularly beyond Marmaras, where, as the name suggests, marble quarrying continues. The nunnery of Archangelos perches on a sheer precipice, but beyond an even more vertiginous view meets the eye. Silver-grey and ochre cliffs drop sheer for hundreds of metres into a mirror-surfaced bay. You accelerate round a corniche and the effect is not dissimilar to a big dipper. Suddenly the earth and sea seem very far below you.

Then, very quickly, the landscape settles down to undulating foothills with olive groves. Just past the turn-off for Astris there is a white sand cove with excellent swimming, shade trees and a fish restaurant at the water's edge.

The western route starts at Limenaria, the island's second village, and can be covered at a leisurely pace, and − allowing for detours into the interior − in two hours. As you approach Limenaria you will see a sign to Theologos, coming up just after the turn off to Potos beach is indicated.

Theologos was founded by refugees from Constantinople in the fifteenth century and its sheer inaccessibility made it for a long time the capital of Thasos. The island was plagued by pirates up to the beginning of the last century, and coastal settlements were reduced to ashes again and again and their inhabitants enslaved.

Refugees, with an especially sharpened instinct for survival, appreciated a position blessed with good water and, as in the case of Panaghia, good cover as well as clear visibility. The road follows the valley up through olive groves which give way to high pasture. Whitewashed Macedonian houses with stone-shingled roofs suddenly appear at the very edge of the tree line. The setting seems barren and forbidding but the impression is dispelled the moment you enter the village.

Mountain streams gurgle through myriad channels and culverts, irrigating small gardens with apple and pear trees, vines are carried on trellises over tiny patios and, unbelievably, at this altitude, there are pomegranates.

The road narrows to the width of a mule track as it climbs but just as you think it is going to peter out, it takes another twist and comes out at another small platea with a tree-shaded café.

Regaining the coast road the way you came you drive into Limenaria past a picturesquely derelict stuccoed house in the Moorish style with huge century plants outside. This, together with a larger folly fashioned as a mock chateau, which stands on a bluff overlooking the waterfront, are reminders of the great gold rush in the island before the First World War. It was a fruit of the Kaiser's fantastic conception of himself as the Sword of Islam, which stretched to economic aid for the Turks, like the plan for a Berlin-Mecca railway. German miners were put up in Thasos in some luxury to prove Herodotus right, but his gold eluded them.

Limenaria is a clean, modern village with many C and D class hotels and rooms to rent. Its assets are in full view, a narrow horseshoe of a town beach which juts out under the balconies, and terraces of fish restaurants and cafés.

Beyond Limenaria a long white shingle beach stretches two kilometres to the Pefkari campsite. It is an area just for lazing and sleeping and eating for a few drachmae a day − the western coast is generally the cheaper side of the island. Round Kefalas point, the land begins to rise and forms a corniche with fine views of Halkidiki. The road regains the sea at Skala Kalirachis, but swimming is from a shale beach with boat houses every few metres.

On to Prinos, the stopping place for direct ferries (several sailings a day). It is hardly worth a stop; the narrow beach is seaweed-clogged and provision lorries loading and unloading from the ferries career with alarming abandon up and down the front.

Four kilometres up the coast is Skala Rachoni, the beach area for the little mountain village of the same name. Despite the 'skala' the beach is not recommended for swimming, but the landing has several good fish restaurants and one can enjoy one's meal sitting under a vine trellis and watching the swallows skimming low over the sea.

Rachoni itself, a white-stuccoed hamlet 20 minutes' drive into the interior, has rooms for rent and is an ideal place to stay for those with cars as beyond its skala good swimming can be found at several rocky covers. Here, the coastline has a feel of the rocky east coast, but it is not nearly so precipitous. All the way round the north-westerly point as far as Glyfada, with its fine sand cove and large, pine-screened hotel, are enticing little inlets in the rocks, ideal for scuba diving. Glyfada also has a campsite on the beach with a restaurant.

And so back through olive groves to Thasos town. Perhaps one diversion should be mentioned, that to Aghios Georgios, the turn off for which is just before Skala Rachoni. Here is preserved the house in which Mehmet Ali, the future Khedive of Egypt, was fostered by a Greek family named Karapanayiotis. Later, when he was wanted for murder, Mehmet Ali 'went to ground' there with his old foster father and never forgot the debt he owed to him. When the Khedive ruled Egypt he sent a felucca to bring the family to join him, but discovering that the patriarch had been betrayed to the Turks and hanged from a plane tree in the village square he had the betrayer hanged from the same tree. Later Mehmet Ali received other members of the family with great honours and when the Sultan offered him a reward for his help in putting down a revolt in Arabia he claimed Thasos. His protection lasted only a short time but for it the Thasians did enjoy exemption from the heavy taxes they had hitherto paid.

Guide to Hotels etc.

Thessaloniki

Thessaloniki has the range of hotels you would expect in a major trade centre. English is spoken in almost all of them by some staff.

Hotels

Makedonia Palace Alexander the Great Avenue — tel. 837-520.
Luxury class; directly on sea front; conference centre; fine cuisine and roof-top restaurant; fully air-conditioned; outdoor swimming pool.

Elektra Palace 5a Aristotelous Square — tel. 232-221.
Large A class, set in one of the most attractive squares in the city, close to tourist offices and to shopping streets and markets with abundant cafés and nightlife. Air-conditioned; has good restaurant.

Capsis 28 Monastiriou Road — tel. 521-321.
Large, B class, catering to commercial and tourist trade; close to the railway station and on the direct bus route for a five-minute ride into the centre of town. A feature of this hotel is a very pleasant roof-top swimming pool and bar with dancing in the evenings and a good place to rest and recover after the midday heat. Open to non-residents; air-conditioned.

Olympia 65 Olympou Street — tel. 235-421.
C class, ultra-modern conversion of older hotel with open-plan bar and dining area; close to the city market, coppersmiths and antique shops; very convenient to the old city and the centre; good value.

Hostels
YMCA, YMCA Square — tel. 225-277.
YWCA, 11 Aghias Sofias Street — tel. 276-144.

Camping
Akti Thermaikou (NTOG) — tel. 0392-51360.
Asprovolta (NTOG) — tel. 0397-31249.

Guide to Hotels

Beaches

Akti Thermaikou (at Aghia Triada; 27 kilometres by road from city, or can also be reached in season by boat from the foot of the White tower).
Aretsou (5 kilometres, bus No. 5).

Tourist office

Greek National Tourist Organization, 8, Aristotelous Square
tel. 222-935 and 271-888

Travelling

Doucas Tours, 8 Venizelou Street — tel 224-100
Largest of the tour companies; comprehensive services to: Pella, Philippi; Mount Athos; Meteora and Halkidiki.
Palandijian travel and tourist agency, 11 Vass. Constantinou Avenue — tel. 26177.

Car Hire

Hertz, 4 Venizelou Street — tel. 224-906 or airport — tel 419-851.
Ace, 7 Nease Paralias Street — tel. 811-880.

Buses

Local bus service is frequent and very inexpensive and has the great advantage of operating in siesta time when it is difficult to find a taxi.

Long-distance buses offer a very good service and we have found the staff very patient and helpful, making it possible to take extensive journeys without the language. For information it is best to ask at the NTOG in Aristotelous Square since there are different bus stations for destinations.

Ordinary Restaurants

Makedonia Palace — for luxury and a continental cuisine; roof-top restaurant. Many of the cafés in Aristotelous Square offer a good, light meal in an attractive setting.

There are a great number of moderately priced restaurants in the centre of the city, two of which we enjoyed were:
The Great Constantine, Olympos 82, near Dikastirion Square, and
Sparta, Aristotelous 82, near the tourist office.

Do not worry about the menu being all Greek; you will be invited into the kitchen to choose from one of the bubbling pots.

Wine

Macedonia has vineyards producing fine wines which are not generally known abroad. Naoussa is the main centre of production for reds and one of the interesting offshoots of the Porto Carras development is the distinguished Château Carras white.

Reds

Cambas — (the Pella or Athos) — like a good Beaujolais.

Naoussa — Boutari; robust, like a Côte du Rhone.

Whites
Porto Carras — Château Carras; Blanc de Blancs (both like good Alsatian wine).

Tsantilis of Halkidiki produces some very good wines and one of the best of the retsinas. The best brandy we found was Cambas.

Fish Restaurants
The best fish restaurants are located at Krini, which is the closest bathing area and marina for the city, easily reached by local bus No. 5, which runs along the sea front. It is approximately a 20-minute ride and well worth it. There are a great number of moderately priced restaurants but do remember the price of the fish depends upon the weight.

Edessa — hotels

Helena, 4 Dimitriou Rizou.
Xenia, 41 Philippou Paradissos.

Veria — hotels

Villa Elia, 16 Elias (very friendly, English-speaking manager. It is on the main street).
Polytimi, 35 Megalou Alexandrou.

Florina — hotels

Lygnos, 3 Tagmatarhou Naoum Street,
New Xenia, follow signs — on hilltop just outside town.

Kastoria — hotels

Kastoria, 122 Nikis Avenue (beautiful lakeside position, open in season, no restaurant).
Xenia du Lac, Dexamenis Square.

Kavala — hotels
Hotel Lucy — tel. 031-832600.
Very pleasant hotel, ultra-modern, fully air-conditioned, indoor pool and good bathing beach. Restaurant. Very helpful, English-speaking manager. It is situated round the headland from the centre of the city. There is a frequent local bus service, No. 4, which takes 10 minutes to the town centre.
Tosca Beach; bungalow complex, 6 kilometres from Kavala.
There are hotels around the harbour offering good accomodation.
Tourist information office, Eleftherias Square — tel.051-22425.
The city has a number of excellent fish, restaurant around the habour. At the harbour ferries depart for Thasos and many other northern Aegean islands.

Halkidiki

The peninsula lies one-and-a-half hours' drive from Thessaloniki.

Hotels

As befits the new holiday frontier of Greece, the peninsula has 50 hotels with about 10,000 beds, and 14 camp sites, with 7000 camping spots. The accommodation ranges from large hotels providing a complete environment to bungalow developments.

De luxe class

Akti Meliton Beach (Porto Carras); 834 beds; 17 suites; open April to December.

Sithonia Beach (Porto Carras); 456 beds; open April to October − pools, marina, golf course.

A class

Athos Palace (Kassandra); 1130 beds large swimming pool; beach area which it shares with Pallini Beach; all sporting facilities. Nightclub, disco, sauna, indoor pool, gym.

Pallini Beach; 938 beds, 98 bungalows, 42 suites; own pool; all sporting facilities.

Akti Sani (Kassandra); 436 beds in bungalows.

Kassandra Melathron (Kassandra); 357 beds.

Mendi; 311 beds.

B class

Gerakina Beach; an accommodation with a difference. Set in a large olive grove with luxurious gardens; it successfully merges the modern resort hotel with the character and life we go to Greece to find.

It has 503 rooms with 955 beds; 39 suites and bungalows; a restaurant and a Greek taverna; dancing, displays of folk dancing, sauna, indoor pool, children's playroom and cinema; tennis courts; outdoor pool; all sporting facilities.

There are numerous other B and C class hotels, which offer good accommodation. The above are those of which we have personal experience and can recommend. Halkidiki has local bus services (for information it is best to inquire at your hotel desk.) It is possible to travel to all of the towns and around the peninsulas to the very beautiful beaches but do go forearmed with the schedules, so that you don't miss the last bus back.

Thasos

The ferry goes from Kavala, which can be reached by bus from Thessaloniki (the station is 59 Langadas Street, and the journey takes three hours). The ferry takes an hour to Prinos (from Kavala) or 45 minutes from Keramoti, near Kavala.

Hotels
Makryammos; A class; set in more than 100,000 square metres of pine woods and gardens, with undoubtedly the best beach on the island; with a good restaurant and bar/disco, tennis courts, outdoor pool, all sporting facilities. It comprises bungalows set into the hillside, some with their own stone stairs down to the sea. It is suitable for families and people wanting to relax without going outside the complex; ten bungalow suites and 200 bungalows, each with two beds — tel. (0593-22101/2).
Xenia; B class; on the front of Thasos town.
There is a good selection of C class hotels in the town.
    Limenaria also offers a wide selection of moderately priced hotels.

Travelling
Buses The main bus depot is found on the front of Thasos town, from where you can take a bus to almost any coastal point on the island (see the schedule for times).
Hire cars Auto Service Thasos (tel. 21535).

Bibliography

Introduction
 Leake, William Martin, *Travels in Northern Greece*, 1835
 Baynes, Norman and Moss H., *Byzantium*, Oxford, 1949
 Vacalopoulos, Apostolos, *History of Macedonia*, Institute for Balkan Studies, 1973
 Mitsakis, K, *Macedonia throughout the Centuries*, Thessaloniki, 1975
 Hammond Prof. N.G.L., *History of Macedonia*, Vol. I, Oxford at the Clarendon Press, 1973

Royal Tombs
 Andronicos, Manolis, *The Royal Graves at Vergina*, Athens, 1978
 Andronicos, Manolis, *Vergina*, Karamos Guides, 1972
 Bruno, Vincent, *Form and Colour in Greek Painting*, Thames and Hudson, London 1977
 Price, Martin, *Coins of the Macedonians*, British Museum Publications, 1974
 Pliny, *The Natural History*, Loeb Classics, Heinemann
 Hammond, N.G.L. and Griffiths, G.T. *History of Macedonia*, Vol II. Oxford, at the University Press, 1973

Thessaloniki
 Vacalopoulos, Apostolos, *A History of Thessaloniki*, Institute for Balkan Studies, 1972
 Molho, S., ed., *Monuments of Thessaloniki*
 Xyngopoulos, A., *The Mosaics of the Church of St Demetrius at Thessaloniki*, Thessaloniki, 1969
 Rossiter, Stuart, ed., *Greece*, Blue Guide, London, 1977
 Ware, Timothy, *The Orthodox Church*, Pelican, London, 1964
 Weitzmann, Kurt, *The Icon*, New York, 1978
 Dietz, E. and Demys, Otto, *Byzantine Mosaics in Greece*, 1931
 Talbot-Rice, David, *Byzantine Art*, Penguin, 1968

Western Macedonia
 Comnena, Anna, *The Alexiad*, Penguin, 1979
 Touratsoglou, John, *Lefkadia*, Keamos Guides

Touratsoglou, John, *Heraclea Lyncestis*, Board of Heraclea, Bitola, 1973
Broussalis, Peter, *The Prespa National Park*, The Hellenic Society for the Protection of Nature, Athens, 1975

Philippi and Kavala
O'Sullivan, Firmin, *The Egnatian Way*, David and Charles, 1972
Collart, Paul, *Philippi*, Strasburg, 1937

Halkidiki
Schroder, Raymond S. J., *Ancient Greece from the Air*, Thames and Hudson, 1974
Livy, *The Roman History*, Loeb Classics

Mount Athos
Lancaster, Osbert, *Sailing to Byzantium*, John Murray, 1972
Kadas, Sotiris, *Mount Athos*, Athens, 1979

Thasos
Ecole Française d'Athenes, *Guide de Thasos*, Paris, 1968
Wynne-Thomas, Joan, *Legacy of Thasos*, Springwood Books, 1978

Index